"Entry into a new space can be daunting. It can be challenging to encounter the thought, imagery, language, and themes of the Gospel of John. Dorothy Lee is a helpful guide for this Gospel, supporting first-time readers and offering new insights for advanced readers. While exploring the major themes of John, Lee points out connections with the thought and writings of the ancient world and offers stimulating reflections for contemporary readers. This will be an excellent companion for classes and reading groups seeking a deeper understanding and appreciation for the Gospel of John."

—*R. Alan Culpepper,* dean and professor emeritus of New Testament, McAfee School of Theology, Mercer University

"In her characteristically insightful manner, Professor Lee contributes a powerfully evocative volume on the Gospel of John to the NWBT series. Taking her cues from the Gospel's prologue (1:1–18), she explores distinctively Johannine themes across the narrative through beautifully accessible prose that excites the senses. Her love for this story is evident as she provides a gateway that leads readers of all levels deeply into John's particular telling of the Good News."

—*Sherri Brown,* professor of New Testament, Creighton University

"With her characteristic accessibility and attention to narrative nuance and detail, Dorothy Lee provides an accessible and enjoyable overview of John's theological themes. Lee grounds her study with attention to historical and literary contexts without ever losing focus on the Gospel itself. She is an encouraging guide who invites us into John's theological

thicket by providing us clear paths to navigate. This book will be a welcome addition to classrooms and churches alike!"

—*Alicia D. Myers,* associate professor of
New Testament, Baylor University

"What a joy to read such a lucid and sensitive insight into the Gospel of John! Dorothy Lee has a formidable background in classical and patristic literature, which she seamlessly weaves into her analysis. Taking the prologue (1:1–18) as her key, Lee leads the reader through the entire Gospel, relating the themes introduced in the prologue to the narrative that follows. She looks back to an ancient text and then consciously relates its implications to the present world and the experience of believers today. Pastors and teachers will find this volume a gem, while academics will recognize the wealth of scholarship needed to write with such authority. Thank you, Dorothy, for this outstanding contribution to our appreciation of John."

—*Mary Coloe,* professor emerita, University
of Divinity, Melbourne, Australia

"Dorothy Lee has provided an accessible and enjoyable explanation of the key themes in the Gospel of John. Attentive to both detail and the big picture, she takes readers on a tour of the spiritual depths and glorious heights of John's witness to Jesus as the Word made flesh. An indispensable resource for anyone wishing to learn about the Gospel according to St. John."

—*Rev. Dr. Michael F. Bird,* Deputy Principal,
Ridley College, Melbourne, Australia

"Dorothy A. Lee combines a lifetime's passionate and erudite study of the Gospel of John with a poetic sensibility to provide a thorough and nuanced reading of its main themes. These themes are explored through a careful reading of the narrative, avoiding the tendencies to atomise or decontextualise which often affect such studies. Careful reflections on the themes' relevance to historical and contemporary theological concerns round off each treatment. Professor Lee's deep scholarship, lightly worn, deftly elucidated, and generously shared, ensures that this volume deserves to become a vade mecum."

—*Fergus King,* Farnham Maynard Associate
Professor in Ministry Education, Trinity
College, University of Melbourne, Australia

"World-class scholarship, deep theology, and a Christian spirituality for our century come together with clarity and accessibility in this superb opening up of John's Gospel. Dorothy Lee has distilled for us the wisdom of decades spent engaging with the overflowing meaning of this glorious text. This book consequently, like the Gospel of John itself, can teach and inspire a wide range of readers."

—*David F. Ford,* Regius Professor of Divinity
emeritus, University of Cambridge

JOHN

4 WORD BIBLICAL THEMES NEW

JOHN

DOROTHY A. LEE

NIJAY K. GUPTA, SERIES EDITOR

ZONDERVAN ACADEMIC

John, Volume 4
Copyright © 2025 by Dorothy A. Lee

Published in Grand Rapids, Michigan, by Zondervan. Zondervan is a registered trademark of The Zondervan Corporation, L.L.C., a wholly owned subsidiary of HarperCollins Christian Publishing, Inc.

Requests for information should be addressed to customercare@harpercollins.com.

Zondervan titles may be purchased in bulk for educational, business, fundraising, or sales promotional use. For information, please email SpecialMarkets@Zondervan.com.

Library of Congress Cataloging-in-Publication Data

Names: Lee, Dorothy A., author.
Title: John / Dorothy A. Lee.
Description: Grand Rapids, Michigan: Zondervan, [2025] | Series: New word biblical themes: new testament | Includes index.
Identifiers: LCCN 2024051507 (print) | LCCN 2024051508 (ebook) | ISBN 9780310126911 (paperback) | ISBN 9780310126935 (ebook)
Subjects: LCSH: Bible. John--Criticism, interpretation, etc.
Classification: LCC BS2860.J62 L34 2025 (print) | LCC BS2860.J62 (ebook) | DDC 226.5/06--dc23 /eng/20250106
LC record available at https://lccn.loc.gov/2024051507
LC ebook record available at https://lccn.loc.gov/2024051508

Unless otherwise noted, Scripture quotations are taken from the New Revised Standard Version Bible. Copyright © 1989 National Council of the Churches of Christ in the United States of America. Used by permission. All rights reserved worldwide. · Scripture quotations marked CEB are taken from the Common English Bible. Copyright © 2011 Common English Bible. · Scripture quotations marked ESV are taken from the ESV® Bible (The Holy Bible, English Standard Version®). Copyright © 2001 by Crossway, a publishing ministry of Good News Publishers. Used by permission. All rights reserved. · Scripture quotations marked KJV are taken from the King James Version. Public domain. · Scripture quotations marked NABRE are taken from the *New American Bible, revised edition.* Copyright © 2010, 1991, 1986, 1970 by the Confraternity of Christian Doctrine, Inc., Washington, DC. Used by permission of the copyright owner. All rights reserved. No part of the New American Bible may be reproduced in any form without permission in writing from the copyright owner. · Scripture quotations marked NASB are taken from the New American Standard Bible®. Copyright © 1960, 1971, 1977, 1995 by The Lockman Foundation. Used by permission. All rights reserved. www.lockman.org. · Scripture quotations marked NIV are taken from The Holy Bible, New International Version®, NIV®. Copyright © 1973, 1978, 1984, 2011 by Biblica, Inc.® Used by permission of Zondervan. All rights reserved worldwide. www.Zondervan.com. The "NIV" and "New International Version" are trademarks registered in the United States Patent and Trademark Office by Biblica, Inc.® · Scripture quotations marked NJB are taken from *The New Jerusalem Bible.* Copyright © 1985 Darton, Longman & Todd, Ltd. and Doubleday, a division of Bantam Doubleday Dell Publishing Group, Inc., Garden City, NY. · Scripture quotations marked NLT are taken from the Holy Bible, New Living Translation. Copyright © 1996, 2004, 2015 by Tyndale House Foundation. Used by permission of Tyndale House Publishers, Inc., Carol Stream, Illinois 60188. All rights reserved. · Scripture quotations marked RNJB are taken from *The Revised New Jerusalem Bible.* Copyright © 2018, 2019 Darton, Longman & Todd, Ltd. and Doubleday, a division of Bantam Doubleday Dell Publishing Group, Inc., Garden City, NY. · Scripture quotations marked NRSVue are taken from the New Revised Standard Version Updated Edition. Copyright © 2021 National Council of Churches of Christ in the United States of America. Used by permission. All rights reserved worldwide. · Scripture quotations marked REB are from the Revised English Bible. Copyright © Cambridge University Press and Oxford University Press 1989. All rights reserved. · Scripture quotations marked RSV are taken from the Revised Standard Version of the Bible. Copyright © 1946, 1952, and 1971 National Council of the Churches of Christ in the United States of America. Used by permission. All rights reserved.

Any internet addresses (websites, blogs, etc.) and telephone numbers in this book are offered as a resource. They are not intended in any way to be or imply an endorsement by Zondervan, nor does Zondervan vouch for the content of these sites and numbers for the life of this book.

All rights reserved. No part of this publication may be reproduced, stored in a retrieval system, or transmitted in any form or by any means—electronic, mechanical, photocopy, recording, or any other—except for brief quotations in printed reviews, without the prior permission of the publisher.

Cover design: Tammy Johnson
Interior typesetting: Sara Colley

Printed in the United States of America

25 26 27 28 29 30 /TRM/ 8 7 6 5 4 3 2 1

To my Johannine friends:
Brendan Byrne, Mary Coloe, Frank Moloney
with gratitude

Contents

Series Preface xiii
Acknowledgements xv

1. Introduction to John 1
2. John and Christian Theology 23
3. Word and Wisdom 44
4. Life and Light 68
5. Temple and Glory 93
6. Witness and Believing 117
7. Birth and Family 139
8. Law and Revelation 162

Subject Index 189
Scripture Index 199

EDITORIAL BOARD

Series editor: Nijay K. Gupta
Zondervan Academic editor: Katya Covrett

CONTRIBUTORS

1. Matthew | Patrick Schreiner
2. Mark | Christopher W. Skinner
3. Luke | Rebekah Eklund
4. John | Dorothy A. Lee
5. Acts | Holly Beers
6. Romans | Michael J. Gorman
7. 1 Corinthians | Todd D. Still
8. 2 Corinthians | David E. Garland
9. Galatians | Nijay K. Gupta
10. Ephesians | Andrew K. Boakye
11. Philippians | M. Sydney Park
12. Colossians/Philemon | Jarvis J. Williams
13. 1–2 Thessalonians | Jeanette Hagen Pifer
14. 1–2 Timothy, Titus | Lucy Peppiatt
15. Hebrews | Cynthia Westfall
16. James | Craig L. Blomberg
17. 1 Peter | Jeannine K. Brown
18. 2 Peter, Jude | Shively T. Smith
19. 1–3 John | Alicia D. Myers
20. Revelation | David A. DeSilva

Series Preface

In 1982, F. F. Bruce's 1–2 Thessalonians commentary was among the first volumes to appear in the now highly esteemed Word Biblical Commentary series (1982–). A handful of years later, the Word Biblical Themes series began publication with Leslie Allen's Psalms and Ralph Martin's Philippians volumes, both printed in 1987. The WBT series was designed to supplement the WBC by offering short discussions of the most important themes in each biblical book. While the WBC volumes were technical and lengthy, focusing on an audience of scholars, the WBT series was meant to distill the key messages of biblical texts to help students and pastors as they present Scripture's testimony to form churches today.

Over the last forty-five years the Word Biblical Commentary series has almost reached completion of its fifty-two volumes, and some older volumes have been revised. However, the original Word Biblical Themes series only managed to produce fifteen volumes between 1987–1991. Therefore, we are pleased to now carry on the original vision of this supplement series with *New* Word Biblical Themes, allowing a new generation of scholars to explore the most crucial theological themes in each book of Scripture. These concise guides will inform and enhance Bible study, Christian teaching, and faithful preaching of the Word of God.

The New Word Biblical Themes offers the following features:

- Reliable research from a diverse group of expert scholars
- An up-to-date academic summary of basic issues of background, structure, and content for each biblical book
- Focused study of each biblical book, discussing the most important theological themes
- Insight into the "big picture" of a book of the Bible by understanding what topics and concerns were most important to the biblical writers
- Thoughtful reflection on theological and moral issues facing the church today by showing readers how the biblical writers approached similar issues in their day
- Reading recommendations for those who want to explore topics in more depth

We hope that readers will be blessed by the expertise of the series contributors, enlightened by concise and clear thematic discussions, challenged by fresh ideas and approaches, and encouraged in their own reading of the Bible as a text full of wisdom.

Nijay K. Gupta

Acknowledgements

In the beginning there were always stories.

First there were the children's stories, then the biblical ones (Abraham and Sarah, Moses and Miriam, David and Goliath), then the novels: Kenneth Grahame, Robert Louis Stevenson, Charles Dickens, Jane Austen, C. S. Lewis, Dorothy L. Sayers, and Paul White. My father was a busy pastor, but he always had time for reading stories.

Then, in early adulthood, the full glory (I use the word advisedly) of John's story of Jesus broke over me and I've never looked back. This story has always been my favorite, even though at this stage of my life I've read many other stories, sacred and secular, and told them and read them to my children and grandchildren as well as to my students. But I've never tired of John's story. And I've come to believe that this Gospel is all story from start to finish—even the discourses are part of it. This story is truly compelling in spite of rough edges and contains a beginning, middle, and end, as Aristotle dictated, having an absorbing plot, lively characters, engaging imagery, and a message to live by.

So, the opportunity to explore the themes of this Gospel which arise from John's story was too good to be missed. With John's Gospel, I sometimes feel like the Water Rat in *The Wind in the Willows* who says dreamily (just before crashing the boat into the riverbank): "there is *nothing*—absolutely nothing—half so much worth doing as simply messing about in boats."[1] I don't much care for boats, but I do care for John's Gospel and the pleasurable and enriching hours I've spent simply messing about in its story.

I need to thank many people in this endeavor: my coworkers at Trinity College for their inspiration and support, especially the Dean, Bob Derrenbacker, and my colleagues, Fergus King and Christopher Porter, for all the Johannine conversations; my daughters, Miriam and Irene, for literary advice along the way; my grandchildren, Jemima, Theo, Harriet, and Wilfred for delightful interruptions; my friends, particularly Muriel Porter, who read this book through and ironed out its creases; Nijay Gupta, who enlisted and encouraged me to write this book in the first place; and Daniel Saxton, who worked tirelessly on the manuscript. Finally, I am especially grateful for my three New Testament colleagues who have been with me almost from the start of my Johannine journey, and this work is dedicated to them: Professor Brendan Byrne SJ, Professor Mary L. Coloe IBVM, and Professor Francis J. Moloney SDB, all connected to the University of Divinity. Their friendship and love of John's story is a constant joy to me.

---

1. Kenneth Grahame, *The Wind in the Willows* (London: Book Club Associates, 1908), 12.

CHAPTER 1

Introduction to John

Apart from the text itself, nothing in the traditional background material surrounding the Gospel of John is particularly stable or transparent. At one level, what we do *not* know seems at first to represent more than we *do* know. Who wrote it and to whom, in what place and context, and at what time: these elements are unknown and we can only guess their answers. But before we despair, we need to note that what we do have—in spite of what we do not—is inexhaustible. The Gospel is indeed a pool in which an infant can paddle and an elephant can swim.[1] As we consider something of the scholarly estimations about the mysteries behind the writing of this Gospel, we will find that what we have far outweighs what we lack.

AUTHORSHIP

We do not know for certain who the author of this Gospel is. The name "John" is a common one, and only some later traditions (in the second century) identify this name with John the apostle, the brother of James, whose father we know to be Zebedee and whose mother is likely to be Salome (see

---

1. The saying has been attributed to both Augustine and Gregory the Great; see Paul N. Anderson, *The Riddles of the Fourth Gospel: An Introduction to John* (Minneapolis: Fortress, 2011), 1–6.

Mark 15:40/Matt 27:56). The same John is also held to be the author of the Johannine epistles and the book of Revelation. This tradition goes back to Irenaeus, bishop of Lyons, one of the early defenders and definers of the Christian faith (c. 130–c. 200 CE).[2]

A complicating factor in determining authorship is the figure of "the disciple whom Jesus loved," who appears in several episodes in the second half of the Fourth Gospel. We gain several impressions of this disciple throughout the Gospel:

a. He is an eyewitness of Jesus's ministry and may be identified with the unnamed disciple of 1:35 who is first a disciple of John the Baptist; he and Andrew change their allegiance from the Baptist to Jesus.

b. He has particular insight into Jesus's death and resurrection and is a primary witness to those events, along with the holy women—an insight that seems to exceed that of Simon Peter (19:26–27, 35–37; 21:7).[3]

c. He is named as the "author" of the Gospel (21:24), although it is not clear where his responsibility lies in the processes of composition.

d. He has most likely died before the completion of the Gospel (21:23).

Some maintain that the beloved disciple is identical to the author of the Gospel who is identical to the apostle John,

---

2. Irenaeus, *Against Heresies* II.22.5, in *Ante-Nicene Fathers*, ed. Alexander Roberts, James Donaldson, and A. Cleveland Coxe, vol. 1 (Buffalo: Christian Literature, 1885), https://www.newadvent.org/fathers/0103222.htm. See Lorne Zelick, "Irenaeus and the Authorship of the Fourth Gospel," in *The Origins of John's Gospel*, ed. Stanley E. Porter & Hughson T. Ong, JS 2 (Leiden: Brill, 2016), 239–58.

3. For the view that John's eyewitness language is metaphorical and theological rather than literal, cf. Andrew T. Lincoln, *The Gospel According to Saint John*, BNTC (London: Continuum, 2005), 17–26.

Introduction to John

the son of Zebedee,[4] though this view is contested. It is true that in Acts 3–4 we see the apostles Peter and John working together in mutual ministry, which would fit with John's Gospel where the two are sometimes side by side (e.g., at the Last Supper and the empty tomb). On the other hand, the "sons of Zebedee" are only mentioned explicitly in one context in John's Gospel (21:2). Given that we know the apostle James was martyred in 44 CE (Acts 12:1–2), it seems astonishing that the apostle John would make almost no mention of his brother in the main parts of the Gospel.

The question of the identity of the beloved disciple is sometimes distinguished from that of the author. Did the beloved disciple write most of the Gospel (John 1–20) while someone else—one of his disciples—completed it after his death (John 21)? Or was the beloved disciple not the literal author but rather the teacher of the community and the primary eyewitness source of the stories found in the Gospel, while someone else put together the Gospel in its current form?[5]

Part of this debate revolves around the question of what "write" means. We know that New Testament authors did not usually write their texts in a literal sense but employed a scribe (an "amanuensis") to do so: someone with the necessary implements and skill (see, for example, Tertius in Rom 16:22). So we are likely not speaking of literal writing. But is it possible that the evangelist was the composer of the Gospel, using the stories learned at the feet of the beloved disciple, whose identity is never made explicit in the Gospel? It could be said that such a person is less likely to refer to himself as

---

4. See esp. Craig S. Keener, *The Gospel of John: A Commentary*, vol. 1 (Peabody, MA: Hendrickson, 2003), 1.81–139.

5. For a summary of the authorship question, see Tom Thatcher, "The Beloved Disciple, the Fourth Evangelist, and the Authorship of the Fourth Gospel," in *The Oxford Handbook of Johannine Studies*, ed. Judith M. Lieu and Martinus C. de Boer (Oxford: Oxford University Press, 2018), 83–100.

"the disciple whom Jesus loved" and more likely that a disciple of his would do so. We will see in chapter 7, however, that there is another way of explaining this anonymity.

There are two other possibilities for authorship in addition to the apostle John, whether we assume that the beloved disciple and the evangelist count as one person or two. One of these views postulates that since the Gospel itself gives us no direct indication of authorship, an unknown Christian leader wrote the book. The community for which the Gospel was written would know perfectly well the identity of the beloved disciple and the author. This seems an unlikely view: it is hard to know how a text with no known leader's name behind it would gain notice and popularity in the wider church.

At this point, we need to bear in mind that the ancient world viewed composition very differently from us. It did not put the same emphasis on originality and singular authorship. Some of Paul's letters, for example, are written in collaboration with several other people (though we usually ignore them) and one letter even arises from a group of Christians in addition to Paul (Gal 1:2). Furthermore, not all scholars agree that Paul wrote all the letters in his name, though he is probably their ultimate source. The ancient world was not as concerned to pinpoint individual authorship with the same fervor we display. However, the second-century church wanted to be confident that these writings could be traced back to an apostle, either directly or indirectly, as it worked out its own identity around the developing canon of sacred writings.[6] Nevertheless, a text can be deemed "apostolic" in its content without necessarily having one of the twelve apostles as its proven author or source. The evangelist's authority "did

---

6. John Behr (*John the Theologian & His Paschal Gospel: A Prologue to Theology* [Oxford: Oxford University Press, 2019], 44–63) argues that the evidence for the apostle John in the early witnesses beyond the New Testament is minimal.

Introduction to John 5

not derive from being part of the twelve but rested instead on his own relationship to the Lord."[7]

There is a second possibility to consider: that the John who is the Gospel's author is another "John,"[8] a presbyter mentioned by Papias of Hierapolis. Papias was a second-century bishop (c. 60–130 CE), whose work we know through the great bishop and church historian Eusebius (c. 260–340 CE). This John is particularly associated with the Roman province of Asia Minor (modern Türkiye), where the Gospel was likely written.[9] Although Papias does not regard this "John" as the author of the Fourth Gospel, there is evidence of another person, a potential candidate for the beloved disciple or the evangelist (or both). Other possibilities have also been canvassed: that "John" the beloved disciple and/or evangelist is Lazarus or Thomas or even a self-concealed female disciple.[10]

In summary, the authorship of this Gospel is hidden from us.[11] Apart from the inscription "according to John," we have no contemporary evidence of the author's identity. We can be reasonably sure that the beloved disciple was an intelligent and believing eyewitness to the ministry of Jesus. He was perhaps very young and outside the circle of the twelve apostles, but was still closely connected to Judea and Jerusalem and lived to a ripe old age. If he is also the unnamed disciple at 18:15–16, which seems likely, he would have had connections with the

---

7. Behr, *John the Theologian*, 63.

8. Marianne Meye Thompson, *John: A Commentary* (Louisville, KY: Westminster John Knox, 2015), 17–22.

9. See Richard Bauckham, *The Testimony of the Beloved Disciple: Narrative, History, and Theology in the Gospel of John* (Grand Rapids: Baker Academic, 2007), 33–91.

10. For a discussion of the options, see Mary L. Coloe, *John 1–10*, WC (Collegeville, MN: Liturgical, 2021), liv–lviii. See also the helpful chart in Gabriel-Mary Fiore, *Spirituality in John's Gospel: Historical Developments and Critical Foundations* (Eugene, OR: Pickwick, 2023), 225.

11. For further details on this, see Fiore, *Spirituality in John's Gospel*, 215–80.

6 John

high priest's family and would thus be able to gain admittance for Simon Peter into the high priest's courtyard—an otherwise inexplicable feature. There are later traditions that John of Ephesus came from a priestly family: he is one "who leaned on the Lord's breast, who was a priest wearing the mitre, and martyr and teacher" and who "sleeps at Ephesus."[12]

It is important in all this speculation to remember that the twelve apostles were not the only disciples of Jesus, as readers of the Gospels sometimes assume. Apart from anything else, John's Gospel only refers to "the twelve" in two narrative contexts (6:67, 70; 20:24) and never speaks of "the apostles." In addition to the many Galilean women disciples who followed Jesus to Jerusalem (see Luke 8:2–3)—an aspect featured in John's emphasis on women's discipleship—there were other male disciples who were also part of the large company of those attached to Jesus and who travelled with him for at least some of his ministry. Luke, for example, speaks of Jesus sending out seventy-two disciples (Luke 10:1–12, 17–20). For Paul, there were more than just twelve apostles; and we know that, of this wider group (which included Paul himself), one at least was a woman (Junia, Rom 16:7).[13]

DATING AND VENUE

If we continue along this speculative route, we come to the question of dating. Opinions in the past have varied from very early (pre-60 CE) to very late (second century CE). Most scholars these days would date John to sometime in the 90s. There are several reasons for this conclusion. In the first

---

12. Quoted from Polycrates in Eusebius, *Ecclesiastical History*, trans. J. E. L. Oulton, LCL 265 (Cambridge, MA: Harvard University Press, 1965), III.xxxi.3.

13. Dorothy A. Lee, *The Ministry of Women in the New Testament: Reclaiming the Biblical Vision for Church Leadership* (Grand Rapids: Baker Academic, 2021), 151–54.

Introduction to John

place, John cannot be dated too late as we have a small papyrus fragment of the Gospel which comes from the second century, perhaps even from the first decades of that century. That puts a late dating out of the question. An early dating is equally unlikely, as the Gospel sometimes equates "Jews" and "Pharisees" (e.g., John 9) in a way not possible before 70 CE and the destruction of the Jewish temple by the Romans. In that conflict, much of the diversity of Judaism disappears and only Pharisees and Christians remain to pick up the pieces and reorganise Jewish faith and practice.[14]

Early church tradition tells us that the Gospel was finally produced in Ephesus, although there is evidence of specific Palestinian knowledge in the origins of the Gospel, especially around Judea. There seems no particular reason to doubt Ephesus as the final destination of Johannine groups of Christians.[15] Ephesus was a leading city in the ancient Roman-Hellenistic world and in the province of Asia Minor. It was a trade center second only to Rome and had its own harbor and diverse religious traditions, likely including a Jewish community. The main deity of the city was the goddess Artemis, and the Artemisium, the temple of Artemis, was one of the seven wonders of the ancient world. A famous library was located there, the Library of Celsus (built in 110 CE after the writing of John), as well as several philosophical schools. Ephesus also became an early site for the development of emperor-worship by pagan (i.e., non-Christian and non-Jewish) magistrates and merchants who owed so much of their livelihood and prosperity to Roman imperial power.

---

14. On the dating and the issues surrounding it, see Stanley E. Porter, "The Date of John's Gospel and Its Origins" in *The Origins of John's Gospel*, ed. Stanley E. Porter & Hughson T. Ong, JS 2 (Leiden: Brill, 2016), 11–29.

15. For a helpful discussion of the issue of venue, see Keener, *Gospel of John*, 1.142–49.

8 John

Ephesus was a major center of early Christianity and appears many times in the New Testament. It is associated with the apostle Paul (who wrote 1 Corinthians from there) and with Timothy (who ministered there); it is also one of the seven cities mentioned in the book of Revelation. All of this makes Ephesus a likely location for the Fourth Gospel's composition, though it is possible that the fledgling Johannine group originated in Jerusalem and moved to Ephesus at some point in its history following the Jewish War (66–73 CE).

AUDIENCE

We know as little about the Gospel's audience as its authorship. That they were Greek-speaking is clear. That they were Jewish is also likely, given the stress on Jewish ritual and the temple as well as wider Old Testament traditions. The Gospel of John is steeped in these traditions, known particularly from the Septuagint (LXX), the Greek translation of the Old Testament which stems from the third and second centuries BCE. Pagans from the Greco-Roman world may also have been members of the Johannine group (or groups), given the evangelistic thrust of the Gospel (20:31). It is also probable that women were held in high regard, including as leaders among the Johannine Christians—if indeed the prominent place of women disciples within the text is a faithful reflection of the community behind it.

However, it is more significant to recognise that "Jewish" and "Greco-Hellenistic" are not mutually exclusive categories. All Judaism was influenced, to a greater or lesser extent, by Greek (Hellenistic) ideas and culture. We know from first-century CE Jewish writers such as the philosopher Philo (20 BCE–c. 50 CE) and the historian Josephus (c. 37–100 CE) that Jewish people were largely hellenized in language and

Introduction to John

culture while still maintaining their monotheism and Jewish religious traditions.

If the Fourth Gospel is enmeshed in Greco-Roman culture, it is equally embedded in Judaism.[16] We think of Judaism and Christianity as separate religions today, but in the first century CE Christians were a sect of Judaism (like the Pharisees) and laid claim to the same Old Testament traditions and covenant identity. It is unlikely that Christians separated decisively from Judaism following the Jewish War with Rome, as has been argued in the past; the split between the two groups was much more gradual. The Fourth Gospel sees itself as the inheritor of Judaism and Jewish faith in rivalry with the synagogue (that is, the Pharisees). If so, John's Gospel still lies within the wide bounds of Judaism. That certainly makes a great deal of difference to the way we interpret references to *Ioudaioi* ("Jews") throughout the Gospel, especially given that almost all the characters are Jewish and that the Johannine Jesus asserts "salvation is of the Jews" (4:22), as we will see in chapter 8.

How do the four Gospels relate to each other—and, more specifically, how does John relate to the Synoptic Gospels? For a number of decades in the twentieth century, many scholars thought John was separate from the other three Gospels and that any influence from the Synoptic tradition must have been early in the period of oral tradition.[17] But more recently, scholars have become convinced of direct links between John and the Synoptic Gospels, especially that of Mark.[18] John

---

16. For an outline of the environment and values of the ancient world and the early church, see David A. deSilva, *An Introduction to the New Testament: Contexts, Methods & Ministry Formation*, 2nd ed. (Downers Grove: IVP Academic, 2018), 9–81, 82–116.

17. See, e.g., Raymond E. Brown, *An Introduction to the Gospel of John*, ed. F. J. Moloney (New York: Doubleday, 2003), 6–7.

18. See especially the collection of essays in Eve-Marie Becker, Helen K. Bond, and Catrin H. Williams, eds., *John's Transformation of Mark* (London: T&T Clark, 2021).

also assumes knowledge of the Synoptics on the part of his readers: such as the name of Jesus's mother (never named in John), the baptism of Jesus by John the Baptist in water, or even the institution of the Eucharist.

The main question is whether this knowledge is more dependent on one Synoptic Gospel than another (on Mark, for example) and whether John's reason for writing is competitive or complementary. Is John trying to assert the superiority of the Johannine Gospel over the other Gospels, correcting them on various points in the process, or is he trying in a more reconciling spirit to supplement them: to tell stories they do not have or to present a different theological outlook—establishing, in the process, the Johannine tradition as authentic? The latter view makes more sense in terms of the ancient world, where writing was not driven by the same competitive spirit as in the modern world. In the end, the "four-fold Gospel" of Irenaeus holds both traditions together—the Synoptic and the Johannine—in a spirit of complementarity that recognizes the gifts and graces each brings to the New Testament portrait of Jesus.

When taken to extremes, the older view that John was independent of the Synoptic Gospels had the effect of turning Johannine believers into a sectarian community, cut off from Judaism, the rest of the Christian church, and ultimately the world.[19] This view has now been challenged. John does have an awareness of other Jesus believers (e.g., 10:16) and he has a distinctive focus on mission.[20] The disciples are sent out by the risen Christ who breathes on them the power of the Spirit

---

19. Wayne A. Meeks, "The Man from Heaven in Johannine Sectarianism," *JBL* 91 (1972): 44–72.

20. For further details on this theme, see Michael J. Gorman, *Abide and Go: Missional Theosis in the Gospel of John*, Didsbury Lecture Series (Eugene, OR: Cascade, 2018).

Introduction to John

(20:22) to carry on the mission he has brought as the "Sent One" (e.g., 4:34; 5:36–37; 6:29, 44, 57; 7:16; 8:16–18; 9:4, 7; 12:49; 14:24; 17:21).[21] The reaction against the sectarian view of the Fourth Gospel has sought to question whether we can speak in any sense of a discreet "Johannine community."[22] However, if we have a more porous understanding of John's Gospel, with its openness to other Christians, to Judaism, and to dialogue with the Greco-Roman world, it is legitimate to speak of the Christ groups in Ephesus as a Christian community—or, rather, several Christian communities meeting in house churches—out of which this Gospel has emerged and to which it speaks.

GENRE

A good deal of work has been done in recent decades on what kind of writing John's Gospel actually is: what type of literature it belongs to. The Greek is simple and the vocabulary limited, suggesting a writer whose first language may not have been Greek, although he is at home with it. Previous generations saw John's writing as very late and theological rather than historical, with little interest in Jesus's biographical details. It is true that John does not write with a modern, chronological view of time,[23] but that does not mean he is dismissive of the actual history. Only John the evangelist tells us that the first disciples of Jesus were initially disciples of John the Baptist (1:35–42), only he gives a three-year ministry

---

21. Paul N. Anderson, "The Having-Sent-Me Father: Aspects of Agency, Encounter, and Irony in the Johannine Father-Son Relationship," *Semeia* 79 (1999): 33–57.

22. See the series of essays on this question in *The Johannine Community in Contemporary Debate*, ed. Christopher Seglenieks and Christopher W. Skinner (Lanham, MD: Lexington/Fortress Academic, 2024).

23. Douglas Estes, "Time," in *How John Works: Storytelling in the Fourth Gospel*, ed. Douglas Estes and Ruth Sheridan (Atlanta: SBL, 2016), 41–57.

to Jesus, and only he gives us the name of the slave whose right ear Peter cuts off (18:10). These and other details attest to the grounded nature of this Gospel in history.

These factors also indicate that, like the other Gospels, John belongs, at least partly, in the category of biography: not in the modern sense but in the ancient understanding.[24] Biographies in the ancient world were not written to capture a neutral sense of history but to improve and edify the reader. The best-known biographer of the ancient world was Plutarch (46–119 CE), who wrote *Parallel Lives* of distinguished Greeks and Romans.[25] As a philosopher following the tradition of Plato, Plutarch wrote with a disposition to virtue and a fierce polemic against rival philosophical schools. There is nothing impartial in his writings. Similarly, the Gospels take a partisan attitude from the start, which they identify with truth: John writes to give rise to faith and life (20:30–31), Mark writes as "good news" (Mark 1:1), Matthew sees time as having its culmination in Jesus (Matt 1:1–17), and Luke writes to provide assurance of faith to Theophilus (Luke 1:4). The Gospel of John qualifies in this sense as ancient biography, seeking to arouse and strengthen faith.

At the same time, the Fourth Gospel also lends itself to other genres in the ancient world. One example is that of dramatic narrative, which is a feature of the long stories in this Gospel and integrally involves dialogue and action. This is as much a way to tell the story of Jesus as ancient biography. Therefore, John's Gospel represents a mixed genre of literature, which adds to its complexity and dynamism.[26]

---

24. Richard A. Burridge, *What Are the Gospels? A Comparison with Graeco-Roman Biography*, 3rd ed. (Waco, TX: Baylor University Press, 2018).

25. Plutarch, *The Parallel Lives*, trans. Bernadotte Perrin, 11 vols., LCL (Cambridge, MA: Harvard University Press, 1962–1967).

26. Howard Attridge, "Genre," in *How John Works: Storytelling in the Fourth Gospel*, ed. Douglas Estes and Ruth Sheridan (Atlanta: SBL, 2016), 7–22.

NARRATIVE OUTLINE

John's Gospel falls most easily into two segments, famously designated by Raymond E. Brown as "the Book of Signs" (John 1:19–12:50) and "the Book of Glory" (John 13:1–21:25).[27] This is a neat division and not without basis in the text, but therein lies the problem: it is a little too neat for John's "tangled thicket" style where sections interlace and overlap, one folding into another.[28] For instance, the Easter events comprise the greatest of all the signs and John's summary at the end of the first Easter narrative seems to make that point: "There are many other signs which Jesus did . . ." (20:30). Additionally, the first major section of the Gospel is filled with the theme of glory, from the incarnation itself (1:14) to the signs and works of Jesus's ministry (2:11).

The major division between John 12 and John 13 is clear enough. John 13:1 acts as more than an introduction to the footwashing (13:2–30); it serves as a "mini-prologue" to the second half of the Gospel with its focus on the divine purpose of Jesus's departure, centered on his enduring love for "his own." Also, within the two main sections there are subdivisions, even if these themes overlap. The first part, for example, has a section that begins and ends in the public arena at Cana in Galilee (2:1–4:54), while the following chapters (John 5–10) commence with "a feast of the Jews" and maintain the same focus (5:1). Yet the healing at 4:46–54

---

27. Raymond E. Brown, *The Gospel According to John*, vol. 1, AB 29 (New York: Doubleday, 1966), 1:cxxxviii–cxxxix, followed by a number of recent commentaries (e.g., Francis J. Moloney, *The Gospel of John*, SP [Collegeville, MN: Liturgical, 1998], 23–24).

28. Ruben Zimmermann, "Imagery in John: Opening up Paths into the Tangled Thicket of John's Figurative World," in *Imagery in the Gospel of John: Terms, Forms, Themes, and Theology of Johannine Figurative Language*, ed. Jörg Frey, Jan G. van der Watt, and Ruben Zimmermann (Tübingen: Mohr Siebeck, 2006), 1–43.

14   John

connects to the healing in 5:2–9a, while the threat to Jesus at
10:31–39 provides important background to the narrative of
John 11. The second half of the Gospel divides itself between
Jesus with his closest disciples in the private arena (the Last
Supper and resurrection narratives, John 13–17, 20–21) and
Jesus in the public sphere in the trial and crucifixion narrative
(John 18–19).

Putting all these elements together yields the following
structure in two parts, which includes the presence of *chiasms*
(i.e., structures derived from oral tradition that form a circular pattern) in some narratives:

I. Descent: Incarnation and Ministry, John 1:1–12:50
    Beginnings (1:1–51)
      • Prologue: incarnation of Word (1:1–18)
      • John the Baptist and gathering of first disciples
        (1:19–51)
    Cana to Cana (2:1–4:54)
      • First Sign: wedding (2:1–11)   **A**
      • Cleansing of temple (2:12–25)   **B**
      • Two Jewish leaders: Nicodemus and the
        Baptist (3:1–36)   **C**
      • Samaritan woman and temple worship
        (4:1–42)   **B**¹
      • Second Sign: healing (4:43–54)   **A**¹
    Feasts of Judaism (5:1–10:42)
      • Jesus's Sabbath work (5:1–47)
      • Bread of Life narrative: Passover (6:1–71)
      • Tabernacles narrative: water and light (7:1–8:59)
      • Man born blind narrative: water and light (9:1–41)
      • Parable of sheepfold and dispute: festival of
        Dedication (10:1–42)
    Climax of Public Ministry (11:1–12:50)

Introduction to John

- Raising of Lazarus, plot, and anointing (11:1–12:11)
- Entry into Jerusalem (12:12–19)
- Coming of "hour" (12:20–36)
- Conclusion to public ministry (12:37–50)

II. Ascent: Departure, John 13:1–21:25

Last Meal with "His Own" (13:1–17:26)

- Making God known: footwashing (13:1–30)   **A**
- Jesus's departure (13:31–14:31)   **B**
- Abiding and hatred (15:1–16:4a)   **C**
- Jesus's departure (16:4b–33)   **B**[1]
- Making God known: prayer (17:1–26)   **A**[1]

Passion, Death, and Burial (18:1–19:42)

- Jesus's arrest in garden (18:1–11)   **A**
- Trial before high priest and Pilate (18:12–19:16a)   **B**
- Jesus's crucifixion and burial in garden (19:16b–42)   **A**[1]

Resurrection Appearances (20:1–21:25)

First narrative

- Appearance to Mary the Magdalene (20:1–18)   **A**
- Giving of Spirit (20:19–23)   **B**
- Appearance to Thomas (20:24–29)   **A**[1]
- Purpose of Gospel (20:30–31)

Second narrative

- Jesus appears to seven disciples (21:1–14)
- Simon Peter and beloved disciple (21:15–19)
- Beloved disciple and writing of Gospel (21:20–24)
- Conclusion (21:25)

There are several problems with John's narrative that are somewhat concealed by this outline. Most conspicuously, many

16　　　　　　　　　　　John

argue that John 21 reads like a later addition to the Gospel, a kind of postscript to the text.[29] The reason for this view is that John 20:30–31 seems to form a conclusion to the Gospel: the Spirit has already been given (20:19–23) and, on either side, Mary the Magdalene (20:1–18) and Thomas (20:24–29) have attained full Easter faith. It also seems strange to find the seven disciples going fishing, as if they had not yet met the risen Lord or been given their commission for mission (21:1–14).

This issue is not unique in John's narrative style. There are other seeming inconsistencies in the plot. For instance, the prologue contains language that does not appear elsewhere in the Gospel (e.g., the concept of grace), raising the question of whether it was originally part of the Gospel or perhaps a hymn of the early church added to the Gospel. Also, Jesus goes up to Jerusalem at John 5:1, then is suddenly and rather confusingly crossing the Sea of Galilee at John 6:1, from where he returns to Jerusalem at 7:10, this time secretly. Additionally, Jesus's farewell discourse is divided by an injunction to "let us go from here," suggesting the ending of the discourse (14:31), yet his speech continues unabated and without notification at 15:1. Finally, material from John 14 and John 16 seems strikingly similar and repetitive.

How are we to account for these apparent inconsistencies and points of awkwardness? One real possibility is that the Gospel was composed in more than one edition. The subsequent editions would have enlarged an original shorter Gospel (possibly oral) and included a second version of the

---

29. E.g., Francis J. Moloney, "John 21 and the Johannine Story" in *Anatomies of Narrative Criticism. The Past, Present, and Futures of the Fourth Gospel as Literature*, ed. Tom Thatcher and Stephen D. Moore (Atlanta: SBL, 2008), 237–51. For the view that John 21 is integral to the Gospel, see Jo-Ann Brant, *John*, Paideia (Grand Rapids: Baker Academic, 2011), 263–90.

last discourse (16:4b–33) and an additional resurrection narrative (John 21).

At the same time, we also need to take into account the very careful way these materials were added. The farewell discourse, as it now stands, has an overarching narrative shape within the Last Supper: "making God known" forming the bookends of a chiastic structure (as seen in the outline above) with the theme of love and hatred at the center (15:1–16:4a).[30] John 21 also has significant points of correspondence with the rest of the Gospel. This commonality includes the bread and shepherd imagery (21:9, 15–19) as well as Simon Peter's and the beloved disciple's consistent characterization: their rivalry at one level yet also having different and complementary roles (21:18–24).

John's Gospel is not a modern novel where anomalies are smoothed out to create a more consistent surface. Allowance needs to be made in ancient writings for what we might see as rough parts of the plot. This kind of "narrative fluidity" is an aspect of the novels of antiquity as well as the Gospels and the apocryphal literature of the second century CE and beyond.[31] The texts themselves are often varied and uneven, some of which can be explained by manuscript transmission and translation into other languages, but some of it goes back to the largely oral nature of publication and reception in the ancient world.

While we cannot go so far as to claim that oral composition is fluid while written composition is stable—there is a spectrum on which both oral performance and literate

---

30. Moloney, *The Gospel of John*, 370–71, 477–79.

31. See Christine M. Thomas, "Narrative Fluidity as a Generic Characteristic," in *The Acts of Peter, Gospel Literature, and the Ancient Novel: Rewriting the Past* (Oxford: Oxford University Press, 2003), 72–86.

composition lie, with stability and fluidity in both[32]—we can allow for the relative fluidity of all forms of ancient literature. Even the text of the Fourth Gospel is not quite as stable as our English translations suggest: there are a number of manuscripts and papyrus fragments that lie behind it, with a diversity of alternative readings. These factors help explain aspects of the Johannine text that look uneven and disjointed to us.

The focus on narrative is an important point in a book that deals with Johannine themes. The heart of John's Gospel is narrative, not thematic discourse. Even those parts of the Gospel often dubbed as "discourse" are more usually part of dialogues that have an overall narrative flow (for example, the Tabernacles narrative, 7:1–52 and 8:12–59). The Johannine plot is both enhanced and made possible by the literary devices that sustain and support it: the rich imagery and symbolism, the irony, the characterization, the examples of foreshadowing, the shape and movement of the plot, and all the other literary devices such as paradox, parallelism, antithesis, diction or tone, reversal, and recognition.[33] To extract themes from the narrative of the Gospel risks giving the literary devices secondary if not negligible status, when in fact they themselves are the bearers of meaning.

Nevertheless, there is a vital place for the study of themes within a narrative. True, this type of study is an extrapolation from the narrative, but it is a necessary step in taking us back to the story in a deeper and more conscious way. Paul Ricoeur speaks of a three-stage process in interpreting a text. We begin with a "first naivety" where we experience the narrative

---

32. Note particularly the later addition of the woman caught in adultery to the Johannine text (7:53–8:11).

33. For further details on the literary devices of the Gospel, see esp. R. Alan Culpepper, *Anatomy of the Fourth Gospel: A Study in Literary Design* (Philadelphia: Fortress, 1983).

Introduction to John

for the first time, with all the emotional responses we might conceivably have: enchantment, bewilderment, surprise, or even repulsion. The second stage is where we take a step back and study aspects of the text at a cognitive level: its background, context, shape, and themes. The third stage is the most important: we return to the text with a "second naivety," open once more to what it has to offer and how it touches us affectively. However, this time we come with a knowledge we did not originally possess.[34] Study of the themes of John's Gospel thus holds an important place—as long as we return thereafter to the narrative of the Gospel and place ourselves before it with an open heart.

THE SHAPE OF THIS BOOK

As part of the New Word Biblical Themes series, this study approaches the Johannine text from the perspective of its themes, recognizing that these belong in a narrative context. The themes themselves are garnered from the prologue to the Gospel (1:1–18), either explicitly or implicitly, since the prologue is generally recognized as a kind of musical overture to the whole Gospel. It sets the scene, giving the reader access to a level of knowledge that the characters who encounter the Johannine Jesus do not themselves possess. It acts, in other words, as the theological key to the Gospel, anticipating its major themes and imagery as these unfold through the ensuing narrative.[35]

For this reason, it makes sense to draw themes from within

---

34. Paul Ricoeur, *The Symbolism of Evil*, ET (Boston: Beacon, 1967), 347–57.

35. On the links between the prologue and the Gospel, see R. Alan Culpepper, "The Prologue as Theological Prolegomenon to the Gospel of John" in *The Prologue of the Gospel of John: Its Literary, Theological, and Philosophical Contexts*, ed. Jan G. van der Watt, R. Alan Culpepper and Udo Schnelle, WUNT 359 (Tübingen: Mohr Siebeck, 2016), 3–26.

the narrative structures of the Gospel itself—and particularly from its overture—in order to identify the core ideas and symbols rather than impose a list of external themes. Most of these themes are explicit in the prologue, though a couple are strongly implied without being stated. Often these themes appear in a series of pairings, though not always of the same kind. They are dualities but not binary ones. We begin, therefore, with the Word of God as the Gospel itself does. We will explore the Gospel's background, its Johannine meaning, and its significance, bearing in mind the Old Testament and the Jewish setting, particularly in relation to holy Wisdom (Christ).

The following chapters pursue other themes from the prologue: imagery of light and life, which have their origins in creation (chapter 4); temple and glory, which appear at the point of the incarnation (chapter 5); witness and believing, incorporating the ministry of John the Baptist and the faith of believers (chapter 6); birth and family, which speak of the regaining of identity as children of God and the relationship of Father and Son (chapter 7); and, finally, the law and revelation as they stand together rather than in opposition, the one pointing and leading to the other (chapter 8).

Admittedly, some Johannine themes do not appear in the titles of the chapters. There is no chapter dedicated, for example, to love, or abiding, or freedom, although all are key Johannine themes. Nor is there a chapter heading dedicated solely to Father-Son imagery, nor one to the work of the Spirit-Paraclete. The chapter headings do not in themselves cover every Johannine theme, but these major images and motifs are found in all the chapters. For example, although love is not mentioned explicitly in the prologue, it is implied from beginning to end: in the relationship between the Word and God—the Son and the Father—and in the attachment of believers.

In exploring the paired themes of the Fourth Gospel, we find considerable overlap across the chapters. Each smaller narrative contains more than one theme, so this study will return sometimes to the same story again and again, each time from a different angle. The raising of Lazarus, for example, exemplifies several Johannine themes. As the central narrative of the Gospel's plot, this story is explored more than once to draw out its theological and spiritual meaning. Such repetition or revisiting is inevitable in this type of thematic study. In the end, the reader is enabled to return to the Gospel story with an enriched understanding of its meaning and is able to enter more deeply into the narrative flow.

One final note on the English text: Translations from the Gospel of John are my own, striving for as literal a rendering as possible within the bounds of comprehensible English. From time to time, however, I interact with the main English translations. Within the tradition of the King James Version (KJV) are the New Revised Standard Version Updated Edition (NRSVue) and the English Standard Version (ESV), both contemporary updates of the Revised Standard Version (RSV); alongside is the updated New American Standard Bible (NASB). Translations which are outside the KJV tradition include the New International Version (NIV), the New American Bible Revised Edition (NABRE), the Revised New Jerusalem Bible (RNJB), and the Revised English Bible (REB). All these translations are based on recent study of Greek New Testament manuscripts, which has been conducted across the ecumenical spectrum.[36] For those with limited or no knowledge of the Greek text, consulting several reputable English

---

36. The New King James Version (NKJV) is not included because it is based on the Textus Receptus, an out-of-date edition of the Greek New Testament, ignoring the manuscripts and papyrus fragments which have come to light since the KJV and its English predecessors were first translated.

translations can be a helpful substitute—especially those that lie outside our own traditions, as they are more likely to challenge our presuppositions.

FURTHER READING

Bauckham, Richard. *The Testimony of the Beloved Disciple: Narrative, History, and Theology in the Gospel of John.* Grand Rapids: Baker Academic, 2007.

Brant, Jo-Ann A. *John.* Paideia. Grand Rapids: Baker Academic, 2011.

Brown, Sherri, and Francis J. Moloney. *Interpreting the Gospel and Letters of John: An Introduction.* Grand Rapids: Eerdmans, 2017.

Culpepper, R. Alan. *Anatomy of the Fourth Gospel: A Study in Literary Design.* Philadelphia: Fortress, 1983.

Moloney, Francis J. *The Gospel of John.* SP. Collegeville, MN: Liturgical, 1998.

Thompson, Marianne Meye. *John: A Commentary.* NTL. Louisville, KY: Westminster John Knox, 2015.

CHAPTER 2

John and Christian Theology

John's Gospel has made a major contribution to Christian theology through the centuries. It possesses the most sophisticated theological understanding of the relationship between God and Jesus, using the core metaphorical conjunction of "Father" and "Son," which was particularly significant in the early debates of the first Christian centuries. It brings a unique perspective to theological issues such as eschatology and the Spirit, which have likewise had great influence. In contemporary study it contributes to theological discussions on creation, gender, and ethics. John has made perhaps the most vital contribution to theology of any of the Gospels and, together with them, is placed early within the New Testament canon. This placement is not because of the Gospels' supposedly earlier dating (the earliest writings are those of the apostle Paul) but because they incorporate in narrative form the entire life, ministry, death, and resurrection of Jesus.

We customarily speak of "the Gospel of John," but that moniker is in fact inaccurate. The title of the Gospel is "according to John," and it is one of four manifestations of the one "Gospel." The phrase "according to" is of vital importance because it reminds us that John's Gospel is not the only witness to the life-giving advent of Jesus Christ. The good news itself, for the early church, consisted of the Four

23

24 John

Gospels, each of which brings a different perspective to bear on the saving significance of Jesus in his life, ministry, death, and resurrection. Even in the early centuries, the differences between John and the other Gospels were noted and the diversity vigorously defended. It is no coincidence that, among the four living creatures associated with the evangelists (Rev 4:6b–11; Ezek 1:4–25), the early church connected John with the eagle, soaring high into the heavens.[1]

The significance of the Fourth Gospel to the basic structuring of what came to be "orthodox" theology—enshrined in the Nicene Creed (325, 381 CE)—is evidenced from the number of commentaries during the early centuries.[2] Four, in particular, stand out among them. Origen's massive commentary on John (c. 226–29 CE), much of which unfortunately has not survived, argued against certain Gnostics that the Jesus of this Gospel was both divine and human. John Chrysostom wrote a commentary, which was basically a series of homilies on the Gospel (386–94), aiming to refute the Arian heresy (which denied the full deity of Christ) and to offer pastoral encouragement to Christians. Cyril of Alexandria wrote a commentary on John that was largely doctrinal and concerned with refuting heresies, particularly in relation to Jesus (425–28). Finally, Augustine of Hippo delivered a series of 125 homilies on John called the "Tractates" (delivered in the period after 416 CE), which combined theological and allegorical interpretations of the Gospel; these sermons were often interrupted by comments and questions from the congregation. These and other commentaries attest to the

---

1. For further details on this, see Richard A. Burridge, *Four Gospels, One Jesus? A Symbolic Reading*, 2nd ed. (Grand Rapids: Eerdmans, 2005), esp. 133–63.

2. William Lamb, "Johannine Commentaries in the Early Church," in *The Oxford Handbook of Johannine Studies*, ed. Judith M. Lieu and Martinus C. de Boer (Oxford: Oxford University Press, 2018), 416–36.

importance of the Fourth Gospel from the end of the second century onwards and its centrality in the doctrinal formulations of the early church.[3]

GOD AS THE CENTER OF JOHN

While Jesus is unquestionably the main character in the Johannine narrative, God is at the theological center of the Gospel. This factor is of key importance in subsequent theological debate. The Fourth Gospel, in other words, is *theo*-centric rather than *Christo*-centric.[4] There is not a competition, of course, but in terms of later theology it is vital to make the distinction. From the opening verses it is clear that God stands at the heart of things. The word "God" (*theos*) occurs three times in the opening two verses in careful juxtaposition (1:1–2):

A   the Word was "*towards*" **God** (in the beginning
      of creation)
B   the Word *is* **God**
A[1]   the Word was "*towards*" **God** (from the beginning)

English translations usually translate "towards" as "with," but this is a rather weak rendering of the Greek preposition *pros*. It has the sense of being "turned towards" or even "face to face." The REB translates it, in its first instance, as "in God's presence," which captures something of the nuance. This preposition brings a sense of relationship and

---

3. Joel C. Elowsky, ed., *John 1–10*, ACCS NT IVa (Downers Grove: IVP Academic, 2006), xxvii–xxxvi.

4. C. K. Barrett, "Theocentric or Christocentric? Observations on the Theological Method of the Fourth Gospel" in C. K. Barrett, *Essays on John* (London: SPCK, 1982), 1–18, and Marianne Meye Thompson, *The God of the Gospel of John* (Grand Rapids: Eerdmans, 2001), 227–40.

intimacy between God and the Word, but also denotes the precedence of God from before creation. The Word's own being is God-sourced, God-oriented, and God-directed. In tune with Genesis 1, God's dynamic word, which brings the universe into being, is the projection of God's creative voice. Yes, creation happens through the Word, but nonetheless the chief actor behind creation is God, who is the ultimate source of all life.

Throughout the Fourth Gospel the role of God as the primary actor in the drama of salvation is carefully and consistently unfolded. The advent of Jesus is itself the result and manifestation of the gracious divine love for the world and the desire to rescue human beings, no matter the cost (3:16). The divine giving of Jesus is in fact God's *self*-giving. God is the sender of Jesus (3:17), and it is God's mission which Jesus carries out and God's will for which he both hungers (4:34) and thirsts (19:28). The Johannine Jesus also possesses authority over life and death, but, again, it is God's authority that he bears (5:19–23).

How has this core Johannine perspective influenced subsequent Christian theology? Perhaps the most obvious aspect is the implicit awareness in the history of the Christian church that John's Gospel is grounded in the God of the Old Testament. That means it is one voice in a larger chorus that has its origin in the revelation of the God of Israel in and through the story of creation and salvation: from Abraham and Sarah through Moses and David to the prophets.

There is a preference today in scholarly circles to speak of the "Hebrew Bible" rather than the "Old Testament" because of the wish to avoid the implication that this first section of Scripture is irrelevant and obsolete. This is an important point for subsequent church history, even though "old" need

John and Christian Theology

not imply anything more than precedence in age and time.[5] In the second century CE, Marcion seems to have excised the Old Testament and parts of the emerging New Testament from Scripture. According to the early Fathers and Mothers in this period, for Marcion the God of the Old Testament cannot be the God of Jesus Christ. There are thus two Gods: one inferior and violent, and the other the God and Father of Jesus Christ. The main inspired writings are those of the Gospel of Luke (with omissions) and the Pauline letters. Marcion—although we only know his views from those who opposed them—wanted to separate Christianity from its roots in Old Testament faith and practice.[6]

As early church leaders in the second century quickly realized, such views, if left unchallenged, had serious implications for Christian faith. In dislocating Christian theology from its Jewish heritage, these views sought to lead the church away from an emphasis on the God of Israel to an exclusive focus on Jesus and his new God. Marcion's views (whether or not they were understood) were declared heretical and he was banished from the church in Rome, forming his own churches based around his understanding of the gospel. Origen's commentary on John, particularly the prologue,

---

5. Early Christians used the wider canon of the Old Testament, which included the Apocryphal/ Deuterocanonical books: such as Wisdom, Sirach, 1 and 2 Maccabees, and Judith. As we saw in the previous chapter, they also, for the most part, read the Old Testament in its Greek version, the Septuagint, which was likely translated for the Jewish community in Egypt in the third and second centuries BCE. On the Septuagint, see Jannes Smith, "What Is the Septuagint?," *Bible Odyssey*, accessed October 16, 2024, https://www.bibleodyssey.org/passages /related-articles/what-is-the-septuagint-and-why-does-it-matter/. Because the Bible of the New Testament church was largely that of the Greek Septuagint, I prefer to use the term "Old Testament" rather than "Hebrew Scriptures."

6. See Henry Chadwick, *The Church in Ancient Society: From Galilee to Gregory the Great*, OHCC (Oxford: Oxford University Press, 2001), 89–92; for a contextual view, see Judith M. Lieu, *Marcion and the Making of a Heretic: God and Scripture in the Second Century* (Cambridge: Cambridge University Press, 2015), esp. 433–39.

endeavored to counteract this theology by demonstrating the unity of the God of the Old Testament and the God of Jesus.[7]

Through interaction with such "heretical" movements, the early church was able to confirm the place of the Old Testament and Jewish faith as the mother of Christianity—a mother it could never relinquish. John's emphasis on the centrality of God—the God of Israel, the God of the temple in Jerusalem and all its feasts and festivals, and the God of the ancient Jewish Scriptures—was vital in promoting a wider vision of God, grounded in the past story of God's revelation in both creation and Israel.[8]

JESUS CHRIST

John's Gospel played an even greater role in the formulations of the fourth and fifth centuries as they began to work through the meaning and significance of Jesus's identity in relation to God.[9] These were controversial times for the church. The rise of Arianism in the fourth century avowed belief in the divinity of Christ, albeit as a lesser deity to God the Father. Arius was a presbyter from Cyrene in Libya who believed in the subordination of the Son to the Father: for him, there was a time when the Son did not exist. His views were popular in his day and in following generations;

---

7. See Mark Lindsay, "The Interpretation of John Through Key Moments of Church History," in *The Enduring Impact of the Gospel of John: Interdisciplinary Studies*, ed. Robert A. Derrenbacker Jr., Dorothy A. Lee, and Muriel Porter (Eugene, OR: Wipf & Stock, 2022), 105–23.

8. On Jewish and Christian identity in the second century, see Laurence D. Guy, *Introducing Early Christianity: A Topical Survey of Its Life, Beliefs and Practices* (Downers Grove: IVP Academic, 2004), 13–16.

9. For a summary of John's Christology, see Udo Schnelle, "The Person of Jesus Christ in the Gospel of John" and Jean Zumstein, "The Purpose of the Ministry and Death of Jesus in the Gospel of John" in *The Oxford Handbook of Johannine Studies*, ed. Judith M. Lieu and Martinus C. de Boer (Oxford: Oxford University Press, 2018), 311–30, 331–46.

they were based on texts such as John 14:28: "The Father is greater than I."

The issue was resolved at the ecumenical Council of Nicaea in 325 CE when the church decided against Arianism and affirmed the full and eternal divinity of the Son. The great theologian of the day was Athanasius (c. 296–373 CE). Later in the same century, the Cappadocians (Gregory of Nyssa, Gregory Nazianzus, Basil, and the women associated with them[10]) confirmed the equality of divinity within the three persons of the Trinity.

In its Christological affirmations, the Nicene Creed, followed by the declarations of the fourth ecumenical council at Chalcedon in 451 CE, was profoundly influenced by the theology of the Fourth Gospel. While Arius might quote John 14:28, the Creed and Chalcedonian Declaration drew their inspiration in large part from the prologue of the Gospel with its assertion of the Word as part of the being of God from before creation (1:1–2, 18). Other passages in John's Gospel established for them the equality of divinity between the Father and the Son: "making himself equal to God" (5:18) and "the Father and I are one" (10:30). The supposedly "subordinationist" passages, such as 14:28, were seen as signs of the incarnation, where the Son placed himself under obedience for his earthly life. Insight into the heavenly intercession of the Son to the Father, including their mutuality and equality of love and belonging, was to be found in Jesus's prayer in John 17, drawing the believing community into the same divine circle of love and unity.

There is a more contemporary twist to this debate. The Western tradition, unlike the Eastern, has in more recent

---

10. See Carla D. Sunberg, *The Cappadocian Mothers: Deification Exemplified in the Writings of Basil, Gregory, and Gregory* (Eugene, OR: Pickwick, 2017).

30 John

centuries tended to hold a subordinationist view of the Son's relationship to the Father. While not wishing to deny the eternal divinity of the Son, some have in effect compromised that divinity by a hierarchical ordering of the relationship between Son and Father. The recovery of the doctrine of the Trinity, along with the influence of Eastern theology, has challenged this kind of subordinationism, which had its origins in Origen and Tertullian in the debates leading up to Nicaea. It stands over against the firm conviction of Athanasius and the Cappadocians that the Son and Father, along with the Spirit, are coequally divine. No hierarchy exists within the Trinity, although there is a procession of Father, Son, and Spirit, evident particularly in the Farewell Discourse, which a later generation (and particularly Maximus the Confessor, c. 580–662) saw in terms of "perichoresis," a divine dance in which each Person circles the other in an affinity of love and being.[11]

A more modern variant of this debate has centered around the issue of the relationship between men and women. The subordination of women to men in the home and the life of the church is said to be grounded in the subordination of the Son to the Father. The debate is fierce particularly among Reformed and evangelical theologians.[12] Over against this perspective, others have argued that the subordinationist view is a denial of the New Testament evidence—particularly the Gospel of John—along with the Councils of Nicaea and

---

11. For further details on this theological imagery, see Jürgen Moltmann, "'God in the World—the World in God': Perichoresis in Trinity and Eschatology" in *The Gospel of John and Christian Theology*, ed. Richard Bauckham and Carl Mosser (Grand Rapids: Eerdmans, 2008), 369–81.

12. See, e.g., Wayne Grudem, "Biblical Evidence for the Eternal Subordination of the Son to the Father," in *The New Evangelical Subordinationism? Perspectives on the Equality of God the Father and God the Son*, ed. Dennis W. Jowers and H. Wayne House (Eugene, OR: Pickwick, 2012), 223–61.

Chalcedon, which confirm the equality and mutuality of the Son and Father in Christian theology. This equality of divinity confirms full gender equality in the church, the home, and everywhere else.[13]

THE SPIRIT

Although the deity of the Holy Spirit was never questioned in the same way as that of Christ, the full personhood of the Spirit within the Holy Trinity was not formally confirmed until the Nicene Creed. This perspective, again, was influenced in large part by the Fourth Gospel's presentation of the Spirit as the "Paraclete" ("Advocate" or "Comforter"). The Farewell Discourse shows the Holy Spirit as personal and engaging in personal activities. The Paraclete will abide with the community and be the presence of Jesus (14:17), the Paraclete will teach and remind the community (14:26), the Paraclete will bear witness to Jesus (15:26) and convict the world (16:8), and the Paraclete will lead the disciples into all truth, speaking what he hears and glorifying Jesus (16:13–14).

Can we, therefore, speak of the Fourth Gospel, with its subsequent influence on the creeds and councils of the church, as "trinitarian"? The answer is both "no" and "yes." On the one hand, the term "Trinity" (*trias* in Greek, *trinitas* in Latin) did not emerge till the second century CE with Tertullian (160–220 CE), who first coined it. Moreover, the debates about whether the Son was "of like substance" or "of the same substance" as the Father are not part of the New Testament evidence: not even the Gospel of John raises this

---

13. For a history of the debate, see esp. Kevin Giles, *The Rise and Fall of the Complementarian Doctrine of the Trinity* (Eugene, OR: Cascade, 2017). See also Catherine Mowry LaCugna, *God for Us: The Trinity and Christian Life*, rev. ed. (New York: HarperCollins, 1993).

issue. In this sense, the formal doctrine of the Trinity is a later manifestation, an authorized development of what emerges originally from the Fourth Gospel and elsewhere in the New Testament. It endeavors to answer questions thrown up by the New Testament and to develop themes already implied in the New Testament's various writings.

On the other hand, it is hard to see where else the New Testament could have gone in light of John's explicit theology of incarnation, a theology that relates not only to Father and Son but also incorporates the Spirit (3:3–8; 6:63; 7:39; 20:22).[14] The questions with which the later church wrestled are implied particularly (though not exclusively) in the theology and Christology of the Fourth Gospel. In what way can the Word be said to be preexistent, in relationship with God and also sharing God's being (1:1–2)? What does it mean to say that the Son lies in the Father's embrace (1:18)? How has the Son become human, and what implications does this have for Jesus's identity in his life and ministry (1:14)? How is Jesus's death to be reconciled with that identity (6:51; 10:17–18; 19:34–37)? How and where do Father, Son, and Spirit connect to each other, if each speaks and listens to the other (16:13)? And how can the risen Jesus be acclaimed "Lord and God" (20:28)? From this angle, the relationship between Father, Son, and Spirit in the narrative of the Fourth Gospel outlines the shape and form of the future doctrine of the Trinity.[15]

The questions themselves push the Fourth Gospel in a trinitarian direction, which is very different from the

---

14. See J. C. O'Neill, *Who Did Jesus Think He Was?*, BIS 11 (Leiden: Brill, 1995), 74–93.

15. For an outline of the different scholarly approaches to the emergence of the Trinity, see Matthew W. Bates, *The Birth of the Trinity. Jesus, God, and Spirit in New Testament & Early Christian Interpretations of the Old Testament* (Oxford: Oxford University Press, 2015), 12–40.

alternative: an adoptionist view.[16] Adoptionism is the belief that Jesus the human being was adopted by God as divine at an early point in his ministry: either at his baptism by John the Baptist when the Spirit descends on him (1:29–34) or at the resurrection.[17] It is hard to sustain an adoptionist view in light of Jesus's great prayer in John 17: "Father, in relation to what you have given me, I desire that where I am they too may be with me, to see my glory which you have given me, because you loved me before the founding of the world" (v. 24). This passage, along with the prologue, validates the Johannine theological notion of the Son as present with God from all eternity. As we have already seen, this Christological insight has made its way into Christian understandings of orthodoxy: "The personality of the Spirit and the precise coordination of Spirit, Son, and Father are expressed here [in John's Gospel] in a way that is unsurpassed in the New Testament and in a way that provided the foundations for the subsequent formation of creeds."[18]

This view is confirmed by the way in which Jesus is not only the true worshiper but also the object of worship in the Fourth Gospel. The tension between the two is vivid in the cleansing of the temple, located early in Jesus's ministry. In that episode, Jesus as true worshiper reclaims the temple for the authentic worship of God (2:14–16) and, equally, as the object of worship, identifies the temple with his own body (2:18–21). The Spirit is also incorporated into this

---

16. Bates, *Birth of the Trinity*, 76–79.

17. For this latter view, see, e.g., Michael Peppard, *The Son of God in the Roman World: Divine Sonship in Its Social and Political Context* (New York: Oxford University Press, 2011) and Bart D. Ehrman, *How Jesus Became God: The Exaltation of a Jewish Preacher from Galilee* (New York: HarperOne, 2014).

18. Jörg Frey, *The Glory of the Crucified One: Christology and Theology in the Gospel of John*, ET (Waco, TX: Baylor University Press, 2018), 344; Frey describes John as "proto-Trinitarian" (368–72).

34   John

understanding through the Paraclete's distinctive personhood in the Fourth Gospel and the many parallels between
Jesus and the Johannine Spirit, who is portrayed as "the
personal presence of Jesus with the Christian while Jesus
is with the Father."[19] On this basis, the Nicene Creed in its
third section maintains that "with the Father and the Son
[the Spirit] is worshiped and glorified."

THE LAST THINGS AND THE CHURCH

John's perspective on eschatology ("the last things") is unique
among the New Testament writings in the emphasis it brings.
While the Fourth Gospel shares with other parts of the New
Testament belief in the return of Christ and the future resurrection of the dead (5:28–29; 6:39; 16:22–23), it also has an
unusually strong focus on resurrection life that can be attained
in the here and now. This is based on the identity of the
Johannine Jesus as "the resurrection and the life" (11:25–26),
a life that begins in present experience and is victorious over
death, both in the present and in the life to come.

The emphasis on the anticipation of God's future in the
"now" of believing existence connects also to John's ecclesiology: that is, his understanding of the church. Unlike the
Gospel of Matthew or the writings of Paul, John does not use
the actual word "church" (*ekklēsia*), but there is a strong sense
of community flowing through the Gospel: a community
that grounds itself in both word and sacrament. This sense
of community begins in the pronoun "we" at 1:14, where the
newborn children of God (1:12–13) together turn their believing gaze to the glory of the Word-made-flesh. It concludes

---

19. Raymond E. Brown, *The Gospel According to John*, vol. 2, AB 29A (Garden
City, NY: Doubleday, 1966), 2.1139. See chapter 8 for further details on the role
of the Spirit.

John and Christian Theology

with the same pronoun "we" after the resurrection narratives, where the community attests to the beloved disciple as the truthful witness to its tradition (21:24).

The history of the church has seen fierce debate over the meaning, significance, and number of the sacraments. Some of this conflict has involved the Fourth Gospel, which has been variously interpreted on both ends of the spectrum as either containing explicit sacraments or being anti-sacramental and so referring to none. The issue arises primarily from the fact that John gives no account of the institution of the Eucharist in his account of the Last Supper and narrates instead the story of the footwashing (13:1–30).

Yet John, unlike the Synoptics, does not depict the Last Supper as a Passover meal. If anything, he wants to make the link with Passover stronger: Jesus dies on the day of Passover at the hour when the paschal lambs are sacrificed, so that he is truly "the Lamb of God who takes away the world's sin" (1:29). Instead, John draws the Eucharist into the second of the three Passover references in his Gospel: the Bread of Life narrative (John 6).[20] Yet, although explicit symbolic references to drink and to blood imply it (6:51–58), the focus is not primarily on the Eucharist but on the spiritual relationship with the Johannine Jesus, the Bread of Life, through his death and resurrection, which the believing community experiences through both word and sacrament.[21]

There is little to inform us how the believers of John's Gospel structured and organized themselves in their worship and missional life. But one point has become clear over the

---

20. For the diverse arguments on this question, see Brown, *The Gospel According to John*, 1.284–85, and Craig S. Keener, *The Gospel of John: A Commentary*, vol. 1 (Peabody, MA: Hendrickson, 2003), 1.689–91.

21. For a historical overview of this passage (which sees it as both spiritual and sacramental), see Frederick Dale Bruner, *The Gospel of John: A Commentary* (Grand Rapids: Eerdmans, 2012), 437–45.

36 John

last few decades: women are strongly featured in the narrative of the Fourth Gospel as eminent disciples of Jesus, suggesting also their presence as models and leaders within the community behind the Gospel. Several female characters have emerged as critical to the Johannine narrative in its portrayal of discipleship:[22]

- The mother of Jesus is given a prominent place at the beginning and end of Jesus's ministry, nurturing the faith of the disciples (2:1–11; 19:25–26).
- The Samaritan woman comes to faith and bears witness to Jesus in an apostolic way to her fellow villagers (4:28–29, 39–42).
- Martha and Mary of Bethany proclaim Jesus's identity in both word and deed (11:17–27; 12:1–8) and recognize in faith his death and resurrection.
- Mary the Magdalene is the key witness to the resurrection, the "apostle of the apostles," proclaiming the message to the other disciples (20:17–18).[23]

This rich portrayal of women disciples has played a significant role in the impetus and biblical warrant for belief in the equality of women and men before God and the vocation of women, alongside men, to be not only disciples but also leaders in the church.

---

22. See Susan Miller, *Women in John's Gospel*, LNTS 676 (London: T&T Clark, 2023), Holly J. Carey, *Women Who Do: Female Disciples in the Gospels* (Grand Rapids: Eerdmans, 2023), 155–84, and Dorothy A. Lee, *The Ministry of Women in the New Testament: Reclaiming the Biblical Vision for Church Leadership* (Grand Rapids: Baker Academic, 2021), 117–47.

23. As we noted in the last chapter, the story of the woman caught in adultery is omitted here: though likely to be historical, it does not belong in John's Gospel but was added later. For further details on this passage, see Gail R. O'Day, "John 7:53–8:11: A Study in Misreading," *JBL* 111 (1992): 631–40.

LANGUAGE AND IMAGERY

John's Gospel has played an important role in more recent debate on the male language and imagery so prominent within the text. Some forms of feminism might see John's Gospel as patriarchal, wedded to masculine images of God that portray a male deity with his male offspring. The prominence of the Father-Son imagery (more so than anywhere else in the New Testament) has created this perceived problem with the Fourth Gospel. Women have asked how their own experience can connect to imagery that is so dominantly masculine in its portrayal of revelation.[24]

John's Gospel may seem to have created this problem, but it has also seen ways through it, either explicitly or by implication. The Johannine picture of the Father, far from upholding patriarchal patterns of authoritarian power, overturns them. Honor is relinquished and shared, not hoarded, above all in the giving of the Son. It is donated in vulnerable and self-giving love for the world, of which the cross itself is the sublime symbol (3:16–17). The love between Father, Son, and Spirit is not exclusive or inaccessible to outsiders but an open doorway through which all are invited to enter. These aspects challenge patriarchal constructions of power.

The language, moreover, is symbolic, not literal. Here, "symbol" means not an ornament or decoration but an expression of theological and spiritual truth that is beyond the power of analytical words to convey; only figurative language can evoke it. God is not a literal father in the Fourth Gospel—either to Jesus or to believers. For instance, in the dialogue following the feeding of the five thousand,

---

24. On gender readings of John's Gospel, see Colleen M. Conway, "Gender and the Fourth Gospel," in *The Oxford Handbook of Johannine Studies*, ed. Judith M. Lieu and Martinus C. de Boer (Oxford: Oxford University Press, 2018), 220–36.

38   John

the crowd shows its increasing limitations by defining Jesus
narrowly as "the son of Joseph, whose father and mother we
know" (6:42). The people cannot understand that Jesus is
also—symbolically and even more fundamentally—the true
Bread from heaven (6:41, 48, 51). The symbolism points to
both authorship, authority, and love in order to portray God
as the divine source of Jesus's life and the source, by exten-
sion, of the life of believers.

The maleness of Jesus has been a particular problem
more broadly in Christian theology. "Can a male Savior save
women?" is the question feminists have asked.[25] Once again,
the Fourth Gospel can provide an answer. Yes, it confirms
the maleness of Jesus, particularly through the use of sonship imagery, but here again there are mitigating factors
in this Christology. John introduces the incarnation at 1:14
in the language of "flesh," where the stress is on the bodily
and material reality of Jesus rather than his maleness (and
not even exclusively on his humanity). This aspect brings
a universality to the incarnation, which has implications
for women's theology. There is a solidarity to fleshly reality
that Jesus possesses in this Gospel, which extends to women
and beyond. The early church understood this truth very
clearly: Gregory Nazianzus famously said: "*that which is not
assumed is not healed*" (*to . . . aproslēpton kai atherapeuton*).[26] In
other words, Jesus takes on a cosmic humanity—as well as
a specific one—that incorporates female as well as male,

---

25. For further details on these issues, see Dorothy A. Lee, "Feminist
Theology," in *Jesus in History, Thought, and Culture: An Encyclopedia*, ed. Leslie
Holden, 2 vols. (Santa Barbara, CA: ABC Clio, 2003), 1.281–88.

26. Marcelo P. Souza, "'That Which Is Not Assumed Is Not Healed': St
Gregory the Theologian's Letter 101," *Luminous Darkness: Reflections on Theology,
Philosophy and History*, February 9, 2021, https://luminousdarkcloud.wordpress.com
/2021/02/09/famous-although-not-last-words-that-which-is-not-assumed-is-not
-healed-st-gregory-the-theologian-and-sundry-unsalvific-heresies-a-brief-account/.

Gentile as well as Jew, and all the other divisions created by space, time, and culture.

The metaphor of Jesus's sonship refers to that unique and sublime relationship to deity in which he is enmeshed from all eternity, though it also connects to his human maleness, which is an element of the particularity of his humanity. By entering into that sonship—that "filiation," to use a more technical and less gendered term—believers too become children of God, their status dependent on that of Jesus.[27] This point becomes clearer when we take into account the momentous significance female discipleship and witness has in this Gospel, as we observed in chapter 1.

A related issue is the exclusively male language and imagery that is used in church and academic life to speak of God. John's Gospel has again had a perspective to contribute to this debate. John's portrayal makes room for feminine language and imagery in divine revelation. Johannine scholarship has pointed to the feminine imagery of Wisdom/Sophia in the presentation of Jesus as the Word, as we will see in chapter 3. This may not be obvious to the modern reader, but the ancient hearer or reader, immersed in the Old Testament, would not have missed or mistaken it. Apart from its synonymous link to the Word, it is particularly apparent in images of hospitality where Sophia is the gracious host at the table, offering the gift of herself through images of food and wine: she is both the giver and the gift. This symbolism is intrinsic to John's Christology and presents a feminine face to God and Jesus in the Gospel that feminist scholarship has welcomed.[28]

---

27. Dorothy A. Lee, "Jesus' Spirituality of [Af]filiation in the Fourth Gospel," *Religions* 13 (2022): 647, https://www.mdpi.com/2077-1444/13/7/647?type=check_update&version=1/.

28. See, e.g., J. Massyngbaerde Ford, *Redeemer Friend and Mother: Salvation in Antiquity and in the Gospel of John* (Minneapolis: Fortress, 1997) and Mary L. Coloe, *John*, 2 vols., WC 44A & 44B (Collegeville, MN: Liturgical, 2021).

SPIRITUALITY AND ETHICS

John's Gospel has had a significant impact on the development and experience of Christian spirituality. Long ago, Clement of Alexandria famously described the Gospel of John as "the spiritual Gospel" (150–215 AD).[29] There is deep truth in this statement, but, at the same time, John's spirituality cannot be divorced from his understanding of the body and flesh. This understanding is apparent particularly in the seven "I am" sayings of the Gospel and their metaphorical significance as they draw on creation and embodied human life:

- "I am the Bread of Life" (6:35).
- "I am the Light of the World" (8:12; 9:5).
- "I am the Gate for the sheep" (10:7, 11).
- "I am the Good Shepherd" (10:11).
- "I am the Resurrection and the Life" (11:25–26).
- "I am the Way, the Truth, and the Life" (14:6).
- "I am the true Vine" (15:1).[30]

John's spirituality is enfleshed, grounded in creation, incarnation, and resurrection along with the created goodness of matter and materiality which, in the Johannine worldview, has an integral place in the future restoration of God.[31]

---

29. Quoted by Eusebius, *Ecclesiastical History* 6.14.7.

30. On the 'I am' saying both with a predicate and without, see Sherri Brown and Francis J. Moloney, *Interpreting the Gospel and Letters of John: An Introduction* (Grand Rapids: Eerdmans, 2017), 166–68, and Felix Just, "'I AM' sayings in the Fourth Gospel," The Johannine Literature Web, April 11, 2018, https://catholic-resources.org/John/Themes-IAM.htm.

31. For further details on this theme, see Gabriel-Mary Fiore, *Spirituality in John's Gospel: Historical Developments and Critical Foundations* (Eugene, OR: Pickwick, 2023), esp. 163–66, and Stephen C. Barton, *The Spirituality of the Gospels* (Eugene, OR: Wipf & Stock, 1992), 113–43.

Spirituality has become popular in recent decades in Western thinking and is often placed in a separate category of its own. But it is (or at least needs to be) closely tied to the theology which underpins it. It is significant that the Eastern Church does not separate the two but sees theology and mysticism (or spirituality) as two sides of the one coin. In this sense, spirituality can be seen to be both objective and subjective: referring, on the one hand, to the actual content of the Gospel in its teaching and narration and, on the other hand, to its subjective apprehension in the hearts and lives of its readers.

At the basis of Johannine spirituality is an understanding of the Spirit-Paraclete who connects to the hearts, minds, and spirits of readers through a relationship centered around abiding, enabling them to grasp spiritual meaning and leading them "into all truth" (16:13) and transformation of life. The Spirit enables the abiding-in-love of the Father and the Son (14:23). This spirituality is profoundly personal without being individualistic and is therefore linked in a broader way to the community of believers who abide on Jesus as the Vine (15:1–8).[32] It is personal, concerned with discipleship, transformative, mystical, and grounded in the experience of the beloved disciple.[33]

An earlier generation of Johannine readers argued that John had no ethics beyond the simple love command as a sign to the unbelieving world: "love one another as I have loved you" (13:34–35). More recent studies, however, have demonstrated the presence of ethics across the Gospel, especially in the narrative characterizations.[34] The figures of the hostile

---

32. Dorothy A. Lee, *Hallowed in Truth and Love: Spirituality in the Johannine Literature* (Eugene, OR: Wipf & Stock, 2012), 143–49.

33. Fiore, *Spirituality in John's Gospel*, 362–63.

34. Sherri Brown and Christopher W. Skinner, eds., *Johannine Ethics: The Moral World of the Gospel and Epistles of John* (Minneapolis: Fortress, 2017).

authorities ("the Jews," Caiaphas, Judas, and Pontius Pilate) all display characteristics that go directly against Johannine ethics, whereas other characters exemplify them. Apart from Jesus himself, characters such as Mary of Bethany, the holy women, and the beloved disciple at the foot of the cross (12:1–8; 19:25–27) show exemplary valor in their conduct, pointing to self-giving and courageous ethics as well as love of Jesus's true disciples: they are those who "bear fruit" and "keep my commandments" (15:8, 10). In this sense, spirituality and ethics belong together, the one nurturing and inspiring the other.

A further issue is whether Johannine ethics extends also to creation and thus to moral issues of ecology in light of the devastating effects of climate change. While the Fourth Gospel is not explicit about creation and its despoiling—which is, after all, a contemporary rather than ancient issue—there are implications flowing from John's understanding of creation and redemption that are relevant here. For example, John the evangelist emphasizes that "all things" are brought into being by God (1:3). Moreover, as we have noted, the divine Word becomes "flesh" in solidarity with all living creatures. Putting these points together leads to an understanding that creation is not excluded from the redemptive will of the Johannine God and that blessings flow to the whole creation from human redemption. On these and related questions we are looking at trajectories which have their ultimate source in the Johannine text but are drawn out in new contexts for new situations—in this case, that of ecology where John's perspective has a vital role to play, just as it does on many other theological, spiritual, and moral issues.[35]

---

35. See Dorothy A. Lee, "Creation, Ethics and the Gospel of John" in *Johannine Ethics: The Moral World of the Gospel and Epistles of John*, ed. Sherri Brown and Christopher W. Skinner (Minneapolis: Fortress, 2017), 241–59.

CONCLUSION

This chapter has outlined some of the ways in which the Fourth Gospel has influenced subsequent Christian history, particularly in the development of its core teachings. This Gospel has had a major impact on Christian tradition in various ways, especially in the early centuries of trinitarian debate and consideration of the two natures of Christ.[36] Beyond the formative early period, however, this Gospel has continued to be a significant resource for theological understanding, worship, ethics, personal devotion, and spirituality. Its place in the canon is assured, not just by its early history but by its enduring influence across the Christian church, from East to West.[37]

FURTHER READING

Bauckham, Richard, and Carl Mosser, eds. *The Gospel of John and Christian Theology*. Grand Rapids: Eerdmans, 2008.

Edwards, Mark J. *John Through the Centuries*. BBC. Oxford: Blackwell, 2004.

Elowsky, Joel, ed. *John 1–10* and *John 11–21*. 2 vols. ACCS IVa and IVb. Downers Grove: InterVarsity Press, 2006–2007.

Fiore, Gabriel-Mary, *Spirituality in John's Gospel: Historical Developments and Critical Foundations*. Eugene, OR: Pickwick, 2023.

Ford, David F. *The Gospel of John: A Theological Commentary*. Grand Rapids: Baker Academic, 2021.

Thompson, Marianne Meye. *The God of the Gospel of John*. Grand Rapids: Eerdmans, 2001.

---

36. Frey sees John's Gospel as the climax of New Testament theology (*Glory of the Crucified One*, 347–75).

37. See especially the series of interdisciplinary essays on John's Gospel in Derrenbacker, Lee, and Porter, eds., *Enduring Impact*.

CHAPTER 3

Word and Wisdom

In the beginning was the Word. (1:1)

Our first pairing in this study of Johannine themes is a closely synonymous one, that of Word and Wisdom. These are intricately linked and complement each other throughout the Fourth Gospel. Together they form, in effect, one theme, though with slightly different dimensions. The initial theme of the Gospel is that of "the Word" (*logos*), and it occurs as the first clause in the opening sentence as a distinct title (1:1). Logos contains implicitly the notion of holy Wisdom (*sophia*), which is present in wisdom imagery elsewhere in the Gospel.[1] Both Word and Wisdom are linked to creation and the giving of the Law (Torah).

Throughout the Gospel, there are also frequent references (more than forty in all) to Jesus's word or words, in addition to occasional references to other people's words and, more significantly, the "word of God" in relation to the Old Testament. The references to Jesus's word accompany the sense of hearing—one of the five senses that recur

---

1. For a summary of the sapiential theme in John, see Ben Witherington III, *John's Wisdom: A Commentary on the Fourth Gospel* (Cambridge, UK: Lutterworth, 1995), 18–27; see also Marianne Meye Thompson, *John: A Commentary*, NTL (Louisville, KY: Westminster John Knox, 2015), 37–39.

44

throughout the Gospel[2]—but, as a title for Jesus himself, the Word also connects to the sense of sight ("we *gazed on* his glory," 1:14). These ideas coalesce in the Gospel narrative and are interlinked in the closest possible way: Jesus as the Word and Wisdom of God, the word or words of Jesus throughout his ministry, and the word of God in the sacred writings of the Old Testament.

BACKGROUND: OLD TESTAMENT

The principal background to the concept of the Word is the Old Testament, beginning with the first account of creation. In a highly stylized narration, encompassing six days in a repeated pattern, God creates all that is and rests on the seventh day, generating the first week of created life (Gen 1:1–2:3). Through the narrative design, God's word utters creation into being, names it, blesses it, and pronounces it good. The same word of God brings Israel into being through a series of covenants, which themselves represent the communicating, speaking God and God's saving action.[3] God's word begins with Abraham and Sarah and continues through the ancestral narratives. It is finally revealed in the gift of the law on Mount Sinai, where Moses receives the stone tablets containing God's ten "words" (Exod 20:2–17; Deut 5:6–21), commands that reveal to Israel how to keep its side of the covenant with God: "Then God spoke all these words: I am the LORD your God, who brought you out of the land of

---

2. Dorothy A. Lee, "The Gospel of John and the Five Senses," *JBL* 129 (2010): 115–27.

3. For a brief overview of the covenant motif, see Marvin A. Sweeney, "Covenant in the Hebrew Bible," *Bible Odyssey*, accessed October 16, 2024, https://blog.bibleodyssey.net/articles/covenant-in-the-hebrew-bible/. In relation to John's Gospel, see Rekha M. Chennattu, *Johannine Discipleship as a Covenant Relationship* (Peabody, MA: Hendrickson, 2006), 50–88.

Egypt, out of the house of slavery; you shall have no other gods before me" (Exod 20:1–2).

The same divine word which brings creation and covenant to birth is also the word given to the prophets. In many of the prophetic books, this is a word of both warning and hope, directing Israel to authentic worship of God and to social justice, especially for those who are poor. In some contexts it articulates divine judgement against Israel's failure to keep the covenant, but it does so to effect repentance and a turning back to God. The same word which creates and sustains in the prophetic writings is also the word which, through the covenant, judges and saves:

> Alas for those who devise wickedness
> > and evil deeds on their beds!
> When the morning dawns, they perform it,
> > because it is in their power.
> They covet fields, and seize them;
> > houses, and take them away;
> they oppress householder and house,
> > people and their inheritance . . .
> I will surely gather all of you, O Jacob,
> > I will gather the survivors of Israel;
> I will set them together
> > like sheep in a fold,
> like a flock in its pasture;
> > it will resound with people.
> (Mic 2:1–2, 12)

The wisdom tradition, developed in and beyond the Old Testament, has a number of parallels with that of the word of God, particularly in relation to creation:

> O God of my ancestors and Lord of mercy,
> who have made all things by your *word*,
> and by your *wisdom* have formed humankind
> to have dominion over the creatures you have made,
> and rule the world in holiness and righteousness,
> and pronounce judgement in uprightness of soul,
> give me the wisdom that sits by your throne,
> and do not reject me from among your servants.
>
> (Wis 9:1–4; emphasis added)

In this important text, it is clear that "word" and "wisdom" are synonymous, representing a form of Hebrew parallelism in which the same point is reiterated, though in slightly different language. Here wisdom is identified with the word of creation in Genesis 1, the word by which all things were made. The notion of wisdom also brings with it the sense of order, beauty, and goodness in the formation of the world. Wisdom is both moral and spiritual, related to Torah and the giving of the Law.[4]

The idea of wisdom points in this text to the "dominion" human beings have been accorded in creation, reflecting Genesis 1:26–27. This dominion, far from representing unbridled power to use and abuse, signifies the responsibility humanity has for the rest of creation: a responsibility to be exercised in "holiness and righteousness," showing the same care for all created beings as God does. God's rule is gracious and liberating rather than dominating, ensuring the thriving of all living creatures. Elsewhere in the Old Testament, we find the same idea of God's ruling power as benevolent, gracious, and life-giving (Ps 145:15–17).

---

4. Mary L. Coloe, *John 1–10*, WC 44A (Collegeville, MN: Liturgical, 2021), 2–4.

48 John

Within this tradition, wisdom is personified, even personalized, to reflect an aspect of God's own being, using feminine imagery.[5] Wisdom/Sophia is depicted as the delightful companion of God and agent of creation:

> The LORD created me at the beginning of his work,
>> the first of his acts of long ago.
> Ages ago I was set up,
>> at the first, before the beginning of the earth. . . .
> When he established the heavens, I was there,
>> when he drew a circle on the face of the deep . . .
> when he marked out the foundations of the earth,
>> then I was beside him, like a master worker;
> and I was daily his delight,
>> rejoicing before him always,
> rejoicing in his inhabited world
>> and delighting in the human race.
>> (Prov 8:22–23, 27, 29b–31)

Sophia is also the host who invites people to her table and feeds them bountifully (Prov 8:1–6). Her lavish and beneficent hospitality is so rich and appealing that it makes her guests ever long for more: "Those who eat of me will hunger for more, and those who drink of me will thirst for more" (Sir 24:21). Sophia descends to earth and enables people to enter into friendship with God (Wis 7:27–28). These aspects of word and wisdom from Israel's writings form an intrinsic part of John's Christology and underlie much of the Fourth Gospel's thematic threads, creating connotations that are

---

5. For further details on wisdom writings in the Old Testament world, see Roland E. Murphy, *The Tree of Life: An Exploration of Biblical Wisdom Literature* (Grand Rapids: Eerdmans, 2002).

Word and Wisdom 49

obvious to early recipients of the text but often need explication for contemporary readers.

BACKGROUND: GRECO-ROMAN WORLD

Ideas of *logos* and *sophia* are also present in the Greco-Roman world, under the influence of Greek philosophy. Philosophy is itself literally the love of wisdom and, from Plato onwards, wisdom lay at the center of Greek philosophical thinking. In some traditions *logos* is associated with the capacity for reason. Socrates, who influenced Plato profoundly, was himself a seeker of wisdom who used reason as the basis of his didactic dialogues. In the early dialogues, Plato makes it clear that the pursuit of wisdom is the goal of human existence and surpasses everything else. In Plato's *Apology*, for example, Socrates describes his own pursuit of wisdom as arising from the prophetic words of the oracle at Delphi, who declared that there was no one wiser than he. Socrates's puzzled pondering on this disclosure led him to the conclusion that the oracle was correct in her assessment: his wisdom was unique because it lay in the humble knowledge that he knew nothing:

> So as a result of this scrutiny, men of Athens, I incurred a great deal of enmity of a very harsh and grievous kind, so that from this there have arisen many slanders, and I got this label "wise" [*sophos*]. You see the bystanders think every time that I myself am wise in those matters in which I refute someone else. Whereas the probability is, fellow Athenians, that the god is in truth wise and this is what he means in this oracle: that human wisdom is of little worth, even worthless. And he seems to mean this man, Socrates, adding the use of my name, thus making an example of me, just as if one were to say: "This man is the

wisest among you, you mortals, who, like Socrates, has recognized that he is in truth of no value when it comes to wisdom [*pros sophian*]."[6]

Thanks to these profound thoughts, Socrates came to personify wisdom in the ancient world and epitomized the capacity to draw moral and ethical insights through questioning and reason.

The idea of *logos* was important for Greek philosophy more generally, and was also a portion of the cultural and theoretical mix of which the Gospel of John was part. Middle Platonism, for example, arose in the second century BCE and influenced the writings of the Jewish philosopher Philo of Alexandria (c. 25 BCE–c. 50 CE), in which *logos* "served the separation of the divine and eternal God from the material, sense perceptible world of transitoriness and mortality."[7] Philo, who is almost contemporary with John, is unlikely to have influenced the Fourth Gospel but shares similar concepts within the same Jewish Hellenistic environment.[8]

Stoics, in particular, placed considerable emphasis on the idea of *logos*. The Stoic doctrine of creation was pantheistic and based on two principles: an active principle, which is the *logos* (or the divine), and the passive principle, which is matter (*hulē*). For Stoics, *logos* signifies reason binding all things together into a web of harmony, holding nature in being and representing the divine principle. The purpose of living for the Stoics, and the truest manifestation of wisdom,

---

6. Plato, *Apology*, ed. and trans. Chris Emlyn-Jones and William Preddy, LCL 1 (Cambridge, MA: Harvard University Press, 2017), 23 a–b.

7. Gitt Buch-Hansen, "The Johannine Literature in a Greek Context," in *The Oxford Handbook of Johannine Studies*, ed. Judith M. Lieu and Martinus C. de Boer (Oxford: Oxford University Press, 2018), 145; this essay also traces the more recent history of Greek thought in New Testament scholarship (138–54).

8. Craig S. Keener, *The Gospel of John: A Commentary*, vol. 1 (Peabody, MA: Hendrickson, 2003), 1.343–47.

is the intelligent pursuit of freedom and happiness, which is attained through being in harmony with the *logos*/the divine/nature.[9]

While the Old Testament is dominant as the sacred text of Jesus-believers in the Johannine community, the influence of Greek philosophical thinking also makes its impact, though indirectly. All Judaism by the first century CE was hellenized to some extent: not in the relinquishing of monotheism or adherence to Torah, but rather in its cultural outlook and its use of philosophical ways of thinking. The influence of Plato is apparent in Philo's portrait of Moses as the first true philosopher.[10] For him, too, *logos* and *sophia* are synonymous.

All this means that while John's understanding of *logos* is entrenched primarily in Jewish sacred texts and Jewish thought, it is open to other ways of thinking, particularly to Greek philosophical modes. This dual influence comes via Hellenistic Judaism. Though Johannine ideas of *logos* are different from Greek philosophical traditions that ground all being in reason, a number of circles commonly perceive that *logos* (however defined) describes that which underlies all life, holding it together in being, and has the pursuit of wisdom as the main goal of existence. John's Gospel thus uses common and comprehensible language that has the capacity to appeal and connect to a Hellenistic audience, whether Jew or Gentile. Ideas such as *logos* and *sophia* are part of the culture of the day and recognizable as fundamental conceptions to any hearer or reader—though John invests them with his own distinctive meaning.

---

9. On the distinctions between Stoicism and emerging Christianity, see Fergus J. King, *Stoicism and the Gospel of John: A Study of their Compatibility*, WUNT 2 (Tübingen: Mohr Siebeck, forthcoming).

10. On Philo, see David T. Runia, "Philo of Alexandria," in *Ancient Philosophy of Religion*, ed. Graham Oppy and N. N. Trakakis, HWPR 1 (London & New York: Routledge, 2008), 133–44.

LOGOS AND SOPHIA IN THE PROLOGUE

The Logos is presented in personal terms, having a close yet enigmatic relationship to God (*theos*). The opening verses (1:1–2), already examined in chapter 2, depict each term as significant and the image of the Logos is captured in three aspects. Firstly, the Logos is described as existing "*in the beginning*"—that is, in eternity before creation. The parallel with the opening words of Genesis is striking: "*In the beginning* . . ." (Gen 1:1). This intertextual connection is even more palpable in the Greek translation of the Old Testament, since the definite article ("the") is missing, as in John 1:1: literally, "in beginning." This parallel makes a vital link, not only between the Logos and God but also between the Logos and creation, as the following verses make plain.[11]

Secondly, the Logos is pictured in the opening verse as being in relationship "*with God*," the origin of all that is—the somewhat unusual form of the preposition "with" (*pros*) suggesting an intimacy of connection. As we have seen in chapter 1, it literally means "towards," the phrase "towards God" indicating that the whole being of the Logos is constantly turned to face God and is always in profound relationship with God. The nature of this relationship is expanded in the prologue and throughout the Gospel, forming the basis of John's Christology.

Note also that although Jesus is not yet named at this point in the prologue, his core identity begins in John's Gospel, not at the point of his adult ministry (as in the Gospel of Mark, 1:14–15), nor in his genealogical relationship to Israel and the virginal conception (Matt 1:1–25), nor in the annunciation to

---

11. On Johannine links to creation, see Mary L. Coloe, "Theological Reflections on Creation in the Gospel of John," *Pacifica* 24 (2011): 1–12.

Mary (Luke 1:26–38), but rather before the origins of creation itself. This beginning emphasizes that there is no dichotomy between creation and redemption in John's Gospel; both are the result and work of the same Logos.

Thirdly, the prologue defines the Logos not only as relationally linked to God, but also as sharing the same divine identity: "the Word *was* God." The use of the verb "to be" in the opening clause (*was*), which is used twice in this verse, suggests that the Logos shares in the structure of "being," pointing to an essential correlation with deity. Throughout the prologue, the idea of "being" is distinguished from "becoming," though this is not always visible in the variety of English translations of the verb "to become" (e.g., "was made," "came to be," "came into being," "was created," "became"). It reflects the distinction between the creator as the eternal and unchanging source of all life (the realm of Being), on the one hand, and creation, which is by definition transitory, mortal, and constantly in flux (the realm of Becoming), on the other.[12]

Although it does not do so explicitly, the language at the beginning of the prologue also includes the notion of wisdom. Knowledge of the background just described makes the connection patent to the ancient reader, although it is perhaps not so visible to the modern reader, who lacks knowledge of the layers of connotation.[13] The wisdom of God, as we have seen, is intrinsic to the word of God because God brings order out of chaos and impresses an intelligent and life-giving structure on the world as God creates it. God, in this sense, is the creator, architect, and sustainer of the world

---

12. Frank Kermode, "John," in *The Literary Guide to the Bible*, ed. Robert Alter and Frank Kermode (London: Fontana, 1987), 443–48.

13. See Sharon H. Ringe, *Wisdom's Friends: Community and Christology in the Fourth Gospel* (Louisville, KY: Westminster John Knox, 1999), 46–63.

54 John

whose wisdom is as necessary and creative as his word. We have already noted that Sophia is as much associated with creation as Logos in the Hellenistic-Jewish thinking of the first century CE. We might offer an alternative paraphrase for the opening verse without substantially altering the meaning: "In the beginning was Wisdom, and Wisdom was with God, and Wisdom was God."

The prologue works in a series of three narrative cycles, each of them having as their subject Logos-Sophia, with the first paralleling the third:

A Creation (1:1–5)
  B Believing (1:6–13)
A¹ Incarnation (1:14–18)[14]

The first narrative cycle encompasses in a nutshell the story of creation. The Wisdom-Word is not only intimately associated with God but is also the agent of creation: literally, the one "through whom all things became" (1:3). While partaking in Being, Logos-Sophia is also, and equally, the cause of Becoming. There is thus a kind of self-existence in the Word in company with God, along with a projection of that existence onto the created realm, giving it form and life. Indeed, there is no initial mention of evil in John 1:3. Far from being a coequal force competing with goodness, evil is secondary. The Word-Wisdom of God is the architect of all created life, implying already its pristine goodness and the absence of anything to mar it.

Yet within the same succinct opening narrative, there is a

---

14. For a different and more complex chiastic arrangement of the prologue, see R. Alan Culpepper, "The Pivot of John's Prologue," *NTS* 27 (1980): 1–31; see also Sherri Brown and Francis J. Moloney, *Interpreting the Gospel and Letters of John: An Introduction* (Grand Rapids: Eerdmans, 2017), 181–83.

Word and Wisdom 55

seismic shift in the imagery. From being a created source and therefore good in itself, darkness now becomes associated metaphorically with a major rift in creation, the source or timing of which is never given: the uprising of a hostile force that seeks to overpower the light and replace it with destruction and death. Thankfully, the final word of reassurance in the first cycle declares that this antagonistic power is unable to quench its opponent, ensuring that the light continues to shine unabated (1:5). Light, not death and darkness, will have the last word on creation.

In the second narrative cycle of the prologue, the imagery moves to that of Logos-Sophia as Light (*phōs*), a theme we will explore in more detail in chapter 4. The frame here begins with the believing testimony of John the Baptist, who prefigures the coming of the Light and its rejection by creation. It concludes with the believing of those who do accept the Light—in spite of the tragic rebuff from those created by it—and in so doing become the reborn children of God (1:6–13).

The third narrative cycle begins and ends with explicit reference to Logos-Sophia (1:14–18). At this point the imagery again shifts, becoming clearer and more explicit with the advent of the incarnation. The prologue now introduces the Father-Son language, imagery that will become central to the thematic structure and contents of the Fourth Gospel as core symbols: "And the Word became flesh and pitched his tent among us. And we gazed on his glory, glory as of the only Son from the Father, full of grace and truth" (1:14).

There are two remarkable features to this crucial statement. In the first place, the realm of Being now moves directly and personally into that of Becoming. The Logos, identified with the divine and the eternal, now enters the transitory world of mortality. This represents the crossing of an otherwise impassable gulf, a chasm that no human being could bridge. In the Logos, both Being and Becoming now reside in the one person.

Secondly, the language of the opening verses changes from abstract to concrete, clarifying the strange and paradoxical relationship between the Logos and God at the beginning of the prologue. How can the Word-Wisdom exist in relationship with God and also *be* God at the same time? The symbolism at 1:14 sets out the complex interrelationship in full color. As Son (*huios*), Logos-Sophia both partakes of the being of the Father (*patēr*) and also exists in intimate relationship with the Father.[15] This familial imagery connects to human experience and makes sense of an otherwise inscrutable bond.

The relational and intimate association will be confirmed in the final verse of this cycle (1:18), which brings the prologue back to its beginning in a circular move: the Wisdom-Word is pictured in vivid bodily language as existing "in the embrace" of God (*kolpos*, meaning "lap" or even "womb," 1:18). The phrase is variously rendered in modern English translations: "in the bosom of the Father" (KJV, RSV), "close to the Father's heart" (NRSVue, RNJB), "nearest the Father's heart" (REB), "at the Father's side" (ESV, CEB), "in the arms of the Father" (NASB), or "in closest relationship" with God (NIV). Most of these rightly attempt to retain the physiological nature of the imagery to reinforce the sense of intimacy and union between Father and Son.

Because the Logos functions as a major title throughout

---

15. This assumes that at 1:14 the Father-Son language anticipates key Johannine titles rather than offering a simple comparison; for further details on the symbolism, see Adesola Joan Akala, The *Son-Father Relationship and Christological Symbolism in the Gospel of John*, LNTS 505 (London: Bloomsbury, 2014), esp. 156–64.

the prologue, we might well assume by implication that it is intrinsic to a thematic study of the Fourth Gospel, recurring regularly throughout the Johannine narrative. The situation, however, is more puzzling and complex. Quite apart from the word "Sophia" never being mentioned, nowhere outside the prologue is Jesus named "Logos." We might well ask whether Logos really is a Johannine theme, let alone a significant one. The prologue may have originally been a hymn of the community which was taken over and adapted by the evangelist, as some have speculated.[16] There is a simpler solution, which is found within the prologue itself. Everything that is captured by the concept of Logos, including its wisdom overtones, is transferred to the "Son" title which recurs with frequency throughout the Fourth Gospel. The prologue itself makes the decisive transference of *logos* to *huios*.[17] Similarly, *theos* now becomes identified with *patēr*, although in a less exclusive sense, since *theos* can also be used of Jesus himself, including within the prologue (1:18; also 20:28). We will see more of how this core symbolism of Father and Son works thematically throughout the Gospel in chapter 7.

THE WORDS OF JESUS

While there is no reference to Jesus as the Word outside the prologue, there is frequent mention of Jesus's "word" or "words" (*logoi*) throughout the Gospel. They are first and foremost Jesus's gift to his disciples from the Father: "I have given them your word" (17:14). More than anything, John's

---

16. For a reconstruction of this hymn's possible original form, see Raymond E. Brown, *The Gospel According to John*, vol. 1, AB 29 (New York: Doubleday, 1966), 1.21–23.

17. For further details on the significance of 1:14, see Dorothy A. Lee, "Creation, Matter and the Image of God in the Gospel of John," *SVTQ* 62 (2018): 101–17.

Gospel speaks of "believing" the words of Jesus. For the evangelist, Jesus's words—his teachings, self-revelation, prayers, insights, and verdicts—are all profoundly substantial: they are reflective of, and lead into, a deeper apprehension of reality and truth. Just as God's word "shall not return to me empty, but . . . shall accomplish that which I purpose" (Isa 55:11), so the word and words of Jesus operate as the same incontrovertible conduit to truth and authentic action: "your word is truth" (17:17). The words of the Johannine Jesus, derived from God, are therefore entirely to be trusted: enough to elicit belief and commitment of life.

For instance, as we will see more fully in chapter 6, the Samaritan villagers believe on the basis of Jesus's word, although the woman is the first to bear witness to Jesus,[18] and discover in him "the Savior of the world" (4:41–42). In the next scene, the royal official responds immediately to Jesus's declaration that his son will live and not die; so convinced is he by Jesus's utterance that he at once turns towards home, confident that Jesus's words are sufficient, even at a distance, to bring healing to his son (4:50). His confidence is entirely justified and leads not only the man himself but his whole household to faith (4:51–53). As part of the "Cana to Cana" cycle (2:1–4:54), this scene parallels the wedding at Cana, where the mother of Jesus exhorts the servants to "do whatever he tells you," exhibiting and evoking the same faith in the word and words of Jesus (2:5).

Discipleship begins and ends with belief in the words of Jesus, a theme we will pursue in chapter 7. So formidable and substantial are these words that they even defeat death, bestowing eternal life (*zōē aiōnios*) both in the present and in

---

18. Robert Gordon Maccini, *Her Testimony Is True: Women as Witnesses According to John*, LNTS 125 (Sheffield: Sheffield Academic, 1996), 131–39.

the future beyond death. Indeed, the passage from death to life has already been traversed (5:24), drawing believers into the eternal life of God. Synonymous language for believing is that of "keeping" or "guarding" Jesus's words: "whoever keeps my word will never see death" (8:51). These verbs are significant because some of those who come to faith fall away precisely because of their failure to "keep," treasure, and hold onto the words; instead, they let them go (e.g., 8:31–33). The power and effectiveness of Jesus's words is thus dependent, not only (though primarily) on Jesus's utterance but also on the persistence in faith of those who hear them.

Jesus's words in the Fourth Gospel are also allied to the words of Scripture, the Old Testament.[19] In a significant narrative comment at the end of the cleansing of the temple, the narrator notes that Jesus's disciples "believed the scripture [*hē graphē*, literally, "the writing"] and the word which Jesus had spoken" (2:22). The Scripture reference is the quotation from Psalm 69:9 (69:10 LXX)—"zeal for your house will consume me" (2:17)—which the Johannine Jesus connects to his resurrection using the image of the temple (2:19). These are the two interpretative keys for understanding the cleansing in its Johannine setting, and both keys are given equivalent status. The words of Scripture and the words of Jesus function as parallels, so that to believe the one is to believe the other.

In the same way, the events of Jesus's death and resurrection operate to fulfil the words of Scripture and revelation, a theme we will examine in chapter 8. This fulfilment includes the betrayal of Judas (13:18), the hostility against Jesus (15:18), his capacity to hold together the community of his disciples in all the disarray of his arrest (17:12; 18:9),

---

19. Rekha M. Chennattu, "Scripture," in *How John Works: Storytelling in the Fourth Gospel*, ed. Douglas Estes and Ruth Sheridan (Atlanta: SBL, 2016), 181–85.

60 John

the division of his clothes by the soldiers (19:24), his final thirst (19:28), his unbroken yet pierced body on the cross (19:36–37), and his resurrection from the dead (20:9). Each situation of fulfilment stresses Jesus's obedience throughout: nothing happens outside the divine will, a will to which he gives his wholehearted acquiescence.

Jesus's words in this Gospel include his commands or commandments (*entolē*). The primary focus of the command is love: to love the word of Jesus itself and thereby to enter into the Father's love (14:23). Love is to be the center of the disciples' relationship to one another; this love is grounded in Jesus's own love "to the end" (13:1): "I give you a new commandment, that you love one another" (13:34). In one sense there is nothing new about the command to love others; it is present already in the Torah (Lev 19:18; Deut 10:19). What is "new" is the way in which Jesus fulfills that command through his life and death: "as I have loved you." This word of love binds the community together, both vertically and horizontally. It works as a sign to people in the unbelieving world: disclosing in word and deed a sense of the living, loving presence of God in their midst.[20]

It would be a mistake to conclude from such statements that John's Gospel has no ethics outside the solitary love command, as noted in the second chapter of this study. It is true that love is the central command of this Gospel and the core ethical injunction of Jesus, just as it is the divine motivation behind the incarnation and the cross (3:16–17), a life-giving rather than death-dealing word. John portrays ethics not only in the words of Jesus but also in the actions of the Gospel, which themselves demonstrate its moral and spiritual

---

20. See Francis J. Moloney, *Love in the Gospel of John: An Exegetical, Theological, and Literary Study* (Grand Rapids: Baker Academic, 2013).

values, including that of enemy-love.[21] This ethic involves love but cannot simply be reduced to love within the community. Thus, the authorities' ill-treatment of Jesus himself—in the various attempts to stone him, discredit him, and plot against him (8:59; 10:39; 11:47–53)—reveals the oppression and injustice that is the very opposite of Johannine life-giving ethics. The same is true for the authorities' treatment of the man born blind (9:24–34), which Jesus condemns in the ensuing parable of the sheepfold (10:1–18). In these and other instances, John's Gospel implicitly condemns all that is encapsulated by death, darkness, and untruth. Indeed, Jesus's words can even be depicted as cleansing: capable of making whole and bringing about forgiveness and reconciliation (15:3; 20:23) as well as joy (15:11). Disciples are to "bear fruit" in ethical living and loving relationships with those around them (15:8).[22]

One of the key images that describes this persistent keeping or guarding of Jesus's word is abiding. This is an intrinsic component of discipleship. Here, the link between Jesus as the Logos and the *logoi* of Jesus becomes explicit. To abide in Jesus's words (5:38; 8:31; 15:7) is the same as abiding in Jesus himself and in his love (15:1–9). Here, notions of abiding, obeying, and holding belong together in a relationship of love. Through abiding, disciples are transformed to become friends (*philoi*) of God rather than slaves (*douloi*, 15:12–17). As we will see in chapter 7, disciples belong within the household of God as treasured and beloved children. Therefore, to abide in Jesus's word means to make one's home in him, find

---

21. Michael J. Gorman, *Abide and Go: Missional Theosis in the Gospel of John*, Didsbury Lectures (Eugene, OR: Cascade, 2018), 156–78.

22. See the collection of essays on John's ethics in *Johannine Ethics: The Moral World of the Gospel and Epistles of John*, ed. Sherri Brown and Christopher W. Skinner (Minneapolis: Fortress, 2017).

a center there, rest, and discover the trust which overcomes anxiety and fear. Once again, this abiding or indwelling is mutual. Jesus abides in his disciples as they abide in him (6:56), and he and the Father abide in one another (15:9). Indeed, the Father himself, who has "abiding-places" for believers, makes an abode of love within and among the disciples (*monē*, 14:2, 23). The Spirit-Paraclete is also caught up in the circle of abiding (14:17) and will remind the disciples of the life-giving words of Jesus (14:26).[23]

HOSPITABLE WISDOM

The emphasis on Jesus's life-giving words throughout the Gospel connects to and extends the original title of Logos in the prologue. But the use of wisdom imagery also appears, particularly in contexts that relate to the nurturing gifts of the Johannine Jesus. Here Jesus plays the role of Sophia, with imagery drawn from the wider Old Testament where Wisdom is the host who offers lavish hospitality to those in need: wine for celebration, water for thirst, and bread and fish for hunger.[24]

Several narratives portray this sense of Jesus as divine Wisdom in the role of providing hospitality. The first is the wedding at Cana where Jesus, with seeming initial reluctance, enables the marriage celebration to continue unabated— indeed enhanced—by the quantity and quality of the wine he creates from the stone water jars (2:1–11). This sign is an

---

23. For further details on this motif in John, see Dorothy A. Lee, "Abiding in the Fourth Gospel: A Case Study in Feminist Biblical Theology," in *A Feminist Companion to John*, ed. Amy-Jill Levine, vol. 2, FCNTECW 5 (London: Sheffield Academic, 2003), 64–78.

24. See, e.g., Prov 9:1–6; Sir 15:3; 24:19–21. For further details on this theme, see Judith E. McKinlay, *Gendering Wisdom the Host: Biblical Invitations to Eat and Drink*, JSOTSS 216 (Sheffield: Sheffield Academic, 1996), 38–65; 133–59.

Word and Wisdom 63

act of self-revelation for John, not primarily about Jesus's power over nature but revealing who he is as the divinely human Son (2:11). Jesus shows the same hospitality to the Samaritan woman in his lively dialogue with her: he offers her a quality of water, a form of wisdom, that transcends both the still water of the well and the sacred place of worship (4:7–23). Slowly she comes to recognize both the giver and gift, leading her to evangelize her fellow villagers (4:28–30). The hospitality she receives from Jesus she also shares with others. Here, Jesus is not said to *be* the water of life in this narrative but rather the *giver* of the life-giving flow which, as John will later explain, is in fact the Holy Spirit (7:39). One of the aspects that the Samaritan woman has to grasp is Jesus's identity as the true water-giver—giver of divine wisdom and Spirit—shifting the focus from herself as water-giver to Jesus.

The same is true of the Bread of Life narrative (John 6). Even more explicitly Jesus acts as Holy Wisdom, feeding the 5,000 at the beginning (6:1–15), then, in the subsequent dialogue, revealing himself as the true Bread from heaven, the fulfillment of the manna in the wilderness (6:35, 48, 51). As with the words of the Word, so with the wisdom of Wisdom. In the end, in language that recalls the Eucharist, Jesus is disclosed as Sophia: the giver and the gift, the host at the table, and the food and drink that is served (6:51–58).[25] This giving takes place fundamentally in and through Jesus's death (6:51), so that the wine as well as the bread becomes symbolic of the cross and the paradoxical life Jesus bestows through his self-giving life and death (6:53–56).[26]

---

25. On the sapiential theme running through Jesus's discourse in 6:25–59, see Coloe, *John 1–10*, 168–85.

26. Not all commentators agree that 6:51–58 is eucharistic; for an historical summary of commentators' views over the centuries, see Frederick Dale Bruner, *The Gospel of John: A Commentary* (Grand Rapids: Eerdmans, 2012), 437–43.

64   John

The same picture of Jesus as hospitable host is present in the second part of the resurrection story, where Jesus—in actions that recall the feeding story—feeds the small band of disciples with bread and fish (21:9–14) following the miraculous catch of fish, itself a symbol of mission (21:1–8). This is the basis on which Jesus rehabilitates Simon Peter and commissions him for his mission (21:15–19); the beloved disciple is also in a sense commissioned for the role of witness as the "author" of the Gospel (21:20–24). Hospitality and mission go hand in hand in this Gospel. The Wisdom who feeds and nurtures through word and sacrament is also the Word who forgives and commissions: both are reflections of the Son who is sent from the Father to give life to the world.[27]

REFLECTIONS FOR TODAY

Ancient society was not alone in its search for wisdom: it longed for a word to make sense of created existence, giving it purpose and direction and making a vital connection to a transcendent reality. There is something intrinsically human about such a desire, and it manifests itself in different ways in various cultural settings and contexts. At its core, however, the human spirit in most cultures has evinced a similar longing to locate itself in relationship to the mystery that lies at the heart of all reality.

In the contemporary Western setting, there are a number of significant differences to the world which the Fourth Gospel is addressing. The search for meaningful wisdom is much more individually focused than in the ancient world, which revolved primarily around kinship and community as conveyors of meaning and identity. Furthermore, ancient

---

27. See Gorman, *Abide and Go*, 147–52.

society was implicitly religious—though "religion" is too unhelpful and specific a conception for something that affected every aspect of life and was every bit as communal and political as it was spiritual—whereas religion in the Western world tends to be seen as personal and private.[28]

However, these differences between two worlds need not rule out a vivid sense of connection between the message of John and the modern believer. The two horizons can and do merge for the reader of the Gospel today. Awareness of the differences can warn against interpreting the Gospel in an individualistic and overspiritualized way that sees religious faith as a private matter with no consequences for community and society. John's worldview challenges us as persons who live in relationship with others and with creation; it challenges us in ways that are material as well as spiritual.

John's core message through the conjoint themes of word and wisdom is that true meaning and right living are to be found first and foremost in relation to Jesus. He is the one who creates and confers value in living, who embodies and teaches wisdom, and who speaks the one word of life which human beings long to hear, no matter how difficult it may be to locate or articulate. God, who is manifest in Jesus, is both the giver and the gift itself: the origin and source of meaning and value, their center and their final goal. In one sense, this word is but a continuation of the creative and prophetic word of God in the Old Testament. In another sense, Jesus brings the past to fulfillment, creating something new and fresh from the structures and forms of the old, just as he makes wine from the stone water jars of Jewish purification. God's word continues to create and form, challenge, and bless. But

---

28. On the values of the ancient world apparent in John's Gospel, see Jerome H. Neyrey, *The Gospel of John*, NCBC (Cambridge, UK: Cambridge University Press, 2007), esp. 15–27.

it comes now in mortal form, wearing a human face, becoming part of the very fabric of creation.

In Johannine terms, to love wisdom with all one's being and in humility and openness of heart inevitably leads to Jesus, who embodies divine wisdom and whose profound humility in the incarnation—in taking on mortal flesh and dying on the cross—reaches into the depths of human experience in its hope and longing. It is not hard to imagine how a person like Socrates can be admired due to his own apprehension of wisdom and the humility which accompanied it. The church's evangelism is precisely to portray wisdom in its beauty, mystery, and answer to human longing, inspiring faith in those to whom it is proclaimed.

Yet it would be a mistake to confuse the Word with wordiness and a verbosity that can all too easily obscure the substantial word and its sublime wisdom. Silence is as necessary a part of speech as the different kinds of rest are in musical composition. Music, like speech, is made up of sound and silence as well as movement and stillness. The word of wisdom is like a stone dropped into a still lake, creating ripples that reach the shore. Loquaciousness is the rough wind stirring up the smoothness of the lake, making the dropped stone's effect imperceptible.

The poet T. S. Eliot speaks of the word that is unable to speak because of the absence of silence: "Where shall the word be found, where will the word / Resound? Not here, there is not enough silence."[29] One of the characteristics of our culture is precisely its lack of silence: there is constant noise and endless stimulation of one kind or another. People can live for whole days without a moment's silence:

---

29. T. S. Eliot, "Ash Wednesday," part V, in *The Complete Poems and Plays of T. S. Eliot* (London: Faber & Faber, 1969), 96.

there is no escape from the endless chatter of social media, radio, television, and conversation. C. S. Lewis, for instance, speaks of the grand "Noise" which is a demonic achievement to shut out "the melodies and silences of Heaven," designed to draw people away from critical moments of thoughtful silence and reflection.[30]

The Johannine words which convey Jesus need to be sounded into places of silence and contemplation, into reflective minds and thoughtful spirits. But, above all else, the words of this Gospel need to be uttered with wisdom: with brevity, percipience, and insight and, correspondingly, without coercion, compulsion, or manipulation. The way in which the word is spoken is as significant as the syllables themselves: it is part and parcel of that wisdom which Jesus both conveys and epitomizes. Not the least part of this wisdom is the need for word and silence to go hand in hand, just as word and action do—cooperating together to project an authentic image of Jesus's divinely human plenitude: his grace, truth, and beauty as the incarnate Word and Wisdom of God.

FURTHER READING

Chennattu, Rekha M. "Scripture." In *How John Works: Storytelling in the Fourth Gospel*, edited by Douglas Estes and Ruth Sheridan, 171–203. Atlanta: SBL, 2016.

Coloe, Mary L. *John*. 2 vols. WC 44A, 44B. Collegeville, MN: Liturgical, 2021.

Koester, Craig R. *The Word of Life: A Theology of John's Gospel*. Grand Rapids: Eerdmans, 2008.

Ringe, Sharon H. *Wisdom's Friends: Community and Christology in the Fourth Gospel*. Louisville, KY: Westminster John Knox, 1999.

Witherington, Ben, III. *John's Wisdom: A Commentary on the Fourth Gospel*. Cambridge, UK: Lutterworth, 1995.

---

30. C. S. Lewis, *The Screwtape Letters* (London: HarperCollins, 1942), 119–20.

CHAPTER 4

Life and Light

In him was life and the life was the light of human beings.
(1:4)

Light and life, the next in our series of pairings arising from the prologue, are dominant themes throughout the Fourth Gospel. Strictly speaking, the second of these, life, is a theme while the first, light, is a symbol, but the two are closely allied, the one pointing directly to the other. They make their united appearance early in the prologue and recur throughout the Johannine narrative. Both are associated with significant "I am" sayings in the Gospel (8:12; 11:25–26). While similar thematic imagery is to be found in the Synoptic Gospels (e.g., Mark 8:22–25; 10:46–52), it is not apparent to the same extent as in the Gospel of John. Typical of Johannine dualism, which is both moral and spiritual, light and life are often portrayed in relation to their opposites, darkness and death.[1] Along with their negative counterparts, they are associated also with opposing symbols of blindness and sight. This connection becomes particularly apparent in the story of the man born blind (John 9), where light and

---

1. On John's dualism, see Jörg Frey, "Dualism and the World in the Gospel and Letters of John," in *The Oxford Handbook of Johannine Studies*, ed. Judith M. Lieu and Martinus C. de Boer (Oxford: Oxford University Press, 2018), 274–91.

Life and Light

darkness along with blindness and sight are skillfully interwoven as interconnected symbols of life and death as well as vindication and judgement.

BACKGROUND IN JEWISH AND GRECO-ROMAN THOUGHT

Light and life have their origins in the Old Testament right from its opening page.[2] The first words God utters in forming the world in Genesis 1:3 are "Let there be light," and the initial act of creation is the emergence of light from primeval darkness and void. The whole panoply of life then appears, day after day: the sky (day 2); the land with its vegetation (day 3); the sun, moon, and stars (day 4); marine life and birds (day 5); animals and human beings (day 6); and, finally, the Sabbath (day 7). Light is the first manifestation of life and becomes a core symbol of life in its most fundamental, material sense. God is the source of all that lives and breathes, all that grows and changes, all that thinks and feels, and all that has needs and seeks rest. This is the message of the first creation account in Genesis 1. The advent of sin, narrated in Genesis 2–3, is not part of God's creating and turns the divinely given life, light, beauty, and rest into death, darkness, ugliness, and struggle. However, behind the Old Testament stands God's continuing care for creation, even with human sinfulness, sustaining it providentially from one generation to another and responsible for its growth and flourishing along with its sunshine and rainfall. The same bestowal and sustaining of light and life are evident also in the covenant with God's chosen people, Israel.

---

2. On the God of life in John's Gospel and its relationship to Genesis, see Craig R. Koester, *The Word of Life: A Theology of John's Gospel* (Grand Rapids: Eerdmans, 2008), 30–32 (25–52).

70   John

Light as the summation and representation of the gift of life is understood metaphorically within the Old Testament. In the wanderings through the desert, which represents the movement from death to life, the people of God are guided by a pillar of cloud in the day and a pillar of fire by night (Exod 13:21–22), both representing the light of God's guidance and presence, drawing the children of Israel out of slavery into freedom and life. Light is a symbol of salvation itself, giving security and protection in the gift of life: "the LORD is my light and my salvation" begins Psalm 27. In Psalm 36:9 the link between light and life is direct: "with you is the fountain of life; in your light we see light."

In Judaism, the feast of Hanukkah is particularly associated with light and is often called "the Festival of Lights." It celebrates the rededication of the temple in 165 BCE following the oppression of the Jewish people under the Seleucid king Antiochus IV as well as the rediscovery of life following persecution. The successful rebellion of Judas Maccabeus led to the overthrow of the Syrian oppressors and the establishment of Jewish self-rule.[3] In particular, this victory was celebrated by the dedication of the new altar and the lighting of the great candelabra (*menorah*) in the temple. The tradition arose that there was only enough sacred oil for one day, yet the candles burned undiminished for eight days. Although not an Old Testament feast, Hanukkah became popular and much loved within Judaism, and was linked to the biblical Feast of Tabernacles with its similar emphasis on light and life.[4]

The Old Testament sees God as the source of all life and its providential sustainer, as revealed primarily in the

---

3. For the story, see 1 Maccabees in the Apocryphal/Deuterocanonical Books of the Old Testament.

4. See Gale Yee, *Jewish Feasts and the Gospel of John* (Eugene, OR: Wipf & Stock, 2007), 70–92.

symbolism of light. Yet the notion of life beyond death is slower to develop in Old Testament theology. The dead depart to Sheol and to a shadowy half-life, and there is no developed notion of the soul (e.g., Ps 6:5; Eccl 3:19–21). In later Jewish thinking the idea of resurrection emerges,[5] along with that of the immortality of the soul (Dan 12:2; Wis 3:1–9). Yet these later influences do not represent a huge leap from earlier Israelite theology since God is already depicted as the source of life and renewal, in and beyond mortal life.[6]

Light as a core symbol of life is also widespread in Greco-Roman mythology and philosophy. In Greek literature—for example, Homer's *Iliad* and *Odyssey*—the immortal gods on Mount Olympus dwell in perpetual sunlight, without rain or snow or darkness. Though they are portrayed with human qualities (negative as well as positive) and intervene regularly in human affairs, they share a sublime and endless life. Light signifies the bliss in which they live their lives and the immortality which they share—and it is also manifest in their frequent epiphanies to human beings. In the Homeric epics, light is "identified with the stability and the eternity of the divine world, their secure and tranquil life."[7]

Most famous in the ancient world is Plato's allegory of the cave in his *Republic*, one of the most famous of the Socratic dialogues (c. 375 BCE).[8] The analogy depicts

---

5. For a survey, see Robert Martin-Achard, *From Death to Life: A Study of the Development of the Doctrine of the Resurrection in the Old Testament* (Edinburgh: Oliver & Boyd, 1960).

6. See Dorothy A. Lee, *Flesh and Glory: Symbolism, Gender and Theology in the Gospel of John* (New York: Crossroad, 2002), 213–15.

7. Soteroula Constantinidou, "The Light Imagery of Divine Manifestation in Homer," in *Light and Darkness in Ancient Greek Myth and Religion*, ed. Menelaos Christopoulos, Efimia D. Karakantza, and Olga Levaniouk (Lanham, MD: Lexington, 2010), 91–92.

8. Plato, *Republic, Books 6–10*, ed. and trans. Chris Emlyn-Jones and William Preddy, LCL 276 (Cambridge, MA: Harvard University Press, 2013), VII.514a–518b.

human beings like chained prisoners, in a cave facing a blank wall. They cannot turn their heads. Behind them is a fire and in between the fire and them are puppets on a parapet whose movements cast shadows on the wall through filtered light. These shadows are the prisoners' only access to life. The philosopher, however, can break free of the shadowy realm, turning to see the real objects behind. This allegory reflects Plato's belief that if we remain unenlightened we cannot access reality through the sensory world but can only perceive its shadows. Access to light—to the true Forms and therefore to true life—can only come to those prepared to use reason to reach a vision of reality beyond the senses and the everyday.

Several specific deities are also linked to light in the ancient world. Back in the fourteenth century BCE, the Egyptian pharaoh Akhenaten transformed Egyptian religion to an exclusive focus on the sun god, Aten, as an early form of something like monotheism. While his novel theology did not last and was reversed by his son, Tutankhamen, his attempt to move beyond polytheism indicates an impulse to monotheism even in pagan contexts.[9] In the historical context of the Fourth Gospel, the cult of the Egyptian goddess Isis also became widely popular across the Greco-Roman world. In Apuleius's novel *Metamorphoses* [aka, *The Golden Ass*], written most likely in the second century CE, Isis is depicted as containing the fullness of deity, as mistress of the universe, and as the source of all life in heaven, on earth, and in the underworld. Her miraculous appearance at the end of the novel to bring salvation to its leading character is associated

---

9. Donald B. Redford, "The Monotheism of Akhenaten," *Bible Odyssey*, accessed October 16, 2024, https://www.bibleodyssey.org/places/related-articles/the-monotheism-of-akhenaten/.

with images of light—sun, moon, and stars—which signify her divine power and radiance.[10]

Related images of blindness and sight are also common in the ancient world. In the Old Testament, those who are blind, on the one hand, do not have entry into the temple because of their disability (Lev 21:18–19) and blind or disfigured animals are not to be brought to the temple for sacrifice (Mal 1:8). On the other hand, people who are blind are to be cared for and not impeded in any way in their movements or travels (Lev 19:14), and God will restore their sight in the final redemption of Israel (Ps 146:8; Is 29:18, 35:5; Jer 31:8). Blindness and sight are also metaphors for evil and goodness, and spiritual malaise and covenant living (Deut 28:29; Isa 29:9; 42:16; Lam 4:14).

Various forms of sight impairment are common in the Greco-Roman world. Such disability might even lead, in some cases, to poverty and beggardom, though blind people were not otherwise segregated. Of particular interest is the cult of Asklepios, the god of medicine (usually depicted with a staff on which a serpent coils), who was originally a Greek deity and whose cult became popular in Rome.[11] The center of his cult was the city of Epidauros in Greece. There are stories from the ancient world of blind people being taken there and sleeping in the temple of the god, who then appears to them in dreams with healing power, restoring their sight. Epidauros was thus a place of pilgrimage for many people with disabilities, including that of blindness.

A twist on the theme of blindness and sight in the ancient world is the tradition of great blind poets such as Homer.

---

10. Apuleius, *Metamorphoses (The Golden Ass)*, ed. and trans. J. Arthur Hanson, vol. 2, LCL 453 (Cambridge, MA: Harvard University Press, 1989), XI.1–4.

11. "Asklepios," *Theoi Project*, accessed October 16, 2024, https://www.theoi .com/Ouranios/Asklepios.html.

Here blindness works metaphorically to describe those who may lack physical sight but instead possess a more intense degree of inner sight—insight—along with wisdom and imagination. This imagery represents an ironical overturning of the common view in the ancient world that good health, including sight, was closely tied to moral character.

The widespread theory of vision in the ancient world was that it occurred through "extramission"—that is, by beams of light from the eyes emitted onto various external objects (e.g., Plato; see also Matt 6:22–23). This theory, of course, did not explain why people could not see in the dark. At the same time, though less commonly, some held to theories of "intromission"—that is, that vision was caused by the rays of the sun moving in a straight line and penetrating the eyes (e.g., the Epicurean philosopher Lucretius). This theory was not scientifically validated till some centuries later. The theory of extramission might explain something of the prominence that sight has in the ancient world and its metaphorical importance in literary and philosophical writing, including in the Gospel of John.[12]

LIGHT AND LIFE IN JOHN'S NARRATIVE

The theme of life (*zōē*) is dominant across the Gospel of John.[13] There is hardly a text or a passage that does not either contain or imply this theme and it is markedly present in key passages that reach the heart of Johannine theology. In some ways, this theme parallels imagery of the kingdom or reign

---

12. See Dorothy A. Lee, "The Gospel of John and the Five Senses," *JBL* 129 (2010): 117–20.

13. For a succinct overview of John's understanding of life, see Marianne Meye Thompson, *John: A Commentary*, NTL (Louisville, KY: Westminster John Knox, 2015), 87–91.

Life and Light

(*basileia*) of God in the Synoptic Gospels and even in some sense the idea of the "good news" (*euangelion, euangelizomai*), yet it is a broader concept that stretches across time from beginning to end. As a major theme, it wends its way through narrative and discourse, sign and miracle, and teaching and dialogue in the Fourth Gospel. Just as the kingdom or reign of God is the driving force of Jesus's ministry in the Synoptic Gospels and the inner meaning of the passion story, so the theme of life has a parallel role in the Fourth Gospel.

It is true that *basileia* (kingdom) is found in John's Gospel (unlike *euangelion*, "good news"), but it is only there in two limited and specific places, whereas *zōē* (life) is ubiquitous. In the first context, in Jesus's dialogue with Nicodemus, the idea of the kingdom refers to seeing and entering into eternal life and is synonymous with it (3:3, 5). In the second context, the trial before Pilate—and in spite of the majority of recent English translations—*basileia* is probably better translated as "kingship" rather than "kingdom" (as in the RSV, 18:36).[14] The issue of contention in this scene of the trial is precisely that of Jesus's identity as king (18:33, 37).

The major theme of life is closely allied to the core symbol of light (*phōs*), which is expanded in a number of Johannine narratives.[15] It is one of the seven metaphorical "I am" sayings of the Gospel (8:12; 9:5), as we saw in chapter 1. These go alongside the absolute "I am" sayings, where Jesus speaks of himself as "I am the one" without a metaphor (4:26: 8:24, 28, 58; 13:19; 18:5, 8). These crucial sayings capture something of the identity and saving purpose of the Johannine Jesus in his

---

14. See, e.g., Francis J. Moloney, *The Gospel of John*, SP (Collegeville, MN: Liturgical, 1998), 492–98.

15. On light as one of the three core impersonal symbols in John, see R. Alan Culpepper, *Anatomy of the Fourth Gospel: A Study in Literary Design* (Philadelphia: Fortress, 1983), 189–92. See also Craig R. Koester, *Symbolism in the Fourth Gospel: Meaning, Mystery, Community*, 2nd ed. (Minneapolis: Fortress, 2003), 123–54.

relationship to God as well as the consequences of believing.[16] Both concepts, life and light, are set in polar opposition to death and darkness, which in most cases stand for all that is inimical to God, all that is ungodly and unethical, and all that is ultimately harmful and destructive of created life.[17]

PROLOGUE

In the prologue, life begins in creation itself. As we saw in chapter 3, the Word (*logos*), who is in communion with God and identified as God (1:1–2), is the source of all that exists. Life, therefore, has its origin in the divine Word, from which it will also find its goal. John's opening is a reflection on Genesis 1 ("in the beginning"), where light is the first element created, the primary manifestation of life (Gen 1:3). Crafted before the sun, moon, and stars (Day 4, Gen 1:14–19), light is formed by God who organizes the creation from chaos, dividing light from darkness to generate Day 1. In all this, John makes a distinction between the realms of "being" and "becoming," as we have already discussed: whereas the Word belongs in the domain of "being," "becoming" describes the arena of creation. All that exists has "become" and is thus utterly dependent on "being"—that which *is*—to grant and sustain its flourishing and its lifespan.

This intertextual reading of the first creation account in Genesis (1:1–2:4a) has significant implications for reading John's Gospel, which is grounded, first and last, in a theology of creation. The evangelist's understanding of salvation is

---

16. On the "I am" sayings of the Gospel and their likely background in Deutero-Isaiah (Isa 40:4; 43:10; 46:4), see Catrin H. Williams, *I am He: The Interpretation of 'ANI HU' in Jewish and Early Christian Literature*, WUNT 113 (Tübingen: Mohr Siebeck, 2000), 255–303.

17. On sin and evil in John and its accompanying symbolism of darkness, see Lee, *Flesh and Glory*, 166–96.

built on creation, is a restoration of creation, and therefore by implication incorporates creation in its scope. Soon enough in the Gospel, John will begin to speak of "life eternal" (*zōē aiōnios*, 3:15–16), but the vital link to creation is never lost. The one who created the world redeems it; that which is created by the Word is also redeemed by the Word.

Augustine understands the point well. He sets alongside the miracle of water into wine at Cana the "miracle" of rain falling to water the earth, enabling the grapes to grow, which then become wine. He also parallels the miracle of the raising of Lazarus from the dead with the "miracle" of human beings created by the divine Word: babies emerge from the darkness of the womb each day.[18] The same life-giving God is at work in both instances, faithful to the creation from beginning to end.

While the opening verses of the prologue are in dialogue with Genesis 1 in the emergence of life from primeval chaos, a change then takes place in the basic imagery. Light and darkness are no longer just created phenomena, as we saw in chapter 3, but at 1:5 take on a sudden new and symbolic meaning. They are now at war: "And the light shines on in the darkness, and the darkness did not *grasp* it (*katelaben*)." The verb in the second clause is significant at this point because it has a double meaning (a typical feature of John's style). On the one hand, it means "understood," as in the KJV's translation: "comprehended it not." On the other hand, it can mean "overpower," "overcome," or "extinguish," as in most modern English translations: the NRSVue has "overtake," the ESV and NIV have "overcome," the RNJB "overpower," the REB "master," and the CEB "extinguish." Both meanings are

---

18. Augustine, *Tractates on the Gospel of John* 8:1 (https://www.newadvent.org/fathers/1701008.htm) and 49:1 (https://www.newadvent.org/fathers/1701049.htm).

78 John

present: the darkness has neither understood nor succeeded in overpowering the light.

SIGNS: RESTORATION OF LIFE

The first half of the Gospel offers examples of life as healing and restoration. The signs and works of Jesus's ministry are examples of the gift of life over all the forces of diminishment and death. The "Cana to Cana" cycle of stories (2:1–4:54) is bookended by two corresponding narratives of restoration, both occurring in the same location.[19] They commence and conclude a circular journey that takes Jesus down to Jerusalem where he "cleanses" the temple and meets with Nicodemus (2:13–3:21). From there he goes to the Jordan and we again encounter John the Baptist (3:22–36). Finally, Jesus returns to Galilee and Cana through Samaria (the shorter but less popular route for Galilean pilgrims), where he meets a Samaritan woman and her fellow villagers (4:1–42).

The first of these signs is the miraculous provision of wine at a wedding (2:1–12). The intervention of Jesus's mother draws his attention to the social disaster about to unfold: the lack of wine and the potentially abrupt and shameful ending to the festivities (2:3). Jesus appears at first to cavil at her implicit request and strives to distance both himself and her from the problem ("What is that to you and to me?" 2:4a). He also seems to ignore her undaunted and portentous instructions to the waiters (2:5), but appearances in this Gospel can be deceiving. Instead, John nudges the reader to anticipate the passion when the "hour" will fully and finally come—the "hour" of Jesus's self-revelation on the cross (2:4b; see 12:23;

---

19. Francis J. Moloney, "From Cana to Cana (John 2:1–4:54) and the Fourth Evangelist's Concept of Correct (and Incorrect) Faith," in *Johannine Studies 1975–2017*, WUNT 372 (Tübingen: Mohr Siebeck, 2017), 331–53.

Life and Light

13:1)—while Jesus instructs the waiters to fill with water the stone jars set aside for Jewish purification rites. Water itself is a symbol of life in this Gospel. In changing the water into wine, Jesus not only rescues the host families from shame and loss of face within the community but enables the joyful celebrations to continue unabated.

This, the first sign, is paralleled by the second: the healing of a royal official's son, which also takes place at Cana. From a significant geographical distance (from Cana to Capernaum, about 40 kilometres or 25 miles), Jesus restores the life of a sick child, rescuing the boy from death and his father—most likely a Gentile—from an ocean of grief and loss (4:46–54). In both Cana incidents, the capacity of the Johannine Jesus to give and restore life, in both its literal and metaphorical senses, is not limited by geographical distance or by things outside normal human control. At Jesus's life-giving word, water can change its form to become a superior quality of wine to bless a marriage celebration and mortal illness can give way to unexpected and unprecedented wholeness and healing. In both cases, the gracious bestowal of life brings joy—joy in the face of shame and tragedy—into the ordinary cycles of human life. The word of Jesus has the same dynamic power as the divine word in Genesis 1 which creates and sustains the universe.

The connection between light and life has already emerged in the dialogue with Nicodemus, but the conversation continues after he has receded from the narrative (3:10). Jesus goes on to addresses an unknown group in the plural ("you"), who are most likely represented by Nicodemus.[20]

---

20. In addition, according to Andrew T. Lincoln, "both Jesus and Nicodemus are representative figures, with the former in solidarity with the post-resurrection perspective of the believing community and the latter standing for sympathetic Jews within the synagogue" (*The Gospel According to Saint John*, BNTC [Peabody, MA: Hendrickson, 2005], 148).

The most famous verse from John's Gospel (3:16) occurs in this context, but it is sometimes misunderstood. The background is the exodus and the rebellion of God's people, who are punished by venomous snakes; to save them, God instructs Moses to set up a bronze image of a serpent on a pole so that those seeing it may live and not die (Num 21). Here Jesus is pictured as the serpent lifted up on the cross so that all who gaze on him may find life (3:14; 12:32). God's giving of Jesus is a giving into both incarnation and death: into mortality. The focus here is not so much on the greatness of the divine love but rather on the *way* in which God loves the world: literally "for God loved the world *in this way* . . ." Furthermore, the following verse (3:17), rarely quoted with 3:16, makes clear that God's desire is not for condemnation (death) but rather for the gracious giving of life through Jesus.[21]

By the end of this section, the imagery of birth in the opening verses of the dialogue has folded over naturally into that of light and life (3:19–21). Birth, after all, is about the entry into light after the darkness of the womb. But judgement is also a feature of light, and it operates in an intricate way. God's lack of desire to condemn puts the onus back onto human beings, who engage in a kind of self-judgement by the choices they make and the actions of their lives. The light, therefore, both illuminates and also critically exposes: it brings onto center stage both good and evil, revealing the beauty of the one and the ugliness of the other. It also reveals God as the origin of all goodness and light, and therefore as the source of life to which all are summoned but from which some will shrink. The concluding verse in the first half of the Gospel finds Jesus speaking again of light and judgement,

---

21. Brendan Byrne, *Life Abounding: A Reading of John's Gospel* (Collegeville, MN: Liturgical, 2014), 69–70.

warning of the danger of ending up in the darkness, and finally hiding his light from the public gaze (12:31, 35–36).

The same is true for the story of the disabled man at the pool (John 5), with its focus on disability and the fact that the healing takes places on a Sabbath. Jesus bestows life on one whose life is threatened and diminished by suffering, disability, and poverty. This identification coheres with the prologue, where the word is the source of all created life. In the narrative, the Johannine Jesus has possession over life itself. He can heal on the Sabbath because he possesses divine exemption in relation to the Sabbath. God's ongoing work in creation and providence continues even on the Sabbath, including that of giving life to newborns and judging the dead. Jesus has the power of life in himself, a power that is conferred on him by the Father, who is the ultimate source of life. Thus, Jesus as Son has authority over life and death, to give life and to make judgement on behalf of God (5:21–23).

BLINDNESS AND SIGHT

A further symbolic pairing that is closely connected to light and darkness in John's Gospel is that of blindness and sight. These symbols function at both a literal and metaphorical level. The story of the man born blind exemplifies the theme of Jesus's authority to give life, even on the Sabbath, linking this story to the core symbolism of light and darkness, and blindness and sight, with which it is closely allied (John 9). The story has much in common with the previous healing of disability in John 5. In this context, however, darkness takes on a more nuanced meaning in the Gospel.

Two feasts enclose this story on either side, which are part of the loose thematic section focussing on the feasts and festivals of the Jewish faith (John 5–10). On the one

82   John

hand, it follows the Tabernacles narrative (John 7:1–52; 8:12–59) and employs the two core images of water and light that are intrinsic to the festival. At the same time, it leads into the parable of the sheepfold (10:1–21), which is partly a commentary on the healing narrative and takes place at the Feast of the Dedication (Hanukkah), a feast that also commemorates light.

Strictly speaking, the man himself is not *healed* of blindness because, being blind from birth, he has never possessed sight.[22] As the Light of the world (8:12; 9:5), Jesus creates his sight from nothing, *ex nihilo*, acting as the divine Word through whom "all things were made" (1:3).[23] As a consequence, the man is given access to light for the first time in his life and can emerge from the darkness—in the process also escaping a life of poverty and beggardom, which are the consequences of his disability. In this case, the darkness of the man's physical disability is differentiated from the darkness of sin, which becomes embodied in the authorities due to their rejection of the man himself and Jesus. Both the man and Jesus are vindicated of sin while the authorities, in their presumption of illumination and sight, show themselves to be cloaked in darkness (9:39–41).

The symbolism of blindness works in a unique way in this narrative.[24] There are two kinds of blindness: the blindness of ignorance and the blindness of willful rejection. The

---

22. Joel C. Elowsky, ed., *John 1-10*, ACCS NT IVa (Downers Grove: IVP Academic, 2006), 319.

23. David F. Ford (*The Gospel of John: A Theological Commentary* [Grand Rapids: Baker Academic, 2021], 180–81) sees a parallel in this "I am" saying to the Synoptic story of the transfiguration (Mark 9:2–9/pars.); see Dorothy A. Lee, *Transfiguration* (London: Continuum, 2005), 100–111.

24. On the way in which the symbolism unfolds in this narrative, moving from the material to the spiritual level, see Dorothy A. Lee, *The Symbolic Narratives of the Fourth Gospel: The Interplay of Form and Meaning*, LNTS 95 (Sheffield: Sheffield Academic, 1994), 161–87.

Life and Light

man himself exemplifies the first; he is exempt from sin as the cause of his disability (as a foetus!) as are also his parents (9:3). The authorities, on the contrary, have chosen willful blindness, the blindness which comes from knowingly rejecting the light and therefore choosing to embrace death over life. They choose death not only for themselves but also for the man in their cruel exclusion of him (9:34), and they ultimately set Jesus on the path to death in their treatment of him.

RESURRECTION AND LIFE

The themes of light and life reach a climax in the raising of Lazarus from the dead, an event that occurs four days after his burial, indicating that Lazarus is beyond all mortal reach of recovery. In the "I am" saying at the heart of this story, as revealed to Martha (11:25–26), Jesus speaks of life not only as a gift he confers but also as lying at the core of his identity. As the divine Son of the Father, he embodies life. He is life itself, not with an independent status but as part and parcel of his oneness with the Father, who grants him the same divine access to life so that he, too, is the fountain of life, the spring from whence all creation issues (5:26) and from whom also comes the life-giving Spirit (3:5–6; 7:39).

As a consequence, resurrection in the Johannine worldview is not primarily an end-of-life issue but rather enters with its dazzling radiance into the very heart of human life and created reality. Jesus himself is not only the life; he is also the resurrection, which already implies that resurrection life is capable of dealing with death itself. After all, biological life ultimately ends in death, but resurrection life—eternal life—defeats death. The "I am" saying to which Martha gives enthusiastic assent (though perhaps without understanding

84 John

its full, radical implications; cf 11:39) makes both a christo-logical and an eschatological claim. This saying expresses something definitive about the Johannine Jesus and is equally concerned with God's ultimate reality and its extraordinary degree of anticipation in the present moment within the ministry of Jesus. Death cannot hold sway in Jesus's presence. His voice, and his voice alone, can be heard by those who cannot hear and by the silent dead; he alone can summon Lazarus from the darkness of the tomb into the light of life (11:43).

The Lazarus story contains a significant number of parallels to the passion and resurrection of Jesus. Thomas rightly perceives that journeying with Jesus to Judea—a place of danger and hostility for Jesus—will mean Jesus's death (11:16). Jesus's emotions at the tomb of Lazarus, which have been the subject of scholarly debate for a long time, are as much linked to his own death as to that of Lazarus.[25] His emotional response—his anger and distress—is caused undoubtedly by coming face to face with the intense grief of Mary and the mourners. It snaps him out of his initial joy at the prospect of an increase in belief for his disciples (11:15). While it is possible that Jesus is angry with the disbelief of the mourners, it is more likely, from a Johannine perspective, that his anger is directed against death itself and its devastating effects on human life.

If we include the story of the anointing as belonging to the whole Lazarus narrative (11:1–12:11), then Mary's subsequent actions are a deeply percipient response to both what Jesus has done and the cost of his action in raising Lazarus from death (12:1–8). She acts here as the model disciple, filling the house with the fragrant odor of life in place of the dreadful stench of decay and death at the open tomb (12:3; cf. 11:39).[26] The

---

25. See Brendan Byrne, *Lazarus: A Contemporary Reading of John 11:1–46*, ZS (Collegeville, MN: Liturgical, 1990), 58–60.

26. Lee, *Flesh and Glory*, 197–211.

Life and Light

resultant believing of many of the mourners and bystanders leads Caiaphas, with the assent of the Sanhedrin, to determine the necessity of Jesus's death (11:47–53).

Not only Jesus's death but also his resurrection are foreshadowed in the raising of Lazarus. The tomb with the stone placed against it, the presence of the grave clothes, and particularly the headcloth binding the dead man's face are paralleled in Jesus's own resurrection (20:7). His tomb is enclosed within a rock face and sealed by a large stone. Tears of emotion from Mary are also associated with Jesus's entombment (20:11), as they are with Jesus himself as he approaches the tomb of Lazarus (11:33, 35, 38).[27]

Yet one raising points symbolically to the other. Lazarus's raising is resuscitation; Jesus's raising is resurrection.[28] Lazarus will again die—indeed, his life is immediately under threat soon after his rising (12:9–11). Jesus, by contrast, rises to an endless, deathless life that signifies an explosive transformation of mortality: the overpowering of death itself. The miraculous sign of Lazarus's restoration to life is a symbol of the far greater and cosmic event of Jesus's resurrection, which signifies the turning of the ages, spelling the final demise of death. And Jesus enacts this event of his own accord, because he has been given authority over life itself: "I lay down my own life in order that I might take it up again" (10:17). He speaks these words as the Good Shepherd whose radical care for his sheep is exemplified symbolically in the raising of Lazarus and ultimately in and through his own resurrection. Not even life can be taken away from the one who is the Source of life. At the passion, Jesus surrenders his own life by his own

---

27. On Jesus's complex emotions at the tomb of Lazarus, which include anger as well as grief, see Frederick Dale Bruner, *The Gospel of John: A Commentary* (Grand Rapids: Eerdmans, 2012), 679–80.

28. Byrne, *Lazarus*, 86–89.

unique authority—"he bowed his head and gave up his spirit" (19:30)—just as, on the basis of this same authority, he will release himself from the clutches of death (10:17–18).

The irony of the passion in its bestowal of life is nowhere more explicitly represented than in the wounds of Jesus. These are displayed to the disciples to verify Jesus's risen identity—the continuity with his mortal life despite the astonishing transformation in his bodily presence (20:20). Thomas, in particular, insists on seeing the wounds and utters the highest confession of faith as a consequence (20:25–28). His desire to see and touch these scars, though Jesus commands him to move beyond unbelieving to believing (20:27), is itself the result of insight, though a limited one.[29] Thomas knows that the wounds must be there because they are, paradoxically, the core symbols of life: firstly, of Jesus's own incarnate life and death, and, secondly, of the life that his incarnate life and death convey to those who attach themselves to him. The wounds are ironical symbols of life and of the healing that the Johannine Jesus as Savior offers the world.[30]

In addition to the core imagery of light, there are also "subordinate symbols" associated with light such as torches, lanterns, and fires, which support the key symbolism. Ironically, the arresting party approaches Jesus, the Light of the world, with "lanterns and torches," as well as with weapons and a large contingent of soldiers (18:3). The irony intensifies when Jesus identifies himself ("I am the one") and the soldiers and temple guards, for all their fearful panoply, fall to the ground in awe and dread (18:6). Additionally, the

---

29. On Thomas and his so-called "doubting," see Dorothy A. Lee, "Partnership in Easter Faith: The Role of Mary Magdalene and Thomas in John 20," in *Creation, Matter and the Image of God: Essays on John* (Adelaide, Australia: ATF, 2020), 77–89.

30. Dorothy A. Lee, "The Significance of the Wounds of Jesus in the Fourth Gospel," *Review & Expositor* 120 (2023): 114–26.

charcoal fire at which Simon Peter warms himself before his betrayal of Jesus (18:18) is paralleled by the charcoal fire by which Jesus cooks bread and fish in his risen appearance to the seven disciples—immediately before rehabilitating Simon Peter (21:9): "torches and lanterns . . . are a pathetic substitute for the light of the world and a charcoal fire . . . is a miserable alternative on a cold dark night and a painful reminder in the bright light of a new day."[31] References to night and day also work symbolically: for Judas who enters the darkness of night (13:30) and for those who choose to walk in the light of day before the darkness comes (11:9–10).

REFLECTIONS

Perhaps the most profound theme of this Gospel is that of eternal life, which in John is far more than the promise of unending life beyond death. More radically, it is the gift of a life in the present moment that cannot be defeated by death, or indeed by any other earthly power. Eternal life describes first and foremost a quality that has the capacity to transform our lives in their present contours and shape—and to go on transforming them in and beyond death:

> Eternity undoubtedly includes the notion of endlessness, but also . . . a special quality of life peculiar to the new age. It is this special quality—not endlessness—that is suggested by John's term . . . which might therefore be translated "the life of the new age."[32]

---

31. Clyde Muropa, "The Johannine Writings: Symbolism and the Symbol of 'Light' in the Gospel of John," *AS* 67 (2012): 112 (106–13).

32. John Ashton, *Understanding the Fourth Gospel*, 2nd ed. (Oxford: Oxford University Press, 2007), 402.

Furthermore, this "life of the new age" is intimately linked to the life of creation, as evidenced in the symbolism of light.[33] It is not a separate form of life that supersedes that of creation. Its source is one and the same: the creating and re-creating God, origin of all that is and all that will be. It is the life which issues from Being itself: always contingent and always dependent on its divine source. In the end, and by implication, it is creation itself which is restored by God in the vision of the Fourth Gospel. The life of creation is not set aside or destroyed; rather, it is transformed by the one who has authority over all that exists.

Our world has many competing offers for the authentic and happy life. Much of these are associated with material wealth and comfort—or at least with the presumed access to them. The advertising industry bombards our senses with images of contented people who receive full access to desirable food, drink, security, education, medical supplies, home and furnishings, leisure activities, travel, and secure retirement. These commodities promise stability, a safeguard against catastrophe, an assurance of the perpetuation of youth and beauty, and entry into a fulfilling and rewarding life.

What is not stated in this cultural framework is that behind these material advantages is a significant and terrifying denial of death. Not only are these goods not available to everyone, but their availability is dependent on the endless toil and deprivation of others. No account is made of the cost to those groups who provide the material possessions out of their own poverty and virtual enslavement. For example, sweatshops are the true background of the fashion industry.

---

33. Ford (*Gospel of John*, 181) points out that the symbols such as light, like that of the Word, "connect Jesus with all of Scripture and with the whole of created reality."

Yet no material comfort nor promise of youth will ever ensure against aging, decay, and death. Ernest Becker, for example, speaks of the terror of death that is the tragedy of all mortal life and which our society attempts to deny in various ways, both material and psychological: "Whatever man does on this planet has to be done in the lived truth of the terror of creation, of the grotesque, of the rumble of panic underneath everything."[34]

There is, in this pursuit, a frantic clinging to life—particularly biological life—that is to be prolonged, by whatever means, as much as possible. In effect, medicine and technology hold out promises of everlasting life. The "wellness" industry, built on an illusion that is itself grounded in material prosperity, is another manifestation of this greed for life and the delay of death. Part of the illusion is the way we distance those who are sick, who are elderly, who have mental illness, who live with disability, and who are seeking asylum: hospitals, prisons, detention centers, and aged care homes all keep the threatening "other" at bay. These separate spaces are based as often as not on class, gender, and race, with grave political as well as social and spiritual consequences. We curate and control our lives—what we see and what we do not see—and even our deaths.

At the same time, human beings also evince a desire for death: a wish for the very thing that threatens us. Alongside our crude materialism and our indifference to its sources and implications, we also act in self-destructive ways. Our attitude to the planet is an example of how we destroy that which feeds and nourishes us. Our ecosystems are under threat and many species are endangered. We have pursued life at the

---

34. Ernest Becker, *The Denial of Death* (New York: The Free Press, 1973), 283–84.

cost of the environment, and at the same time we have acted against our own best interests in self-destructive behavior that is exhausting our planet. The state of the environment is part and parcel of the same denial of death. We long for life, no matter what the cost or how artificial and false this longing proves to be, but we also, despite ourselves, pursue death.

Fortunately, John's theme of light, so central to this text, provides a direct challenge to our ideas of life and death. While there is an acceptance of the reality of death for all mortal life, there is also an awareness of life's ultimate transformation in God's new age, which is already at work in the present to overcome the forces of death, whether literal or metaphorical.[35]

Light is a powerful symbol for us today as it was for the ancients. Perhaps we take it more for granted, as easy access to electricity—at least in the Western world—means that we are accustomed to bright light in our homes and cities, by night as well as by day. We forget how dark the nights were in past generations, with the limited light afforded by candles and lamps, and how much more difficult and dangerous travel was at night. Today we have unprecedented access to light and can live and work at hours that suit us rather than follow the natural rhythms of illumination. Indeed, in our cities we can live with relative unawareness of the muted light provided by moon and stars; we are also unaware of the beauty and immensity of the night sky.

Yet light still works for us as a symbol of life. We know well that our lives, and the entire life of creation, are dependent on the light of the sun and its capacity to generate and preserve all forms of life, from the smallest to the greatest. We

---

35. Sandra M. Schneiders sees the Lazarus story as overcoming the fear of death without denying its reality (*Written That You May Believe: Encountering Jesus in the Fourth Gospel* (New York: Crossroad, 1999), 149–61).

Life and Light

associate special kinds of light with significant occasions. We light candles for intimate dinner parties, for soft lighting, for church services, and for birthdays and other celebrations. We do so no longer because we need the light to see or read by, but because of the symbolism attached to it. For Christians, in particular, we see Jesus through the Johannine symbolism as the one who illuminates our lives—who gives meaning, hope, purpose, and guidance. We also find that distinct sources of light, such as sunlight and moonlight, and candlelight and firelight, can take us in imagination to Jesus himself, nudging our consciousness to awareness of how the symbol has transformed our understanding of Jesus and, indeed, of light itself.

Judgement, too, has a place in our understanding of how Jesus functions as the light of the world. Just as in the natural world the light of the sun can burn as well as warm, so judgement has the capacity to sear through the lies of our culture: to expose what is evil and to bring it out of its hidden darkness into the light of day. Our own lives, too, are encouraged to be open to a light that can illuminate our hearts but also test them, challenge them, and reveal the dark places of ignorance and prejudice, the delusions we sometimes live by. In the end, this searing light is a manifestation of divine love: not a judgementalism that leads us to self-loathing and despair but an appraisal that cleanses and renews, heals and invigorates, and draws us into the heart of God's love for us manifest in Jesus.

Finally, the first of the resurrection narratives leaves us with the picture of the risen Jesus present with his wounds, which become in themselves, paradoxically, the source of our healing and joy. There is something profound here for our understanding of God and also of our own selves. If the wounds of the one who is our Lord and our God (20:28) are for the healing of the nations, then our own wounds have the capacity not only to be healed by God but also to have a healing and life-giving capacity for others. They enable us to enter into the suffering of other people, other nations, and other cultures and empathize particularly with the pain and violence they have experienced. Like the risen Christ, we can never in one sense leave our wounds behind. They are always there: stark reminders of our mortal selves, our past pain, and our capacity to reach out to others. They can also become for us symbols of life, even though in many respects they speak to us of death. But they can do so only because of the wounds of Jesus himself, which are always visible in his presence within and among us.

FURTHER READING

Byrne, Brendan. *Come to the Light: Reflections on the Gospel of John.* Collegeville, MN: Liturgical, 2021.

Hamilton, Adam. *John: The Gospel of Light and Life.* Nashville: Abingdon, 2015.

Koester, Craig R. *The Word of Life: A Theology of John's Gospel.* Grand Rapids: Eerdmans, 2008.

Newbigin, Lesslie. *The Light Has Come: An Exposition of the Fourth Gospel.* Grand Rapids: Eerdmans, 1982.

Yee, Gale A. *Jewish Feasts and the Gospel of John.* Eugene, OR: Wipf & Stock, 2007.

CHAPTER 5

Temple and Glory

And the Word . . . pitched his tent among us . . . and revealed his glory. (1:14)

Perhaps the most significant paired theme in John's Gospel, especially in terms of its Christology, is that between temple (*hieron*) and glory (*doxa*). This duality is not one of negative opposition as in the case of light and darkness, which we explored in chapter 4; rather, the two exist in symbiotic relationship to each other, the one pointing to and conveying the other. The temple theme is not explicit in the prologue, though it is strongly implied, but it becomes more developed in the later narratives of the Gospel.[1] It has a particular poignance for Johannine Christians in view of the destruction of the temple in 70 CE. For John, in the material domain of tabernacle and temple, the presence of divine glory emanates to God's people, as it already has done in the giving of the law on Mount Sinai.

The idea of the dwelling place of God in the prologue is also closely allied to that of flesh (*sarx*) as the sense of

---

1. See esp. Mary L. Coloe, *God Dwells with Us: Temple Symbolism in the Fourth Gospel* (Collegeville, MN: Liturgical, 2001) and Alan Kerr, *The Temple of Jesus' Body: The Temple Theme in the Gospel of John*, LNTS 220 (Sheffield: Sheffield Academic, 2002).

materiality where God chooses to abide; paradoxically, it relocates itself in the person of Jesus. The contrast is that the one term, *glory*, refers to divine existence while the other, *flesh*, refers to creation. It signifies the vast gulf that separates Creator from creation, caused not only by evil or sin but by the radically different constitutive nature of each: the independent self-sufficient One who is the source of all being and the secondary, contingent, and dependent nature of all created reality.

TEMPLE BACKGROUND IN JUDAISM

Once again, as with most other themes, John is drawing on Old Testament images and themes as he sets forth the new event in Jesus and confirms its inextricable connection to God's prior manifestation to Israel. In the exodus and the journeyings in the wilderness, God speaks to the children of Israel from the tent of meeting, which Moses has the freedom to enter on behalf of the people. A cloud descends over the tent when God is present and speaking to Moses, signifying the divine revelation and guidance as well as the awe and inscrutability associated with it. Here, substantial divine glory and shifting, finite materiality coalesce in disclosing God's nearness to, and guidance of, his vacillating people.

The sanctuary itself is described as the tabernacle (*skēnē*, Exod 25:9) and the tent of meeting (Exod 40:6), made of linen curtains, which are looped together and are richly colored and decorated, over a frame of acacia wood (Exod 26). At its entrance is the altar of burnt offering (Exod 27:1–8) and inside is the altar of incense (Lev 4:7). Its material aspects are to be tended by the Levites and its cultic ritual by the priests, descendants of Aaron. As high priest, Aaron himself is to approach the innermost shrine once a year to make atonement for the sins of the people: an animal is sacrificed and its blood sprinkled on the mercy seat (Lev 16:1–19). Within the tabernacle resides the ark of the covenant, constructed by Moses at God's direction and depicted as a box or chest. In one tradition it is covered in gold with the mercy seat on the lid, surrounded on either side by two overarching cherubim (Exod 25:10–22); in another tradition it is a simple wooden box (Deut 10:1–5). Inside the ark are the two tablets of the law given to Moses on Mount Sinai (Deut 10:1–5; see Heb 9:1–5).[2]

The ark serves Israel as its movable sanctuary during the wandering in the wilderness and the early settlement period until the building of the temple. The ark itself is regarded as a numinous object able to confer blessing, but it also inflicts death if touched unthinkingly (2 Sam 6:6–11). Within it the presence of God dwells, assuring Israel of the heartening though also fearsome divine presence. While the ark is portable—to be moved on poles by Levites, particularly in times of war or other crises—it is eventually placed in the temple. After the destruction of the temple by the Babylonians, the ark seems to have disappeared.

The temple itself had a chequered history. Assumed to have been built by Solomon in the tenth century BCE, the first temple was destroyed at the time of the exile into Babylon (c. 586/7 BCE) and rebuilt as the second temple in the period of restoration following the exiles' return (516 BCE): a structure reputedly of great beauty and majesty.[3] During the reign of Herod the Great (37–4 BCE) this temple

---

2. Maria Metzler, "The Ark of the Covenant," *Bible Odyssey*, accessed October 16, 2024, https://www.bibleodyssey.org/people/related-articles/the-ark-of-the-covenant/.

3. Shelley Cohney, "The Jewish Temples: The Second Temple," *Jewish Virtual Library*, accessed October 16, 2024, https://www.jewishvirtuallibrary.org/the-second-temple.

96 John

was extensively renovated, a process that took more than forty years and extended into Jesus's lifetime. This temple was destroyed by the Romans in 70 CE.[4]

The second temple was divided into sections, with the court of the Gentiles in the outermost circle. Further in was the court of the women, the court of Israel, and the court of the priests, with the altar of incense and the great candelabra (*menorah*). The holy of holies was the most sacred of all places in the temple, the innermost shrine or sanctuary (*naos*), divided off by a curtain: only the high priest could enter there once a year on the Day of Atonement.

The temple was also understood in an eschatological context. The Old Testament contains prophecies of waters flowing from the temple in the last days. In Ezekiel 47:1–11, the trickling waters from each point of the compass in the temple become deeper and deeper until they turn into a river, which has trees on either side that grow healing fruits. The river itself is life-giving. Similarly, in Zechariah 14:8, "living water shall flow out from Jerusalem" at the end time, turning a city in the desert into a permanent oasis whose security and prosperity is assured. Such texts give the temple a key place in the vision of the final days as the source of life for God's people, Israel.

For devoutly Jewish people, the concept of "glory" was particularly (though not exclusively) tied to the temple, signifying the divine presence at the heart of Jewish cultic life and ritual.[5] In the Old Testament, glory is a significant concept (*kabod* in Hebrew, *doxa* in Greek) associated with the tent of

---

4. For a contemporaneous account of this event, see the Jewish historian Josephus, *The Jewish War Books V–VII*, trans. Henry St John Thackeray, LCL 210 (Cambridge, MA: Harvard University Press, 1928), book VI.

5. For a summary of glory in the Old Testament, see Richard Bauckham, *Gospel of Glory: Major Themes in Johannine Theology* (Grand Rapids: Baker Academic, 2015), 43–50.

meeting, the tabernacle, and the ark of the covenant, as we have seen. When the ark is captured in battle, the glory of God is said to have departed from Israel (1 Sam 4:19–22). Divine glory is equally associated with the giving of the law (Torah) on Mount Sinai and the self-manifestation of God to Israel, as we will see in chapter 8. When the law is bestowed on Israel, Moses asks to see God's glory. However, for his own preservation, he is only able to see the back of God and not God's face (Exod 33:18–23). Glory, in this sense, signifies the imminence of God as "a fiery radiance that can be seen but only in a veiled form, hidden within a cloud."[6] The temple is thus a key (though not the sole) symbolic manifestation of divine glory.

When Isaiah sees God's glory in the temple as part of his call narrative, it represents an epiphany: an experience of the holiness of God that shakes the building to its foundations and fills it with smoke from the altar (Isa 6:1–8). This vision gives Isaiah a profound sense of his own unworthiness because he has seen the majesty of God. However, by being cleansed from the altar of incense, he is able to respond to the call and receive his commission. Though the word *glory* is not explicit in this narrative, it is implied in the temple language and imagery and the sense of overpowering awe evoked in the prophet. Yet the human response to glory in the Old Testament can equally be that of love as well as awe; for example, the psalmist says, "O LORD, I love the house in which you dwell, and the place where your glory abides" (Ps 26:8). In the LXX the phrase is literally "the place of the tent [*skēnōma*] of your glory," signifying the tabernacle and temple as the domain of revelation and salvation.

A significant factor in the life of the Johannine community

---

6. Bauckham, *Gospel of Glory*, 46.

98 John

was the destruction of the temple by the Romans (70 CE), as noted a number of times in this book. Most scholars, as we have already seen, believe that the Gospel was written after this catastrophic event within the Jewish (and therefore the Christian) faith. It is hard to overestimate the effect of this event on Jewish religious and political sensibilities. Apart from the widening implications of conflict with Rome, the loss of the temple and its rituals left a vast hole in Jewish identity and sense of covenant. The temple was the heart of faith and prayer, the place of pilgrimage for the major festivals and the location of various kinds of sacrifice; it was the abode of the high priest and the meeting place of the Sanhedrin, the Jewish Council. A tax was levied for its upkeep (see Matt 17:24–27).

The sack of Jerusalem inevitably also had implications for John's theology, even though there are no direct references to it within the text itself (unlike the Synoptics: e.g., Luke 21:20–24). It is a significant part, however, of the background of the Gospel, which reflects not only the history of Jesus himself in his ministry but also that of the subsequent life of the community. It explains in part some of the emphases in John's Christology, particularly in relation to the temple.[7]

TEMPLES IN GRECO-ROMAN CITIES

In the wider Greco-Roman world, temples were commonplace in ancient cities and reflected the polytheism of antiquity. The Romans were syncretistic and tolerant of various, imported deities, provided that their rites were not too bizarre and that their worshippers were happy to acknowledge Roman deities

---

7. There were also two temples built in Egypt; see Reuven Chaim Klein, "Two Jewish Temples in Egypt," *The Seforim Blog*, January 12, 2019, https://seforim blog.com/2019/01/two-jewish-temples-in-egypt/.

associated with imperialism. Temples were not only places of worship but also of sacrifice and sacred meals, effectively slaughterhouses for the butchery of animals and the location of festive meals where guilds could meet and render honor to their patron deity.[8]

Worship of the Roman emperor as a deity was also popular in Roman Asia. Cities in the region of Asia Minor rivalled each other to build temples to the current emperor, who acted as their divine warden or patron; if successful in building such an edifice, a city was deemed a *neōkoros* ("temple guardian," Acts 19:35). Ephesus eventually erected a "Temple of the Augusti" during the eighth decade of the first century CE in the reign of the Flavian dynasty (69–96 CE).[9] Significantly, according to the Roman historian Suetonius, the Emperor Domitian (81–96 CE), who enthusiastically endorsed the cult of emperor worship, preferred to be named *dominus et deus noster* ("our Lord and God").[10]

In Ephesus, the greatest temple was that of the goddess Artemis. As mentioned in the introductory chapter, the Artemisium was one of the seven wonders of the ancient world, built originally in the sixth century BCE, and was the continuing center of worship and devotion for the city. It was famous for its size, artefacts, and beauty. Inside was the statue of the deity as a maternal goddess, the protector and patron of the city. Her Ephesian worshipers were devout in their adherence to her and, according to Acts, would brook

---

8. On religion in the ancient Roman context, both political and domestic, see Simon M. Jones, "A Supermarket of Faiths," in *The World of the Early Church: A Social History* (Oxford: Lion, 2011), 166–88.

9. Barbara Burrell, "Ephesus as Temple-Warden," in *The Coinage of Ephesus*, ed. K. A. Sheedy (Sydney: Macquarie University, 2005), chapter 10, http://humanities.mq.edu.au/acans/ephesus/chapters/chapter10.htm.

10. Suetonius, *Lives of the Caesars*, ed. and trans. J. C. Rolfe, vol. 2, LCL 38 (Cambridge, MA: Harvard University Press, 1914), VIII.13.

100 John

no challenge to Artemis as their principal, cherished deity (19:23–40). Jewish (and therefore Christian) monotheism constituted a direct assault on Ephesian religious sensibilities.

While the Johannine house churches were largely Jewish and remained under the broad umbrella of Judaism, as we have already noted, there were probably also Gentile converts within them who had once been worshipers of Artemis and adherents of the cult of the emperor. Both Jewish adherents and pagan converts, despite the monotheism of the one and the polytheism of the other, were thus familiar with temple worship, even though the temple in Jerusalem had been destroyed by the time John wrote to that community.

To sum up, temple awareness was intrinsic to life in the ancient Greco-Roman world. Jewish people had the Old Testament Scriptures and memories of temple worship, on the one hand, and pagans had the streets of the ancient city with its many temples, on the other hand. Thus, temple symbolism and ceremony were conspicuous in the everyday experience and imagination of John's readers.

TEMPLE IN THE PROLOGUE AND "CANA TO CANA" CYCLE

Temple language and imagery pervade the Fourth Gospel, sometimes explicitly and sometimes implicitly.[11] The prologue uses temple language and imagery to connote the dwelling place of God. It is particularly associated with the point of incarnation and the revelation of divine glory in Jesus at

---

11. For an outline of different scholarly views on the temple and feasts in the Gospel, see Bruce G. Schuchard, "Temple, Festivals, and Scripture in the Gospel of John," in *The Oxford Handbook of Johannine Studies*, ed. Judith M. Lieu and Martinus C. de Boer (Oxford: Oxford University Press, 2018), 381–95. See also John Behr, *John the Theologian and His Paschal Gospel: A Prologue to Theology* (Oxford: Oxford University Press, 2019), 137–93.

the beginning of the third cycle of the prologue (1:14–18). Unfortunately, the symbolism is almost invisible in English translation, which mostly renders the first of the three main verbs at 1:14 as "lived" (NRSVue, RNJB), "dwelt" (KJV, ESV), "made his home" (NLT), or "made his dwelling" (NIV, REB). While none of these translations is inaccurate, they fail in most cases to convey the subtleties of the text and particularly the imagery underlying it. The Greek verb *skēnoō* has within it the root *tent* (*skēnē*), the Old Testament connotations reflecting Israel's understanding of the divine glory within its ranks in tent, tabernacle, and temple.[12] The evangelist is already indicating here that Jesus himself in this Gospel *is* the true temple of God, the dwelling place of God's glory.[13]

Within the events of Jesus's ministry, the language of glory and temple are present in the "Cana to Cana" narrative cycle of the Gospel (2:1–4:54). Though the wedding at Cana contains the first reference to glory, it is already implied in Jesus's solemn declaration to Nathaniel immediately before: "Amen, amen, I say to you, you will see the heaven opened and the angels of God ascending and descending on the Son of Man" (1:51). The reference here is to Jacob's dream of angels going up and down a ladder reaching to heaven. In flight from the justifiable rage of his brother, Esau, Jacob recognizes the place of his repose as sacred and is filled with awe as a consequence of the dream; it is "the house of God . . . the gate of heaven" (Gen 28:12–17). The imagery of the ladder

---

12. Craig R. Keener uses the translation "tabernacled" here (*The Gospel of John: A Commentary*, vol. 1 [Peabody, MA: Hendrickson, 2003], 1.408–9).

13. The question of whether John's Christology implies a replacement of Jewish faith and practice will be dealt with in chapter 8. In one sense, the Johannine Jesus does replace the destroyed temple in Jerusalem, but, as we will see, that does not imply a full-blown theology of replacement or supersessionism. See Kathleen Troost-Cramer, *Jesus as Means and Locus of Worship in the Fourth Gospel: Sacrifice and Worship Space in John* (Eugene, OR: Pickwick, 2017), 143–45.

102   John

reaching up to God's dwelling while also bringing God's presence down to earth evokes the temple, while the language of the descending Son of Man and the angels reflects the divine glory (Isa 6:2; Dan 7:13; Mark 8:38; 13:26–27/pars.). Jesus's utterance leads directly into the ensuing narratives, where the two themes of temple and glory become explicit.

John makes it clear that the story of the wedding at Cana—despite contentious issues of interpretation[14]—is essentially about the revelation of divine glory in Jesus (2:11). It sets the scene for all the signs of the Gospel and provides the key to their significance. Just as glory is manifest in the incarnation (1:14), so it radiates throughout the words and works of Jesus's ministry as the glorious Son of Man. The water that has become wine signifies the Jewish ritual cleansings, which are the "container" for the new revelation in the Johannine Jesus. From this it is clear that the concept of glory in John is larger than that of the temple: once again, the temple is a "container" for the heavenly glory which both transcends yet also inhabits its earthly contours. The graciousness of God in self-revelation locates itself in a specific time and place without in any sense exhausting it. Temple is thus a symbolic manifestation of divine glory.

The first explicit reference to the temple outside the prologue occurs at the cleansing of the temple, which, unlike the Synoptic versions, occurs early rather than late in Jesus's ministry (2:13–22). There are also differences of detail between the Synoptic and Johannine accounts within the flow of the narrative itself (Mark 11:15–17/pars.). For example, the quotation from Isaiah 56:7 is lacking in John, as is the reference to a "den of thieves"; the Johannine Jesus first makes a whip

---

14. For a discussion that covers the exegetical and background issues, see Keener, *Gospel of John*, 1.492–516.

of cords before driving out the animals, while the issue of contention is not primarily the stealing and dishonesty but rather the buying and selling in itself; and the Old Testament quotation in John's Gospel is from Psalm 69:9 ("zeal for your house will eat [John]/has eaten [LXX] me up").[15]

The most significant difference between the two accounts, however, is found in the second part of the Johannine cleansing (2:18–22). Here, attention moves from Jesus as the passionate defender of God's house (as in the Synoptics) to the temple as symbolic of Jesus's own identity and fate. This material is unique to the Fourth Gospel in the context of the cleansing. In a characteristic example of Johannine misunderstanding, the Jerusalem authorities fail dismally to discern the symbolic nature of Jesus's utterance: "Loose this temple and in three days I will raise it" (2:19). For them, Jesus's words are dangerously subversive (cf. 11:48). The evangelist, therefore, explains the symbolic meaning that the authorities have missed: "he was speaking of the temple of his body" (2:21).

John's Gospel makes a distinctive theological move here in seeing the temple, not only as the dwelling place of God but also identifying Jesus with it. The wider context is the actual dissolution of the temple by the Romans in 70 CE. But, for John, this historical event enables a rich understanding of not only Jesus himself as the fulfilment of the temple and the center of God's abiding presence in Israel, but more specifically his bodily reality, palpable in his suffering death on the cross and the materiality of his resurrection, as evidenced in the showing of his wounds (20:20, 27). The "liberation"

---

15. For more details on the similarities and differences, see e.g., Raymond E. Brown, *The Gospel According to John*, vol. 1, AB 29 (New York: Doubleday, 1966), 1.116–20. Note that a similar metaphor of the destruction and rebuilding of the temple in relation to Jesus himself is found at Mark 14:58/par.

104   John

of the animals in the temple signals also the end of animal sacrifice in the sacrifice of Jesus himself on the cross.[16] As in the parable of the sheepfold, Jesus here has unique, divine authority over life, an authority bestowed on him by the Father: he is the one who both lays down and raises up the "temple" of his own body (10:17–18).

The temple theme is picked up again in the dialogue between Jesus and the Samaritan woman (4:1–42). This time, instead of Jacob's ladder we have Jacob's well (4:5–6), once again emphasizing how deeply embedded in Old Testament faith this Gospel is. While the first scene of the narrative has focused on living water (4:6–15), the second is more concerned with sacred site and specifically the ancestral issue of temple worship (4:20–26), an issue that deeply divides Jew and Samaritan. In the dialogue, the divisive theological question—rightly and properly raised by the Samaritan once she recognizes Jesus's prophetic status—is that of the true site of worship, the authentic "temple mount": Jerusalem or Gerizim. While conceding primacy to the Jewish tradition (4:22), the Johannine Jesus nevertheless relocates sacred site away from contested geographical locations (4:21).

Nowhere in this passage does Jesus overtly identify himself with the temple. Instead, he speaks of worship "in spirit and truth" or, better, "in the Spirit of truth" (4:23–24).[17] However, the Samaritan herself recognizes that this is messianic talk (4:25) and that the new era which Jesus announces ("the hour is coming and now is," 4:21, 23) is bound up with the person of the Messiah (4:25). At this point, Jesus reveals to her his true identity (4:26). Holding together the tension

---

16. On the close intersection between temple and sacrifice in John's understanding, particularly of Jesus's death, see Troost-Cramer, *Jesus as Means and Locus*, 69–94.

17. For this translation, see Brown, *John*, 1.180 (see 14:17; 15:26; 16:13).

inherent in the cleansing episode, the Johannine Jesus, as the locus of worship (the true temple), is both the true worshiper and also the object of worship. His profound connection to, and gifting of, the "Spirit of truth" will later confirm that identity (15:26). While there is no explicit reference to the divine glory in this narrative, it is present synonymously in the language and imagery, particularly that of the Father's seeking of true worshipers and the revelation of Jesus as the "Savior of the world" (4:42).

THE TEMPLE AND ITS FEASTS

The next explicit use of temple and glory language occurs in the following section, which circles the theme of "the feasts of the Jews" (John 5–10). From our perspective in exploring the temple, the most important of these feasts is the Feast of Tabernacles, which is the immediate context for the long narrative of John 7:1–52, 8:12–59,[18] which spills over into the ensuing story of the man born blind (John 9). The Tabernacles narrative consists largely of Jesus's self-revelation and the to-ing and fro-ing of dialogue with the temple authorities which, despite signs of incipient discipleship, climaxes in rejection (8:59).

In this crucial setting, Jesus shows himself to be the embodiment of the temple, based on its two core rituals. In the first place, he summons people to discipleship using water imagery and the promise of the Spirit. This parallels the water ritual of the Feast of Tabernacles, with the pouring of water from the Pool of Siloam onto the altar

---

18. As noted earlier, this omits the story of the woman caught in adultery. Although it is a revered and ancient episode, this story is a later addition to the Johannine Gospel (7:53–8:11); on the narrative, see Gail O'Day, "John 7:53–8:11: A Study in Misreading," *JBL* 11 (1992): 631–40.

106 John

each morning of the feast (7:37–38). Jesus invites the thirsty to come to him to quench their thirst, and the evangelist makes the connection to the donation of the Spirit (7:39). Unlike in the Bread of Life narrative, he does not declare himself to be the water of life—as he is the bread of life (6:35)—but rather the giver of water (7:37; cf. 4:10). These verses echo the vision of Ezekiel of water flowing from the temple on the last days, as we have seen (Ezek 47:1–12). The same water symbolism carries forward to the healing of the man born blind, whose eyes are washed in the same Pool of Siloam and who gains his sight as a consequence (9:6–7).

The second ritual at the Feast of Tabernacles is that of the lighting of the great candelabra (*menorah*) in the evenings, illuminating Jerusalem. Once again, Jesus's utterance is in effect a call to discipleship based, as usual in John's Gospel, on his sublime identity. This time, he refers to himself as "the light of the world," which is, at the same time, "the light of life" (*to phōs tou kosmou/tēs zōēs*, 8:12). The summons is to embrace the light, which will illuminate the darkness. Is this the darkness of sin and unbelief? In the narrative which follows, as we have seen, where the imagery is picked up and extended, the man born blind's darkness (i.e., blindness) is that of ignorance, not sin, for which neither he nor his parents are to be blamed (9:3). His illumination is both physical and spiritual: in his first encounter with Jesus, where his eyesight is not so much restored as created anew; and in his second meeting, where he is illuminated by Jesus, who reveals himself as the Son of Man and is worshiped (9:35–38). However, the narrative has revealed a deeper and culpable blindness in the authorities, who claim sight but are bound in the darkness of rejection and unbelief (9:39–41). This unbelief leads them to abuse the man himself as well as Jesus.

The fundamental irony in all of this is that the authorities,

Temple and Glory

guardians of the temple and responsible for its functioning, reject the very one who is himself the embodiment of the temple. Caiaphas, the high priest, in the plot formulated against Jesus following the raising of Lazarus, is prepared to sacrifice Jesus to protect the people (ironically) from Roman retribution (11:49–50). Note again that, whatever the historical lines of conflict are between Jesus and his opponents, the Johannine context presumes a setting in which the temple and its rituals have been destroyed. In this sense, the Johannine Jesus not only fulfills the rituals and feasts associated with the temple, but also replaces the temple itself.[19]

THE TEMPLE IN THE LAST SUPPER AND PASSION

Explicit references to the temple almost disappear in the second half of the Gospel (13:1–21:25). The focus shifts between private and public: first, on Jesus within the intimate circle of his disciples, set in the private domain, where Jesus and his closest friends have withdrawn from the public sphere as a consequence of its aggression; then to the public arena for the crucifixion; and, finally, back to the private world of the disciples for the resurrection appearances. The only direct allusion to the temple in these chapters is in the passion narrative (18:1–19:42) at Jesus's trial before Annas, the father-in-law of Caiaphas the high priest (18:13–14, 19–23), where Jesus defends the public nature of his teaching in both synagogue and temple (18:20). The Last Supper, which incorporates the

---

19. Note that the Pharisees were in a similar situation after the Jewish War. They "replaced" the temple with the Torah and made it the center of Jewish life and faith. On the Pharisees and Judaism, see Joshua Ezra Burns, "Pharisees and Rabbinic Judaism," *Bible Odyssey*, accessed October 16, 2024, https://www.bible odyssey.org/people/related-articles/pharisees-and-rabbinic-judaism/.

108 John

Farewell Discourse, makes no explicit reference to the temple (13:1–17:26), although the language of glory is apparent, particularly in the two framing sections: the footwashing (13:1–30) and the Great Prayer (17:1–26). Therefore, these chapters seem to stand outside our theme, namely, the interconnection of images of the temple as the manifestation of divine glory.

Yet such an impression would be misleading. The whole of the Last Supper is set within the context of Passover (13:1), which extends to include the passion narrative (18:1–19:42). Indeed, the anointing at Bethany, which is part of the raising of Lazarus (11:1–12:11), occurs six days before Passover (12:1), making the link with the temple implicit and tying it in with the glory language of Lazarus's raising, the last and greatest of the signs in Jesus's public ministry (11:4, 40). Therefore, the Last Supper narrative, with its Passover connection and use of glory language, can be said to continue the motif of Jesus as the temple of God. It is particularly appropriate, for example, that Jesus's ministry—both public and private—concludes with prayer where he stands face to face with God (cf 1:1, 18) as the visible and material manifestation of divine glory while he prepares for his coming death. The implied reader is also prepared symbolically for the crucifixion: to perceive within it the Son's glorious ascent to the Father. In the light of the cleansing of the temple, the Johannine Jesus is to be seen as the "house" in which/whom the Father dwells—himself the place of both prayer and sacrifice.

In the passion narrative, the theological focus rests on Jesus as the Lamb of God. This title is part of the extended metaphor of the temple, incorporating both the feast of Passover and the paschal lamb. This is the third Passover in John's Gospel (cf. 2:13; 6:4). John the Baptist has also already identified Jesus as the Lamb of God who takes away the world's sin (1:29, 36), a title that draws together the paschal

Temple and Glory

lamb, a symbol of liberation, with the sacrificial lambs of the cult in the temple, which deal with sin. Jesus as the Lamb of God is central to the passion narrative, where, in contrast to the Synoptics (who locate the first day of Passover on the evening before the crucifixion), he is crucified on the next day: the day of the feast itself, at the hour when the paschal lambs are slaughtered in the temple.[20]

John emphasizes this theme through characteristic irony in the passion narrative. The temple authorities do not wish to be polluted as they prepare to celebrate the Passover feast. For that reason, they will not enter the governor's headquarters (18:28), and they want the bodies removed from the cross (19:31).[21] Their desire for ritual and ceremonial purity contrasts, painfully and ironically, with the fact that they are collaborating with the colonizing Romans to slaughter the Lamb of God. John also emphasizes the wholeness of the Passover Lamb whose body is not broken (19:36). There is a different kind of irony operating here. Jesus is the perfect and whole sacrifice whose bones are not broken, yet whose side is pierced. This unbroken yet wounded body indicates the profound interconnection between incarnation and passion: for John, it is the primary symbol of the incarnate Jesus and his self-sacrificing, saving death. Through it, Jesus deals with the world's sin once for all, and particularly its rejection of life and its choosing of death and darkness.

The lamb imagery belongs in a wider metaphorical field,

---

20. That is why in the Synoptics the Last Supper, unlike that of John, is a Passover meal (Mark 14:22–25/pars.). On the meaning of "Lamb" in John's Gospel, see Dorothy A. Lee, "Paschal Imagery in the Gospel of John: A Narrative and Symbolic Reading," *Pac* 24 (2011): 13–28.

21. The day is particularly sacred, as the Sabbath falls within the days of Passover celebration: "Leaving the bodies hanging on any day would have violated Jewish custom; leaving them up on a Sabbath was worse; leaving them up on a festal Sabbath was unconscionable" (Keener, *Gospel of John*, 2.1151).

110   John

which incorporates pastoral symbolism in the Fourth Gospel. Jesus is not only the paschal, sacrificial lamb; he is also the gate of the fold and the shepherd of the sheep (10:1–21). The parable of the sheepfold connects partly to Jesus's ministry, especially through the image of the gate, but even more directly to the passion and resurrection.[22] The Shepherd is good precisely in laying down and taking up his life in order to give life to the flock (10:17–18). In both roles, as Lamb and as Shepherd, the passion stands at the heart of Jesus's self-revelation, each pointing—though in different ways—to his saving death, as innocent victim and as divine, authoritative King. The flow from his pierced side also connects to the vision of the eschatological temple in Old Testament prophecies.[23] Once again, Jesus is presented as the true temple of God.

FLESH/BODY AND GLORY

In all this there is an implicit link, already indicated in the cleansing of the temple, between Jesus himself, the temple, and his body. What is the difference between "flesh" (*sarx*) and "body" (*sōma*)? They are, for the most part, synonymous in John's Gospel, since both express materiality. There is also, however, a slight difference of focus. Outside the cleansing of the temple, the word *body* does not reappear in John until the passion and resurrection narratives, where it refers to Jesus's dead body (19:38, 40; 20:12). *Flesh* is used in relation to the incarnation, where it is tied to creation; it can also be used in a neutral sense to refer to the limitations of mortal life (1:13; 3:6; 6:63; 8:15), to the domain of the Son's authority over all

---

22. See Dorothy A. Lee, "The Parable of the Sheepfold: A Narrative Reading of John 10," in *Come and Read: Interpretive Approaches to the Gospel of John*, ed. Alicia D. Myers & Lindsey S. Jodrey (Lanham, MD: Fortress Academic, 2020), 81–95.

23. Coloe, *God Dwells with Us*, 206–9.

created life (17:2), or, most significantly, to the materiality of Jesus himself encountered in his mortality and by faith in the Eucharist (1:14; 6:51–56).[24] So, while they are parallel terms, *body* is used in relation to the passion while *flesh* is the more general term, connecting Jesus to all matter, including that of the sacraments.

What is significant here is that the flesh of Jesus and his body both reflect divine glory in life and in death. This is clear from the incarnation at 1:14, but it is implied in the allusions to Jesus as the temple of God. The temple discloses the divine glory, which in John's terms is the Father's glory— that is, the Father of Jesus as Son. This means that the body of Jesus, crucified and risen, likewise displays the glory of God. Nowhere is this more apparent than in the flow of blood and water from the side of the crucified Jesus (19:34). This scene is the climax of the passion story and is unique to John's Gospel. It expresses the sheer materiality of the incarnation and demonstrates awareness of the literal destruction of the temple. This temple—the body of Jesus—is likewise destroyed but, unlike the Jerusalem temple, it is raised up again. When Jesus's body is raised, and when he appears to his disciples in the resurrection narratives, the symbol of continuity and recognition is the revealing of the wounds which Jesus displays, both to the disciples in general in the upper room and more vividly to Thomas in the following scene (20:20, 25–27).

This imagery is not only profoundly symbolic but also paradoxical: wounds that are fatal cannot possibly be signs of life, still less of any kind of radiance, honor, or glory. Yet in John's Gospel, that is precisely what they are. In the theology

---

24. For further details on flesh in John, see Dorothy A. Lee, *Flesh and Glory: Symbolism, Gender and Theology in the Gospel of John* (New York: Crossroad, 2002), 29–64, and Jörg Frey, *The Glory of the Crucified One: Christology and Theology in the Gospel of John*, ET (Waco, TX: Baylor University Press, 2018), 261–84.

112　　　　　　　　　　　　　John

of the evangelist, they become the primary symbols for the salvation which Jesus achieves through his sacrificial death and resurrection, as also through his incarnation and ministry. Note that it is not the salvation of disembodied souls. It is the salvation of matter: matter created by God and redeemed by God and manifested in the sheer materiality of Jesus himself. Glory, therefore, in John's Gospel is itself saving; it is the divine glory manifest in the flesh, in the body, and in the temple that redeems all matter, restoring it to God.

But there is more occurring here than the continuing revelation of glory. The language shifts from the noun (*doxa*) to the verb (*doxazō*), and we find here a motif of mutual glorification between Father and Son, which signals the inner meaning of the sacrifice of the cross. The body of Jesus, tortured, killed, and mutilated, glorifies God because it reveals the radical love of God in the lifting up and open arms of Jesus (12:32). In doing so, it overcomes in judgement the "ruler of this world" (12:31).[25] Death itself conquers death and, in doing so, glorifies God.[26] In the same way, Simon Peter will glorify God through his death, which will be a sign of the divine life and glory to the unbelieving world (21:19). Jesus himself will be glorified in the cross because of the radical transformation that will restore him to an unending life and to the Father's side (20:17).

TEMPLE, GLORY, AND COMMUNITY

One further aspect of the temple theme in John's Gospel is its effects on the community of Jesus-followers. In the

---

25. On the cross as cosmic victory, see Judith L. Kovacs, "'Now Shall the Ruler of This World Be Driven Out': Jesus' Death as Cosmic Battle in John 12:20–36," *JBL* 114 (1995): 226–47.

26. On the cross as glory, see Frey, *Glory of the Crucified One*, 237–58.

Great Prayer (also known as the High Priestly Prayer, John 17:1–26), Jesus speaks in effect of believers sharing his glory; he prays that they may "be with" him and "see" his glory, which has been given to them (17:21–22). What does it mean for Jesus to donate his glory to his followers? At one level, it denotes the eternal life that Jesus bestows in union with himself and with the Father, a love predicated on the intimate knowledge of God and the recognition of Jesus's Johannine identity (17:2–3).

It may be possible to push this notion further so that the believing community becomes the temple, the dwelling place of God.[27] It would parallel Pauline notions of the church, the household of faith, as the temple of the Holy Spirit (1 Cor 3:16–17). This is a conceivable trajectory from the Fourth Gospel, though it is not explicit in the text. Some of it depends on how we interpret John 7:37–38: will living waters flow from the believer's heart (as in most English translations) or from Jesus's side (19:34)?[28] Given the shape of John's Christology, especially in relation to the temple, the christological reading is as likely as the reference to the mission of believers: both are present in the one symbol.[29] John's theology encourages us to focus on the key christological insight of the Gospel: that the Johannine Jesus is the unique temple of God, the "way, the truth, and the life" to the Father (14:6), and that Johannine believers have as their mission the proclaiming of that identity and life-giving sacrifice.

---

27. E.g., Coloe, *God Dwells with Us*, 176–77.

28. For the former view, see Coloe, *God Dwells with Us*, 125–30; for the latter, see, e.g., Moloney, *John*, 256–57 and Keener, *Gospel of John*, 1.728–30.

29. See Rhonda G. Crutcher, *That He Might Be Revealed: Water Imagery and the Identity of Jesus in the Gospel of John* (Eugene, OR: Pickwick, 2015), 137–42.

REFLECTIONS

The notion of a human being as divine is not new in the ancient world; apart from other characters—heroes in mythology, for example—Roman emperors, beginning with Julius Caesar, had the same claim made of them, and sometimes by them. What is extraordinary is the notion of a human being in his material reality being and replacing a temple—and not just any temple, but *the* temple of the one true God of the Jewish faith. That in itself is an extraordinary christological claim to make, and perhaps only an ancient person familiar with temples on every street corner and a multiplicity of deities could appreciate its truly radical nature.

For those within the Jewish faith, this redefinition of temple was also a challenging and radical conception in light of the destruction of the temple in Jerusalem, the center of Judaism. Here Christians and Pharisees, living and struggling under the umbrella of a traumatized Judaism, took different paths to deal with the tragic reality of the temple's demise. This catastrophe was still undoubtedly alive in the memories of some within the Johannine community. Christian Judaism offered an alternative to Pharisaic Judaism, each holding to the same ancestral traditions to understand a new way of being as a result of the Jewish War. For some Jewish people, as reflected in several of the characters in the Gospel, the Christian way was too shocking and extreme to be admissible. For other Jewish people—as for some Gentiles—it made sense precisely within the traditions and rituals of the Old Testament.

For modern people in developed nations, the situation is rather different. The temple imagery is archaic in a predominantly secular Western society—though that is not necessarily the case for other cultures and traditions outside the

West. In a very different context, the key question revolves around that of worship, understood in a metaphorical rather than literal sense. Who or what lies at the center of our lives, giving them meaning, direction, and purpose? To whom or to what are our energies and desires directed? The answer helps to define the object of our worship, whether that be family and relationships or career and security or status, leisure, and wealth.

The Fourth Gospel offers the Johannine Jesus and the goodness and radiance he embodies as the true center of desire, the only authentic object of worship. Although John's Gospel does not quote it explicitly, what lies behind this is the First Commandment: "You shall have no other gods before me" (Exod 20:3). With Jesus as the locus of worship, other things fall naturally into place. To center our worship on Jesus, on the God who sends him, and on the Spirit who makes Jesus present means that we do not worship other things instead: such as our work, our possessions, or even members of our families. The Bible is clear that worship of God stands at the heart of the life of faith and that worship of other people or other things is not only misguided but even dangerous: for them as well as for ourselves. To revere an object or a person as we are called to revere God puts an unbearable strain on our relationships and threatens their and our well-being. It curtails the freedom that we and they possess to love.

In John's Gospel, Jesus is not only the object of worship but also the true model, the authentic worshiper of God.[30] This does not imply that we imitate Jesus coldly, but rather that we follow him radically on the path that he himself has

---

30. Dorothy A. Lee, "In the Spirit of Truth: Worship and Prayer in the Gospel of John and the Early Fathers," in *Creation, Matter and the Image of God: Essays on John* (Adelaide, Australia: ATF, 2020), 215–36.

forged. Therefore, worship in a Johannine perspective means entry into the divine prayer of the Son to the Father. The worship space into which believers enter is the life-giving sacrificial worship of the Son, who lies at the center of the believing community's life and identity. In this sense he is the temple of God, the dwelling place of divine glory. In this process, "John relocates the place of worship from the (defunct) Jerusalem temple to the person of Jesus."[31] That same relocation of the place and person whom we worship is also a primary challenge for us as readers of the Gospel.

FURTHER READING

Bauckham, Richard. *Gospel of Glory: Major Themes in Johannine Theology*. Grand Rapids: Baker Academic, 2015.

Coloe, Mary L. *God Dwells with Us: Temple Symbolism in the Fourth Gospel*. Collegeville, MN: Liturgical, 2001.

Frey, Jörg. *The Glory of the Crucified One: Christology and Theology in the Gospel of John*. Translated by Wayne Coppins and Christoph Heilig. Waco, TX: Baylor University Press, 2018.

Thompson, Marianne Meye. *The Humanity of Jesus in the Fourth Gospel*. Philadelphia: Fortress, 1988.

Troost-Cramer, Kathleen. *Jesus as Means and Locus of Worship in the Fourth Gospel: Sacrifice and Worship Space in John*. Eugene, OR: Pickwick, 2017.

Um, Stephen T. *The Theme of Temple Christology in John's Gospel*. LNTS 312. London: T&T Clark, 2006.

---

31. Troost-Cramer, *Jesus as Means and Locus*, 114.

CHAPTER 6

Witness and Believing

He came as a witness . . . so that all might believe through him. (1:7)

The two themes of this chapter, witness and believing, are a closely related duo within the narrative of the Fourth Gospel. In one sense the two concepts seem very different. The language of witness or testimony is forensic and deals with the public and political sphere. By contrast, the language of believing is that of personal relationship and community as the basis of discipleship. Yet the one leads to the other in the Johannine worldview: bearing witness to the truth in the Johannine Jesus gives rise to and strengthens faith—or "believing," since John never uses the noun *faith* but always the verbal form *believe*. The two themes are intertwined by virtue of the hostile realities of the world in which the Johannine community finds itself and in which it is called to testify despite the persecution which will inevitably follow. The underlying point is that believing is not an end in itself but is directed to mission and evangelism.

What this means for Johannine understanding is that spirituality and mission go hand in hand within the broader perspective of the Fourth Gospel's ecclesiology—that is, John's understanding of the significance and place of the church in the economy of salvation. This chapter, therefore,

117

under the umbrella of the twin themes of witnessing and believing, covers the Gospel's key perspectives on discipleship, mission, spirituality, and growth in holiness.[1] Spirituality refers here, in the first place, to John's understanding of the work and activity of the Spirit in connecting to the human spirit;[2] only in a secondary sense does it refer to how the reader apprehends the meaning of the Gospel.

OLD TESTAMENT BACKGROUND

The background to the witness theme is clearly forensic: language that has its roots in the Old Testament. Moses is credited with the appointment of judges and the Israelite judicial system to ensure justice among God's people (Exod 18:24–26), based on the giving of the law on Mount Sinai.[3] The book of Judges describes the period before the monarchy when judges—including a female judge, Deborah—were responsible for leadership across the land; this role was later incorporated into the monarchy. Law and justice are an intrinsic part of the covenant.

Alongside the theme of the divine gift of the law runs that of judgement in the Old Testament Scriptures. Many of the prophetic books rail against the two greatest breaches of the covenant: idolatry (against God) and social injustice (against the poor and vulnerable). The prophets proclaim divine judgement against infidelity and disregard for God's law. Judgment is particularly proclaimed against those who

---

1. Gabriel-Mary Fiore (*Spirituality in John's Gospel: Historical Developments and Critical Foundations* [Eugene, OR: Pickwick, 2023], 281–347) understands John's spirituality in terms of mysticism, which he carefully defines.

2. Dorothy A. Lee, *Hallowed in Truth and Love: Spirituality in the Johannine Literature* (Eugene, OR: Wipf & Stock, 2012), 9–12.

3. On law and covenant in the Old Testament, see Amy-Jill Levine, *The Old Testament* (Chantilly, VA: The Teaching Company, 2001), 162–98.

appear religious and do not neglect religious ritual, yet continue to oppress the poor (e.g., Isa 1:11–17; Amos 5:21–24; Mic 3:9–11). Such oracles proclaim God's displeasure with the behavior of those who fail to observe the most fundamental command of the Torah: to love God above all else (Deut 6:5) and to "love your neighbor as yourself" (Lev 19:18).

The theme of God on trial is also found in the Old Testament. In Exodus 17, the Israelites accuse God of freeing them from Egypt in order to annihilate them in the wilderness. The Book of Job uses forensic imagery to depict Job's sufferings and his desire to place God on trial (Job 9), even though that trial is later reversed by God's self-manifestation (Job 40–41). In Deutero-Isaiah, God ironically requests the people to put God on trial: "Accuse me, let us go to trial; set forth your case, so that you may be proved right" (Isa 43:26).[4]

The role of witness is closely allied to that of the trial scene. So important is the role of testimony in the law courts and administration of justice in the Torah that one of the Ten Commandments explicitly forbids giving false witness or testimony against a neighbour (Exod 20:16; Deut 5:20; also Exod 23:1–2). Furthermore, a single witness is insufficient: two or three are necessary for a conviction (Deut 19:15), and the penalty for false testimony is severe (Deut 19:16–19). Not only individuals such as Samuel are witnesses (Sir 46:19), but God also plays the role of witness, knowing the human heart (Wis 1:6) and testifying against those who break the covenant (Jer 42:5; Mic 1:2; Mal 3:5).[5]

Believing is a more prominent theme in the Old Testament,

---

4. See Edmund P. Clowney, "God on Trial," *Christianity Today*, February 24, 1978, 16–17, https://www.christianitytoday.com/ct/1978/february-24/god-on-trial.html.

5. On the legal system in ancient Israel and the Hebrew Bible, see Raymond Westbrook and Bruce Wells, *Everyday Law in Biblical Israel: An Introduction* (Louisville, KY: Westminster John Knox, 2009).

which, like the witness imagery, is closely tied to the covenant. While there is no actual word for "faith" in Hebrew, the notion is present in ideas of trust and the covenant faithfulness of God.[6] In the New Testament, Hebrews 11 captures something of this Old Testament theme, giving an outline of Israel's faith in the list of those who lived by the covenant and trusted the faithful promises of God. This panoply of pre-Christian "saints" begins with Abel and Enoch, moving through the people of God to include Abraham, the great icon and originator of faith in his various trials and tribulations (Gen 12–25), along with Sarah, Joseph, Moses, and Rahab.

THE ROMAN BACKGROUND

While the theme of believing is not of particular relevance in the world of Greco-Roman religion, the use of forensic imagery is present, particularly in the context of oratory. Rhetoric—the art of persuasive speech—was an essential part of the ancient curriculum and was particularly exercised in the law courts. The great Roman orator, lawyer, and philosopher Cicero (106–43 BCE) published a number of his speeches from the courts and was both a formidable defendant and prosecutor. His inventive facility with language in his oratory and other writings did much to influence public opinion in his political career (even though it ended disastrously) and in the subsequent history of Latin.

Language about the law courts is closely tied to the theme of witness, which is essentially forensic and linked to judicial

---

6. Nicholas King, "Faith in the Old Testament," *Thinking Faith*, January 23, 2013, https://www.thinkingfaith.org/articles/20130123_1.htm. Note, in particular, Hab 2:4. According to Walter Brueggemann, faith in the Old Testament is concerned with "steadfast love and faithfulness," which becomes "grace and truth" at John 1:14 ("Faith," in *Reverberations of Faith: A Theological Handbook of Old Testament Themes* [Louisville, KY: Westminster John Knox, 2002], 76 [76–79]).

imagery. In the first century CE, justice was administered in Palestine by both Jewish and Roman judicial systems. Technically, the Jewish ruling body was the Sanhedrin, a body of both priests and elders, which was presided over by the high priest and responsible for religious and judicial matters. The high priesthood was supposed to be a lifelong role, though that changed under Roman hegemony. Caiaphas was the high priest in Jesus's day, yet his father-in-law Annas, a previous high priest, was still alive and continued to hold considerable influence. John's Gospel records a brief appearance of Jesus before Annas after his arrest and no actual trial before Caiaphas and the Sanhedrin, but the meeting of the Sanhedrin earlier in the Gospel following the raising of Lazarus, presided over by Caiaphas, establishes the plot to kill Jesus for reasons of political expediency (11:47–53).

In 63 BCE, the Romans had entered and conquered Palestine, bringing to an end Jewish self-rule under the Hasmonean dynasty, which had lasted for more than a century. Instead, the Roman-appointed Herodian family ruled the land, acting as a buffer between Judaism and the Romans, which lasted until the Jewish revolt against Rome in 66 CE. Judea was a Roman province under the control of a Roman governor, Pontius Pilate, whose authority was exercised without sensitivity to Jewish religious feeling, with minimal justice and often violence.

Such insensitivity and the harsh system of taxation eventually led to the Jewish War (66–73 CE) and the destruction of Jerusalem and the temple by the Romans, as we have already noted in chapters 2, 5, and 6. Thereafter, Judaism changed radically with the demise of key groups such as the Sadducees and the Essenes, while the Pharisees, whose power base was across the country and not confined to Jerusalem, reorganized Judaism around the law rather than the temple and its rituals. The Christians, on the other hand, reorganized themselves around Jesus of Nazareth.[7] The opposition to Jesus in the Gospel of John reflects not only the realities of Jewish life and debate in the 30s but also the post-70 CE context in which Jesus's main opposition among Jewish authorities comes from the Pharisees.

WITNESS AND BELIEVING IN PROLOGUE

The prologue of John's Gospel makes the vital link between witness and believing, presenting these as part and parcel of the community's existence and the basis of its missional activity. The church's role is to bear witness, a role that goes back to John the Baptist, whose ministry interweaves on a more pedestrian level with the lofty and poetic language of the prologue's depiction of creation and redemption (1:1–5). Readers of John often separate these two themes, but they are intrinsically connected, as the structure of the prologue makes plain. The Baptist's witness, which John the evangelist emphasizes, has believing as its fundamental purpose: "he came as a witness to bear witness to the light so that all might believe through him" (1:7).

In the verses which follow John's initial testimony, we return to the theme of the coming of the light and the rejection of "his own" (1:11–12): creation itself fails to recognize its own Creator.[8] The tragedy of rejection, however, does

---

7. On the Roman and Jewish social and political history in the centuries preceding Jesus and the first century CE, see David A. deSilva, *An Introduction to the New Testament: Contexts, Methods & Ministry Formation*, 2nd ed. (Downers Grove: IVP Academic, 2018), 9–81.

8. Is it "the Jews" who reject the Light or the world in general, or both? Most commentators argue that it is a reference to Israel (e.g., Craig S. Keener, *The Gospel of John: A Commentary*, vol. 2[Peabody, MA: Hendrickson, 2003], 2.1398–99), but, given the context of creation in 1:1–5, it may well be a reference to the whole world, which is the domain of the Creator (e.g., Frederick Dale Bruner, *The Gospel of John: A Commentary* [Grand Rapids: Eerdmans, 2012], 27–28).

not have the last word: some people recognize and come to believe through the miraculous labor and birthing of God (1:13). What begins with the testimony of John thus ends with the believing of the "children of God" (1:6–13); it can be set out in a chiastic pattern:

A Believing (6–8)
  B Coming of light (9)
  B¹ Rejection of light (10–11)
A¹ Acceptance of light by children of God: believing (12–13)

The newly birthed children are the "we" who behold the glory of the incarnate Christ, which is a reference to the church, the believing community. Once again John's witness intervenes, alternating prosaically with the more poetic elements of the last cycle of the prologue (1:15). This testimony is explicitly christological in these verses. It is to Jesus, the one who is "first" and the Word, Wisdom, and Son of God to whom John the Baptist bears witness. Such a testimony has believing as its abundant harvest (see 4:35–38). These two themes will be treated separately in what follows, but fundamentally they belong together as two sides of the same coin.

TRIAL MOTIF

Forensic imagery can be traced throughout the Fourth Gospel, particularly in the trial motif.[9] This theme begins with the interrogation of John the Baptist in the opening narrative (1:19–28). First priests and Levites, then Pharisees come to question his identity and the theological basis of his baptismal practice. These would appear to be official

---

9. See esp. Andrew T. Lincoln, *Truth on Trial. The Lawsuit Motif in the Fourth Gospel* (Peabody, MA: Hendrickson, 2000).

124 John

delegations, and their questioning carries more than a hint of hostility. Similarly, confrontational interrogation is also aimed at Jesus following the cleansing of the temple: "What sign do you show . . . ?" (2:18) In other words, by what right do you take these actions upon yourself?

The trial imagery continues beyond the opening narratives. Again and again, Jesus comes up against certain members of the Jerusalem establishment who bring legal accusations against him: that he breaks the Sabbath (5:16; 9:14); that he is uneducated in the law and therefore not qualified to teach (7:15); that his messianic status is undermined by his non-messianic origins in Galilee (7:50–52); that his testimony is invalid because he testifies on his own behalf (8:13); that he is demon-possessed (8:48; 10:20); and that he constitutes a political threat to Rome (11:48–53). Sometimes Jesus is under threat of arrest, but is protected by his popularity (7:30–32, 45–49; 10:39), or spontaneous attempts are made to execute him by stoning on the grounds of blasphemy, which he manages to escape (8:58–59; 10:30–33).

The trial motif also involves Jesus's disciples. The man born blind faces his own interrogation from the Jerusalem authorities, although their hostility ironically draws him to faith (9:24–34). The more they try to make him defame Jesus, the more he supports him and the more courageous is his response. Most of this narrative, except for the outer frames (9:1–7, 35–41), takes place in the absence of Jesus, which may reflect the social and religious experience of the community behind the Gospel in the period after Jesus's departure.[10] The

---

10. E.g., J. Louis Martyn sees the references to "put out of the synagogue" (*aposunagōgos*, 9:22; 12:42; 16:2) as referring to a synagogue ban in which Johannine Christians were effectively excommunicated (*History and Theology in the Fourth Gospel*, 3rd ed., NTL [Louisville, KY: Westminster John Knox, 2003], 35–66). There are historical problems, however, with this view; see Jo-Ann A. Brant, *John*, Paideia (Grand Rapids: Baker Academic, 2011), 166–68.

Johannine Jesus also warns his followers of hatred and persecution from the world (15:18–16:4). Indeed, throughout the Farewell Discourse the theme of peace from anxiety recurs precisely within a context in which the disciples are on trial for their faith in the absence of Jesus (14:25–31; 16:22, 33).

There is considerable debate among scholars about whether John's Gospel is antisemitic or not in its constant reference to "the Jews"; this debate will be further explored in chapter 8. Yet this Gospel places the Romans at the center of Jesus's death. The main trial of Jesus in John's Gospel is before Pilate, and his death is a Roman not a Jewish method of execution. Although some Jewish authorities are implicated—elite groups in Jerusalem associated with the Sadducees and dependent for their continuing power on Rome[11]—the threat to Roman rule is the key issue of contention and is the main reason for Jesus's condemnation. Throughout the Fourth Gospel, the main characters are almost all Jews, including Jesus and his disciples, and the disagreements and hostility throughout his ministry is most likely intramural—that is, within the diverse boundaries of Judaism. Yet, in the end, the Romans are responsible for Jesus's death.

The hearing before Pilate is the main scene in the Johannine trial; there is only a short narrative of Jesus's trial before the high priest (18:19–24). The Roman narrative is carefully constructed in seven scenes with an inside and outside movement, as Pilate shuttles between the Jerusalem authorities outside the governor's headquarters and Jesus within (18:28–19:16a). The characterization of Pilate as judge in these scenes is complex: in moving back and forth

---

11. See Israel Knohl, *The Messiah Confrontation: Pharisees Versus Sadducees and the Death of Jesus*, ET (Lincoln, NE: University of Nebraska Press, 2022), 113–24.

126 John

between the Jerusalem authorities and Jesus, he is facing a dilemma. In the end, however, he chooses the side of injustice and falsehood against truth. He is at best weak and manipulable and at worse malevolent, knowing Jesus to be innocent but appeasing the Jerusalem leaders, whom he despises, in order to save his own skin.[12] His characterization in John illustrates the injustice which forms part of the Gospel's understanding of sin, at the root of which is the great lie, the denial of truth, the deceitful work of "the father of lies" (8:44).

There is a profound irony in the trial motif throughout the Gospel. Not only does the courtroom scenario lead the man born blind, for example, to reassess radically the significance and identity of Jesus, but the trial itself is ultimately overturned across the narrative. This is nowhere better expressed than when Pilate sits on the "seat of judgement" (*bēma*) to pronounce his final verdict on Jesus (19:13); the Greek is ambiguous and it is not at all clear who sits on the judgement seat, Jesus or Pilate. From a narrative perspective it has to be Pilate, of course, but the original wording could also in theory be rendered: "he [Pilate] sat Jesus on the *bēma*." This ambiguity reflects the nature of the real trial in this Gospel. It is Jesus who is the true Judge: who does not judge yet paradoxically whose judgement is true (8:15–16). The Light of the world shines on the unbelieving character of Pilate, as it does on Judas and Caiaphas and all who make judgement against Jesus. Their judgement is finally overthrown because "the ruler of this world has been condemned" (16:11).

---

12. D. Francois Tolmie, "Pontius Pilate: Failing in More Ways Than One," in *Character Studies in the Fourth Gospel: Narrative Approaches to Seventy Figures in John*, ed. Steven A. Hunt, D. Francois Tolmie, and Ruben Zimmermann, WUNT 314 (Tübingen: Mohr Siebeck, 2013), 578–97.

BEARING WITNESS

The trial motif running through the Gospel is the reason that the witness theme is so overt and a major theme.[13] Bearing witness is precisely what is done in a courtroom, and the main conception behind the imagery is that of truth. Three times in the prologue there is reference to truth, in each case in relation to Jesus himself. In the first place, the Word is the "true" light (*alēthinos*, 1:9) in comparison to John the Baptist, the "burning and shining lamp" (*luchnos*, 5:35) who bears witness to the truth. The phrase "grace and truth" (*charis kai alētheia*, 1:14, 17) is used of Jesus twice in the third cycle of the prologue, which defines the way Jesus lives out the truth: with an abundance of grace (1:16), an overflowing of love and mercy.

Later in the Gospel, Jesus will declare himself to *be* the truth in the last of the "I am" sayings in the Gospel (14:6). This truth is life-giving and leads directly to God, who is true (e.g., 3:33; 8:26; 17:3). The Spirit also is associated with truth (14:17; 15:26; 16:13; also 4:24), leading the disciples to the same divine location. Pilate cynically asks "What is truth?" (an odd question from a judge!) even though Truth itself stands before him. The words Jesus utters and the gifts he gives are true, and therefore are both reliable and liberating (e.g., 6:55; 8:32, 45–46).

Indeed, the Gospel narrative itself, from the vantage point of the plot, is bounded on either side by the witness theme and its imagery. This theme bookends the Gospel. John the Baptist is the first witness in the Gospel in his proclaiming of the incarnation and Jesus as the Lamb of God

---

13. James Montgomery Boice, *Witness and Revelation in the Gospel of John* (Grand Rapids: Zondervan, 1970) and Allison A. Trites, *The New Testament Concept of Witness*, SNTSMS 31 (Cambridge, UK: Cambridge University Press), 78–124.

(1:15, 29, 36), while the beloved disciple is the last, bearing witness to Jesus's death and resurrection through his eyewitness testimony (19:35; 21:7) and his composition of the Gospel (21:24).[14] In this continuous sense, the Gospel itself is the witness to Jesus, bearing testimony in the court of public opinion before the values of the unbelieving world.

At the same time, John the Baptist shows the true nature of witness. His actual appearances in the Gospel narrative recede, just as he himself does in the presence of the Bridegroom: "he must increase and I must decrease" (3:30). The same is true of the Samaritan who bears witness to Jesus's identity to her fellow villagers (4:29–30). Upon their arrival at the well, the other Samaritans explain that they initially believed "on account of the word of the woman bearing witness," but now have reached a deeper level of believing in their own meeting with Jesus (4:39–42). Her witness is, in other words, no longer needed and Jesus, the "Savior of the world," now occupies center stage.[15]

Perhaps that is why the beloved disciple is never named in this Gospel. He is the last witness, and the Gospel itself represents his testimony par excellence. His soubriquet as "the disciple whom Jesus loved" gives him, on the one hand, an exalted status as a true disciple worthy of his calling as an evangelist, but his anonymity, on the other hand, undercuts it. He, too, recedes, like John the Baptist and the Samaritan woman, giving way before Jesus, the Lord of life.

We might speak of other disciples also bearing witness to Jesus's identity in the Gospel narrative, such as we find in the

---

14. Dorothy A. Lee, "Witness in the Fourth Gospel: John the Baptist and the Beloved Disciple as Counterparts," *ABR* 61 (2013): 1–17.

15. On the positive confirmation of the woman's faith, as attested by the Samaritans, see Teresa Okure, *The Johannine Approach to Mission: A Contextual Study of John 4:1–42*, WUNT II/31 (Tübingen: Mohr Siebeck, 1988), 168–81.

Witness and Believing

confessions of faith uttered by Simon Peter (6:68), Martha (11:27), and Thomas (20:28). The language of testimony is not explicit in these instances, but it is implied and undergirds the testimony of the community at large. The Farewell Discourse makes it explicit that the disciples themselves are to bear witness to Jesus, with the aid of the Paraclete-Spirit (15:26–27). The evangelist draws on instructions in the Torah about testimony: its role in the revelation of the divine nature and the need for it to be both genuine and corroborated (e.g., Deut 19:15).

Of much greater significance—and frequency in the Gospel—is the testimony offered by Jesus himself. This is not in any sense narrowly focused. Jesus bears witness to himself (though with reservations, 5:31); he can do so because his own identity is truth (3:32–33; 8:14; 18:37) and because the signs and works of his ministry confirm that trustworthy identity (5:36; 10:25). His witness is corroborated by the Father (5:32, 37) and by the Spirit. It is also confirmed by the Scriptures and by those who represent them, particularly Moses (5:39, 45–47).[16] Not only does this count as numerous corroborations in the Johannine world, but it is also extraordinarily weighty, particularly in the context of the increasingly hostile dialogue with members of the synagogue. How is the witness of the Father and the Spirit made palpable, given that neither can be seen? The Johannine answer is all of the above: the Scriptures, the deeds of Jesus's ministry, and the authentic life and love of the believing community—all of which have as their deepest meaning and purpose the revelation of God in Jesus. We will see more of this theme in chapter 8.

---

16. On the role of the Old Testament Scriptures in John's Gospel, see Rekha M. Chennattu, "Scripture," in *How John Works: Storytelling in the Fourth Gospel,* ed. Douglas Estes and Ruth Sheridan (Atlanta: SBL, 2016), 171–86. This theme will be further explored in the last chapter.

There are two further elements to witness in the Fourth Gospel. The first is that the divine witness testifies not only to Jesus's identity but also to the reality of the world in its enslavement to sin and death (7:7; also 16:8–10). A note of challenge is here, which is part of Jesus's role as the Light of the world. The second aspect is that the witness can be, and is, rejected, often on the basis of that challenging testimony. The conflict throughout the Gospel revolves in part around whether Jesus's testimony is to be accepted or not (3:11, 32; 8:14; 10:25). The cross is, among other things, the ultimate symbol of that rejection of truth and of Jesus's witness in John's Gospel: elite Jewish and also Roman authorities collaborating in an unholy alliance to rid the world, ironically, of its only access to truth.

The context of witness is closely allied to that of mission in John's narrative. God is the "having-sent-me-Father" while Jesus is the "Sent-One," commissioned by the Father to carry out the mission of God by bearing witness through his life, death, and resurrection (4:34; 5:36–37; 6:29, 44, 57; 7:16; 8:16–18; 9:4, 7; 12:49; 14:24; 17:21).[17] There is also a corresponding sending out of disciples in the Gospel, as a direct consequence of Jesus's sending and as part of their own bearing witness. In its mission, the community is to be both a sign to the unbelieving world (13:35; 17:23) and sent into it by the Father in the power of Jesus's Spirit (20:23).[18]

---

17. See Paul N. Anderson, "The Having-Sent-Me Father: Aspects of Agency, Encounter, and Irony in the Johannine Father-Son Relationship," *Semeia* 79 (1999): 33–57.

18. Andrew T. Lincoln argues that "world" in John (*kosmos*) always has a negative connotation, including at 3:16 (though most think the reference there is neutral), which for him refers to "the world in its alienation from and hostility to its creator's purposes," and which paradoxically God loves (*The Gospel According to Saint John*, BNTC [London: Continuum, 2005], 154). But John uses terms such as "world" (*kosmos*) in different ways, depending on the context.

BELIEVING

In the Johannine view, believing is the authentic response to divine revelation.[19] To believe in Jesus means to believe in God: "the one who believes in me believes not in me but in the one who sent me" (12:44); "you believe in God, believe also in me" (14:1). The first resurrection narrative closes with the summary words: "these are written that you may come to believe [or go on believing] that Jesus is the Christ/ Messiah, the Son of God" (20:31). In this respect, John sees believing as the one "work" (*ergon*) required by God: "This is the work of God that you believe in the one whom he [God] has sent" (6:29). True believing, in this Gospel, signifies an "unreserved openness to God,"[20] leading to love and worship.

Believing means experiencing the complex character of revelation, which unfolds to disclose who God is in Jesus, who we are as human beings, and what the world is.[21] The story of the Samaritan woman is a good example, since her believing grows as the revelation becomes more explicit: the revelation of her own self (4:29) and of Jesus's messianic identity (4:26). In this sense, believing in John is cognitive as well as affective: it involves the mind as well as the heart. It means to believe in the revealed name of Jesus (17:6), with all that that signifies in terms of content and experience: "And this is eternal life, that they might know you, the only true God, and the one whom

---

19. For further details on this theme, see Sherri Brown, *Come and See: Discipleship in the Gospel of John*, BSCBA (New York: Paulist, 2022), 16–37 and Dorothy A. Lee, *Hallowed in Truth and Love: Spirituality in the Johannine Literature* (Eugene, OR: Wipf & Stock, 2012), 135–40.

20. Sandra M. Schneiders, *Written That You May Believe: Encountering Jesus in the Fourth Gospel* (New York: Crossroad, 1999), 87.

21. Rudolf Schnackenburg, *The Gospel According to St John*, ET, 3 vols. (Tunbridge Wells, UK: Burns & Oates, 1968–1983), Excursus on Faith, 558–75.

132   John

you sent, Jesus Christ" (17:3). Knowledge in this sense is both relational and intelligible.

Believing can also be ambiguous, if not ambivalent, in this Gospel. The dialogue in the Tabernacles narrative (7:1–52; 8:12–59) presents those who initially come to believe (8:31) but eventually reject Jesus and finally take up stones against him (8:59). If based only on signs and Jesus's miraculous powers, believing is weak, vulnerable, and easily lost. Unbelief in this sense is characteristic of Jesus's adversaries who reject the revelation. They consider Jesus heretical and demonic (8:48, 52), sinful (9:24), seditious (11:48), and guilty of blasphemy (5:18; 19:7). In spite of their claim to be the true disciples and inheritors of Moses (5:45–46; 8:39, 41; 9:28–29), the opponents reject the very one to whom, according to John, Moses testifies (1:45).

At the same time, John's Gospel presents believing as a spectrum rather than a strict either-or: "faith is not a one-time event, but a process."[22] Many of the characters of the Gospel need to grow in understanding—they generally start with partial understanding or outright misunderstanding. Some characters or groups move towards believing then veer away from it, as does the crowd in the narrative of John 6. Martha is an example of one who believes and is committed to Jesus, but whose faith grows in dialogue with Jesus (11:21–27). By definition, believing is something that needs to develop through misunderstanding, as the full implications of Jesus's revelation dawn; it can also and equally be rejected in the opposite step-by-step movement.

In this process, teaching and learning play an important role. The word *disciple* (*mathētēs*) means, literally, one who

---

22. On the ambiguity of 20:31, see Gail R. O'Day and Susan E. Hylen, *John*, WBC (Louisville, KY: Westminster John Knox, 2006), 197.

Witness and Believing 133

studies or learns (linked to the verb *manthanō*, "learn"). We generally assume that a disciple is primarily a follower of Jesus, and imagery of following is certainly present in the Gospel. For instance, Jesus explicitly calls Simon Peter to follow him in a different context: into leadership and martyrdom in the resurrection narratives (21:19, 22). Discipleship, however, is even more about learning. In this sense, it is not just something given but rather something that develops into a lifelong commitment: "In this is my Father glorified, that you bear much fruit and *become* my disciples" (15:8). To believe, therefore, is to learn and to plumb the depths of divine knowledge through abiding in love (as we will see in chapter 7). Learning lies at the basis of Johannine spirituality; it is part and parcel of believing.

If disciples are students—learning what it means to believe—Jesus is the Teacher in this Gospel. Although we might more commonly associate this title with the Matthean Jesus, it is also a feature of the Christology of the Fourth Gospel. The first two disciples address Jesus as "Rabbi" at the beginning of John (1:38) and Mary the Magdalene acknowledges the risen Christ as "Rabbouni" ("my Rabbi") when she recognizes him towards the end (20:16); in both cases, the evangelist translates the Aramaic term for "Teacher" into the Greek (*didaskalos*).[23] Jesus admits the rightness of this designation: he is indeed their Teacher, as he is their Lord (*kurios*, 13:13). His teaching, in other words, is intrinsically connected to his sovereignty: his authority over life and death. It has definitive origins because it comes from God (7:16), even though the Jerusalem elite consider Jesus unlearned and unschooled (7:15). With the departure of Jesus following the resurrection, the Spirit-Paraclete enables this teaching to continue in the life of the community: a vibrant calling to mind of Jesus's own teaching in ever-new

---

23. Keener, *Gospel of John*, 1.685–86.

contexts (16:13). John's is a spirituality of pedagogical growth. As Teacher, the Johannine Jesus leads believers to deeper levels of faith, knowledge, and understanding.

The group around Jesus is invariably referred to as "disciples," but this is not confined to the apostles. John makes only a couple of references to "the twelve," who are never called apostles (6:67–71; 20:24). It is therefore difficult to gain any clear apprehension of where the boundaries lie in the group around Jesus. Five individuals are referenced in the opening narrative in addition to John the Baptist (1:19–51), to whom the mother of Jesus is added (2:1–12). Others are included among Jesus's disciples who are not necessarily physical followers: Martha, Mary, and Lazarus are examples (11:1–12:11). One thing is clear: women as well as men are included among Jesus's disciples, and there is no justification in John for restricting discipleship to the twelve apostles. Women in this Gospel are as capable of demonstrating, and developing in, believing; indeed, they often show the true nature of discipleship.[24]

One way of describing the growth of believing in discipleship is that of *theosis* ("deification").[25] This notion is an extrapolation from the Fourth Gospel and never found overtly within its pages. But it is common in the early writers of the church, who speak of God becoming human so that humans may become divine, a theme that derives from 2 Peter: "so that . . . [you] may become participants in the divine nature" (2 Pet 1:4). *Theosis* means growth into ever-deepening union

---

24. On this, see esp. Holly J. Carey, *Women Who Do: Female Disciples in the Gospels* (Grand Rapids: Eerdmans, 2023), 155–84, 185–88; also Dorothy A. Lee, *The Ministry of Women in the New Testament: Reclaiming the Biblical Vision for Church Leadership* (Grand Rapids: Baker Academic, 2021), 75–95.

25. See esp. Michael J. Gorman, *Abide and Go: Missional Theosis in the Gospel of John*, DLS (Eugene, OR: Cascade, 2018), 8–26 and Andrew J. Byers, *Ecclesiology and Theosis in the Gospel of John*, SNTSMS 166 (Cambridge, UK: Cambridge University Press, 2017), 169–223.

with God and participation in the divine character: not to cease being human but in order to share the divine nature in its goodness, immortality, and love. It signifies the progression in holiness (17:20–23). In so doing, believers regain their true identity as creatures formed in the image of God (Gen 1:26–27), becoming true children of God through believing (1:12–13). In this sense, theosis is the end result of believing: the gradual ascent to God by entering more and more fully into the divine glory revealed in Jesus (17:24).

REFLECTIONS

There are a number of implications to John's theology of witness and believing for us as Christians. In the first place, we need to bear in mind that the language of believing and discipleship is primarily ecclesial in the Fourth Gospel. Unlike other parts of the New Testament, such as the Pauline writings or Matthew's Gospel, John's Gospel does not use explicit language of "church" (*ekklēsia*), although the word does occur in the third Johannine epistle (3 John 6, 9). Yet for all that, images of the church are present and of great significance in the Fourth Gospel.[26] The symbolism of the parable of the sheepfold, with Jesus as the Gate and Good Shepherd, is essentially communal, going back to Old Testament imagery of Israel as the people of God (10:1–18; Ps 23; Ezek 34). The same is true for the parable of the vineyard, with Jesus as the true Vine, which is likewise drawn from Old Testament symbolism for Israel (15:1–17; Ps 80:6–18; Isa 5:1–7).

The third ecclesial symbol comes in the second part of the resurrection narratives in the story of the miraculous

---

26. On the church in John's Gospel, see R. Alan Culpepper, "The Quest for the Church in the Gospel of John," *Int* 63 (2009): 341–54.

catch of fish, which the net can barely hold; it is an image of the church in its mission and suggests that the borders are porous. This image also has an Old Testament meaning connected to Israel (21:1–14; Ezek 47:8–10).[27] The collegial nature of discipleship in this Gospel thus presents a significant challenge to the individualism and isolationism of much contemporary Western culture, where community structures are fragile or even nonexistent.

Bearing witness is part of that ecclesial reality. The church's role is to bear witness to Jesus, who is himself the true witness to the Father, as much in actions as in words, just as Jesus's ministry is grounded in his signs and works. Loving action for others is the basis of this mission, as well as teaching on the true nature of God in Christ. Our role is to bear witness in the way John the Baptist does: we are to "decrease in order that he might increase" (3:30). Here John the Baptist acts as a model for the church's mission.[28] It follows that self-promotion, whether personal or ecclesial, has no place in the church's life and witness. In an image-centered culture, it is too easy to become obsessed with outward appearance in the public sphere, an obsession not helped by recent revelations of abuse from within the church itself. Our public character implies the capacity to confess wrongdoing and to be concerned not to exalt or justify ourselves but rather to present the challenging and forgiving face of Christ.

At the same time, John's spirituality manifests itself in personal experience. The Gospel's message is profoundly

---

27. Though a number of scholars consider John 21 a later and sympathetic addition to the Gospel, this study focuses on the final form of the Johannine narrative, regardless of the source history lying behind it. See Keener, *Gospel of John*, 2.1219–24 and Marianne Meye Thompson, *John: A Commentary*, NTL (Louisville, KY: Westminster John Knox, 2015), 431–34.

28. Fergus King, "'De Baptista nil nisi bonum': John the Baptist as a Paradigm for Mission," *MS* 26 (2009): 173–91.

Witness and Believing

personal, even if not individualistic. The promise of the Spirit-Paraclete is given to believers, enabling them to grow into the likeness of Christ (see 1 John 3:2). In an age which is craving spirituality—often set over against "religion" and the institutional church—John's Gospel offers a spirituality that encompasses the depth of human experience, that consoles anxiety and grief, and that promises hope even in the midst of the world's reality of evil and death. The spirituality of Christian faith offers a relationship with the divine life through affiliation with Jesus.

In this sense, the spirituality of believing constitutes a mindfulness of its own: God's mindfulness of us as we become aware of ourselves and the God whose love embraces us. Christians, too, can become caught up in the frantic pace of living that is so much a feature of our society. The practice of meditation finds many fertile sources and resources in the Fourth Gospel to center us around prayer and the presence of the Spirit, drawing us into the life and love of God. John's is a spirituality of fruitful abiding that encourages the silent contemplation of believing ("we *beheld* his glory," 1:14).

St Teresa of Ávila famously speaks of her own experience of meditation in terms of that mystic gaze whose initiative is always with Christ: "Notice him looking at you lovingly and humbly."[29] This meditation captures in a nutshell a Christian, and indeed Johannine, understanding of mindful awareness, which is another way to speak of believing. Such a spirituality enables us to receive Christ in our lives at the deepest level and to strengthen our capacity to bear witness to others in word and deed, whether they stand within or outside the borders of the church.

---

29. For the meditation based on this saying, see esp. Anthony de Mello, *Sadhana, A Way to God: Christian Exercises in Eastern Form* (New York: Doubleday, 1978), Ex. 37, 124–25.

FURTHER READING

Barton, Stephen C. *The Spirituality of the Gospels.* Eugene, OR: Wipf & Stock, 1992.

Brown, Sherri. *Come and See: Discipleship in the Gospel of John.* BSCBA. New York: Paulist, 2022.

Fiore, Gabriel-Marie, *Spirituality in John's Gospel: Historical Developments and Critical Foundations.* Eugene, OR: Pickwick, 2023.

Gorman, Michael J. *Abide and Go: Missional Theosis in the Gospel of John.* DLS. Eugene, OR: Cascade, 2018.

Kelly, Anthony J., and Francis J. Moloney. *Experiencing God in the Gospel of John.* New York: Paulist, 2003.

Winstanley, Michael T. *Symbols and Spirituality: Reflecting on John's Gospel.* Bolton, UK: Don Bosco, 2007.

CHAPTER 7

Birth and Family

> He gave them authority to become God's children who . . .
> of God were born. (1:12–13)

I n this chapter, we explore two linked images in the Fourth Gospel that encompass several themes relating both to God and human beings. Birth and family naturally belong together, but they are used in the Fourth Gospel as symbols for a new identity and a radically new sense of kinship.[1] This theme begins in the relationship between God and Jesus, in the Father-Son imagery which is part of the core symbolism of the Gospel. It extends also to human beings, for whom a new identity is offered that overcomes the gulf separating them from God. The imagery is that of the family of God, often called the "fictive" or artificial family: that is to say, in anthropological terms, "social ties that are neither consanguineal (based on blood) nor affinal (established through marriage)."[2] Such a family's status is not dependent on natural birth or human descent but on the forging of a new connection to God. This relationship has both vertical and

---

1. See esp. Jan G. van der Watt, *The Family of the King: Dynamics of Metaphor in the Gospel According to John*, BIS 47 (Leiden: Brill, 2000), 394–439.

2. Haley Wilson-Lemmón, "Family of God: A Christian Tradition as a Greco-Roman Phenomenon," *Studia Antiqua* 17 (2018): 16.

140   John

horizontal dimensions. Whatever may be inferred about the
actual community behind the Fourth Gospel, the narrative
gives rise to, shapes, and sustains a community based on kinship and covenant.[3]

In many ways, the new identity is a restoration of created
and creaturely identity that was somehow lost in the over-
shadowing darkness. There is already a fundamental difference between God and creation that underlies the prologue,
articulated in the verbal distinction between "being" (*eimi*)
and "becoming" (*ginomai*). This inevitable gulf implies
no fault on the part of creation. It is simply the difference
between that which is eternal by its nature and that which is
created, transient, and mortal. However, the gulf is exacer-
bated by a further division. Though John does not make the
point explicit, it is implied in the prologue and elsewhere in
the Gospel that a tragic loss has occurred, separating human
beings from their Creator and from their true identity as creatures, leading to alienation from God, from others, and from
creation itself.

FAMILY IN THE ANCIENT WORLD

One of the key differences between the ancient and the modern Western world is the nature and significance of kinship.
In contrast to the increasing individualism of Western culture, ancient society was built around the family. Friendship
had its place within that context, as we will see, but the family
was the basic social unit. People's lives were embedded rather
than detached while identity, occupation, and social and economic standing flowed from that embeddedness in kinship.

---

3. For further details on the covenant theme in the Fourth Gospel, see
Sherri Brown, *God's Promise: Covenant Relationship in John* (New York: Paulist,
2014).

Birth and Family

Family was also a wider conception, moving across the generations and beyond the nuclear family to embrace relatives—cousins, aunts and uncles, grandparents, and in-laws as well as the parents and their children. In households with some means, the family included the domestic slaves who were a significant part of the home. If slaves gained their freedom, their connection to the family continued within the broad system of patronage in ancient society. Individuals became part of the household "through analogous means: women through marriage, children through birth [and sometimes adoption], and slaves through purchase or pedigree."[4]

The household was hierarchically ordered in the ancient world and essentially patriarchal. The eldest father/grandfather stood at the top of the pyramid, with members of the household in descending order below him. In the Roman context, the father of the family (*paterfamilias*) had the power of life and death over the household. Women were generally subservient to men, depending on their social status: beneath fathers, brothers, and even sons. The mother of the family (*materfamilias*) had her own status and a degree of authority, particularly above dependent children and slaves. The latter were on the lower rungs and female slaves at the bottom.

According to Aristotle, this pyramid structure was natural: it was based on the different levels of rationality in each group. In ancient Greek society, women and small children were thought to be less capable of reason than adult men, and slaves had even less capacity for rational thought. This social order implied that those with less capacity for reason were responsible to obey those with greater capacity

---

4. Wilson-Lemmón, "Family of God," 17–18.

within the household. Slaves, who had virtually no rights and little capacity for reason, obeyed their owners (male or female), wives obeyed their husbands, and children obeyed their parents.[5]

Slaves could purchase their freedom in some contexts; in others, they were subject to the whim of their owners physically, sexually, and spiritually. They followed the religion of the head of the household, who determined the religious focus and ritual. If a female slave became pregnant, the keeping of her child (who was born a slave) was at the discretion of the *paterfamilias*. The entire economy of the ancient world, and particularly the household, was built on and maintained by slavery, and the constant expansion of the Roman Empire provided a never-ending source of such "merchandise."

Women, at least in theory, were assigned to the household as their primary domain. They could not become citizens nor could they vote. Their realm was supposed to be the private sphere, whereas men were in the public sphere. For the most part, women were not seen to possess civic virtues or capacity, but rather pursued domestic virtues and occupations. However, this picture is not uniform across the ancient world. Roman women could inherit property, unlike Greek women, and slaves could themselves become slaveowners. There were a considerable number of exceptions, particularly among wealthier women, who could play the part of benefactors and contribute in other ways to civic society. One or two philosophical schools accepted women as members, and women of status could wield considerable influence even if they possessed no actual political power.[6]

---

5. See Vernon L. Provencal, "The Family in Aristotle," *Animus* 6 (2001): 3–31.

6. On women in the New Testament world, see Lynn Cohick, *Women in the World of the Earliest Christians: Illuminating Ancient Ways of Life* (Grand Rapids: Baker Academic, 2009).

Birth and Family 143

Children were valued in most contexts—though sons more so than daughters. Female children could be exposed at birth, even those who were not slaves; the order to do so would come from the father of the family. Children followed mostly the trade or profession of their parents. In the context of "cottage industry," women worked within the family to cook and clean, and spin and weave, and taught their daughters the same skills. Schooling was limited by class, wealth, and gender; daughters received much less formal education than their brothers. Children could also be adopted and were given the status of their adopted parents.

Judaism was profoundly influenced by Hellenistic patterns of social behavior and Hellenistic values. Yet there were also differences. Children were considered gifts of God within the covenant community and infanticide was not practiced: it was in direct breach of the seventh commandment. Slaves had some rights: sexual abuse, for example, was considered sinful and they were entitled to the Sabbath rest (as were the domestic animals). In theory, the Year of Jubilee meant their release from enslavement (Lev 25:8–17). While Jewish women remained largely in the domestic sphere, they still belonged within the covenant and some were able to emerge from domesticity as leaders in the context of Jewish social and religious life. The idea of Jewish women as oppressed and domesticated, to be liberated by Jesus in his community of disciples, is a distortion of the reality of Jewish women's lives and ignores the powerful influences on Jesus himself in the context of first-century CE Judaism.[7] As we will see, the Gospel of John has ways of negotiating women's participation and engagement, and even leadership, within the new family

---

7. For further details on this, see esp. Bernadette Brooten, *Women Leaders in the Ancient Synagogue: Inscriptional Evidence and Background Issues*, BJS 36 (Atlanta: Scholars, 2020).

144   John

of believers, which owes its focus largely to Jesus's own Jewish upbringing.

Friendship also belongs within this same social schema. In both Judaism and the Greco-Roman world, friends were highly prized: so much so that they were considered members of the family, able to be incorporated into the core unit of society. The Old Testament has conspicuous examples of friendship, within and beyond familial bonds: Ruth and Naomi (Ruth 1:16–19), and David and Jonathan (1 Sam 18:1–4). Greek and Roman writers, such as Aristotle and Cicero, praise the values of friendship that can cross boundaries within otherwise unyielding social structures.[8] Accepting friends as belonging within the family is an important factor in ancient social arrangements, making possible a somewhat wider definition of the family within various groupings.

There is a further factor to consider in the existence of family groups. Hospitality was a key aspect of ancient society, where obligations towards the stranger were strong. This feature is particularly apparent in Judaism and the Old Testament, but it is also present in the Greco-Roman worldview. Strangers receiving hospitality were treated in a sense as kin, forging new ties closely linked to, but not identical to, the family. Thus, hospitality was also a form of friendship and linked to kinship. The New Testament sense of Jesus's followers as forming a deep "fictive kinship"—that is, an attachment transcending the biological family—arises in part from ancient social prototypes, including that of the acceptance of strangers as guests within the household.[9]

---

8. E.g., Aristotle, *Nicomachean Ethics*, trans. H. Rackham, LCL 73 (Cambridge, MA: Harvard University Press, 1926), books 8 and 9 and Cicero, *On Old Age, On Friendship, On Divination*, trans. W. A. Falconer, LCL 154 (Cambridge, MA: Harvard University Press, 1923), 103–211.

9. As argued by Wilson-Lemmón, "Family of God," 15–25.

IMAGERY OF BIRTH

The prologue makes it clear that a new identity is required for people to become restored to God. Something more, and something divine, is needed in the face of humankind's tragic inability to recognize its own Creator (1:11). This is not a brand-new identity, although the imagery could at first suggest it. John speaks of those who do recognize and receive the Light as being enabled to become God's children. Does this need to imply that creation itself has not already made them children of their Creator? Yet John has already made it clear that "all things" were created by God through the Logos, so that human beings are already God's creatures. John's point is that they have lost that sense of kinship to the One through whom all things became, and so a radical restoration is needed.

John makes three points about this restoration. Firstly, it involves a divinely bestowed gift: "he gave them authority to become children of God" (1:12). Some English translations somewhat shift the meaning by rendering the word *exousia* as "power" (NRSVue, RNJB, NABRE), but others are preferable in using "right" (REB, ESV, NIV) or even turning the verb and noun into "authorized," which is more accurate. The word *exousia* means literally "authority," and it implies freedom as well as capacity; "power" does not quite capture this type of freedom.

Perhaps it is reading too much into the word *exousia* to suggest that the restoration is a rediscovery of the created freedom of God's creatures, which they have somehow forfeited in becoming enslaved. Ignorance of their true nature certainly suggests a form of enslavement, an alienation from the truth of their own existence as well as the truth of their Creator. That theme emerges later in the Tabernacles

146   John

narrative when Jesus speaks of the liberating truth he bestows on his disciples in view of their enslavement to sin (8:31–36).

Secondly, the primary image John uses for the restoration of human identity is that of birth.[10] This image is particularly apt, since it has immediate implications of family. Being born into a family is what gives us our primary identity—indeed, in the ancient world it gives a lifelong identity and a permanent sense of belonging. The implication of this symbolism is that human beings require a new family: a new sense of corporate identity in relation to the Creator. Those who receive this birth become members thereby of God's family, rediscovering in the process their original creaturely identity. Birth implies not only identity but also family.

Thirdly, the prologue makes it clear that a divine miracle is required to effect this transition to a new identity and family. Human beings of themselves are incapable of effecting it. For that reason, John is careful to rule out any human capacity to bring it about. Here, the word order is significant. It happens neither "by bloods [in the plural: meaning by natural descent and physical birth through bodily fluids] nor by the will of flesh [by human desire or means] nor by the will of a man [the male initiative and need for progeny]": in other words, not by any human desire or agency or capacity. Only by God is such a miracle possible, as the final and climatic clause makes plan: "not by blood . . . but of God were born" (1:13). The paradox is that the same God by whose will and word all human beings were made is the same God by whose divine Word all creatures can be remade.

The language of birth and children echoes the Genesis language of image and likeness. Just as human beings are

---

10. On the metaphorical significance of birth, see especially Jan G. van der Watt, *Family of the King: Dynamics of Metaphor in the Gospel According to John* (Leiden: Brill, 2000), 166–200.

made in the divine image in the first creation account (Gen 1:27), so in John's Gospel that image is restored to enable them to regain what was lost. They are children of God—images of God—by right of creation and re-creation, and all from the same gracious and life-giving divine hand.

John develops this imagery more fully in the story of Nicodemus (3:1–21). Here, the symbol of birth is dominant in Jesus's response to Nicodemus's courteous arrival: "Unless one is born from above (*anōthen*), one cannot see the reign [or kingdom, *basileia*] of God" (3:3). It then appears more explicitly: "Unless one is born of water and spirit one cannot enter the reign/kingdom of God" (3:5). The reference to "water and spirit" may indeed have overtones of baptism for the Johannine community (see the baptism theme at 3:22), but it is first and foremost an image of birth, with the breaking of the amniotic sac and flow of "water" (amniotic fluid), along with the infant's crowning and first breath. The same birth imagery is implied in the latter part of this scene after Nicodemus's disappearance, when Jesus speaks of entry into light and life (3:20–21).

In characteristic fashion, Nicodemus misunderstands the initial response of Jesus and speaks (perhaps sarcastically) of entering a mother's womb for a second birth (3:4). But Nicodemus has missed the double meaning in the adverb *anōthen*. It can mean "again," but its literal meaning is "from above," and that is how the Johannine Jesus intends it. In other words, *anōthen* is also a reference to the Spirit, as the ensuing dialogue makes plain (3:6–8). Jesus is saying that the very human processes of birth are symbolic of the spiritual birth needed to enable believers to recover their lost identity as children of God: "that which is born of the flesh is flesh and that which is born of the Spirit is Spirit" (3:6). In this sense, the Spirit is depicted in maternal terms, giving birth to believers through the "labor" of Jesus's ministry. Once again, John emphasizes that the work of restoration is not that of human beings but entirely and wholly of God (1:13).[11]

There are two other references to birth in John's Gospel. In the parable of the woman in labor,[12] Jesus compares the experience of the disciples to that of a mother going through the "hour" of labor to give birth to a child (16:21): "During the prenatal period there is pain in the onset of labour; in the postnatal phase there is joy over the newborn baby."[13] Just as the disciples mourn the absence of Jesus and experience pain and anxiety on account of his passion, so they will rejoice when they see Jesus again (most likely at his future coming but perhaps also with the coming of the Spirit-Paraclete). In the parable, the narrative tells the brief story of the mother's pain of labor resulting in the joyful birth of her child, just as the pain of departure will bring about new life for the disciples. Birth here is a powerful metaphor of suffering and anguish leading to life and joy.

This image of childbirth is particularly apt for the experience of the disciples at this point in the narrative. Their experience of suffering and trauma causes intense distress, which will be transformed into radiant joy. Such an image gives comfort to the disciples in their current context, facing the painful departure of Jesus:

---

11. See Dorothy A. Lee, *Flesh and Glory: Symbolism, Gender and Theology in the Gospel of John* (New York: Crossroad, 2002), 68–71, 147 and Mary L. Coloe, *John*, vol. 1, WC 44A (Collegeville, MN: Liturgical, 2021), 1.92–99. For a different view that sees the imagery as paternal (begetting), see Raymond E. Brown, *The Gospel According to John*, vol. 1, AB 29 (New York: Doubleday, 1966), 1.128–41.

12. On this as a Johannine parable, see Ruben Zimmermann, "The Woman in Labor (16:21) and the Parables in the Fourth Gospel," in *The Gospel of John as Genre Mosaic*, ed. Ruben Zimmermann, SANt (Göttingen, Vandenhoeck & Ruprecht, 2015), 303–39.

13. Zimmermann, "Woman in Labor," 317.

Birth and Family

> Normally, the death of a loved one is such a painfully moving experience that it cannot be forgotten. It is only the birth metaphor that offers an idea of how joy can return. Whereas painful experiences otherwise take deep root in our memories, childbirth is able—not least because of the release of hormones . . . —to make the most horrific events become almost irrelevant only a few hours later . . . Through the actual birth the memory of pain is bathed in new light.[14]

This imagery applies to Jesus himself as well as to his disciples; he is, after all, about to face his own "hour" of pain and labor (2:4; 8:20; 12:23, 27; 13:1; 17:1).[15]

The second passage with a reference to birth (though implied rather than overt) is that of the flow of blood and water from the side of the crucified Jesus (19:34). This is primarily an image of life issuing paradoxically from death, and it is the climactic symbol of the incarnation and the gift of life: "the blood and the water . . . point unmistakably to the theme of life, seen here as God's salvific verdict on the death of the one who has been presented as the divine agent in his mission of witnessing and judging."[16] While there are secondary sacramental overtones here (the work of the Spirit in baptism and Eucharist), this is fundamentally an image of birth, blood and water being part of the processes of childbirth.[17] It is no coincidence that following this scene

---

14. Zimmermann, "Woman in Labor," 335.

15. For further details on this text, including its relationship to Johannine Christology, see Katherine P. Rushton, *The Parable of the Woman in Childbirth of John 16:21: A Metaphor for the Death and Glorification of Jesus* (New York: Edwin Mellen, 2011).

16. Andrew T. Lincoln, *The Gospel According to Saint John*, BNTC (London: Continuum, 2005), 479.

17. Barbara E. Reid, "Birthed from the Side of Jesus (John 19:34)," in Coloe, *John*, 2.494–98; see also J. Massyngbaerde Ford, *Redeemer Friend and Mother: Salvation in Antiquity and in the Gospel of John* (Minneapolis: Fortress, 1997), 194–99.

150 John

Nicodemus's faith comes into the open in his burial of Jesus (19:38–42), as if he has now truly been born "from above."

FAMILY IN JOHN

Imagery of the family, with its emphasis on love, wends its way through the narrative of the Gospel.[18] It begins, as we have seen, with the birthing of God's children through the labor of the divine Spirit. But the primary expression of this metaphorical language is in the relationship between God and Jesus. As we saw in our discussion of Word and Wisdom, the somewhat more abstract language of the opening verses, which set out the relationship between the Logos and God, comes into full color with the third cycle of the prologue. Although it is presented as a simile in 1:14, the language of Father and Son takes over the Logos terminology, presenting one of the core metaphors of the Fourth Gospel. "Father" is the main title for God in the Gospel, while "Son" is the main title for Jesus (including "Son of God" and "Son of Man"[19]), expressing the intimacy of union between them (10:30); this familial relationship stands at the heart of Jesus's spirituality in this Gospel.[20] This metaphor also expresses the sense of authorship of the Father as the source of life in sending the Son into the world with the divine seal and authority (5:19–21, 36–37; 6:27; 12:49; 17:21). Indeed, Jesus speaks on numerous occasions self-assuredly of "my Father," implying a

---

18. van der Watt, *Family of the King*, 304–19.

19. The two titles are closely tied to the absolute designation of "Son" in John, but do not stand for Jesus's humanity and his divinity: "Son of God" is a messianic title referring to the king (Ps 2:7), while "Son of Man" is most likely a higher title, denoting the one who exercises judgement on God's behalf (Dan 7:13–14).

20. Dorothy A. Lee, "Jesus' Spirituality of [Af]filiation in the Fourth Gospel," *Religions* 13 (2022): 647, https://www.mdpi.com/2077-1444/13/7/647?type=check_update&version=1.

unique relationship of love and trust that attests to his exalted identity (e.g., 2:16; 5:17; 6:32; 10:18; 15:8).[21]

Although grounded in the prologue, Jesus's relationship to God as his Father is nowhere more explicit than in his prayer at the end of the Farewell Discourse (John 17). Here Jesus stands before the Father as Son, praying on behalf of his disciples, present and future, who are the children of God. He is indeed "turned towards" the Father, just as he is before creation as the Logos-Son (1:1–2; 17:24). In praying for the disciples, Jesus draws them into his own relationship with the Father, a relationship that will nurture and protect them, guarding them in the circle of his love for the Father. At the same time, not only does the prayer look back to the prologue,[22] but it also looks forward to the crucifixion. Here we find Jesus's ascent to God in prayer, just as he will ascend on the cross and return to the Father, the one a symbol of the other. The prayer, in other words,

> is that spiritual ascent to God which is the inward reality of all true prayer. And this ascent in prayer carries with it all those who are included in the intercession which is, again, inseparable from all true prayer. In thus praying, Christ both accomplishes the self-oblation of which His death is the historical expression, and "draws" all men after Him into the sphere of eternal life which is union with God . . .[23]

The *anabasis* (ascent) of the prayer, in other words, points forward to and reflects the *anabasis* of the cross, which is

---

21. For further details on this metaphorical language, see Adesola John Akala, *The Son-Father Relationship and Christological Symbolism in the Gospel of John*, LNTS 505 (London: Bloomsbury, 2014), esp. 193–213.

22. Akala, *Son-Father Relationship*, 186–92.

23. C. H. Dodd, *The Interpretation of the Fourth Gospel* (Cambridge, UK: Cambridge University Press, 1953), 419.

152   John

the Son's self-offering to the Father for the salvation of the children of God.

Yet Jesus's ascent to the Father is evident not just in the prayer but also on the cross due to their intimately close connection. Jesus's whole life, in one sense, is an ascent to God because he stands always in prayerful union with God—so much so that he does not need to verbalize intercessions (11:41–42): "In view of the complete unity between the Father and the Son there is no need for uttered prayer at all."[24] Earlier in the Gospel, in the context of birth imagery, Jesus uses the symbolism of the bronze serpent (3:14–15; Num 21:4–9) to speak of the way in which he gives life to those who believe. Throughout his ministry as well as climactically on the cross, Jesus is the Serpent as well as the Lamb of God: gazing on him is the only way to salvation and life (1:14; 12:21; 19:37). His ascent to the Father is a quality of his life as well as his sacrificial death and resurrection. The language of ascent is language that incorporates not just the final departure of Jesus and his return to the Father, as in Luke (Luke 24:50–51; Acts 1:9–11); it encapsulates the life, ministry, death, resurrection, and final departure of the Johannine Jesus.

The notion of family in the Fourth Gospel derives directly from the relationship between the Father and the Son. In becoming children of God, disciples enter into that divine circle of covenant love through the regenerating power of the Holy Spirit. The creation of the family of God is grounded in the incarnation, with its roots in the Old Testament and the experience of Israel. But it reaches a climax on the cross when the mother of Jesus and the beloved disciple are given to one another by the crucified Jesus (19:26–27). This is one in a

---

24. C. K. Barrett, *The Gospel According to St John: An Introduction with Commentary and Notes on the Greek Text*, 2nd ed. (London: SPCK, 1978), 402.

series of symbols that reiterate the paradoxical saving and life-giving significance of the cross in Johannine theology. One aspect of this salvation, which overthrows sin and evil and renews the whole of creation, is the forming of community from the death of Jesus. Here again, Jesus gives life through death, life in communion with others. The beloved disciple and the mother of Jesus become family. Jesus's words to each of them ("Behold your son! . . . behold, your mother! . . .") are highly significant here:

> Jesus employs a revelatory formula . . . and performance language. Like a marriage declaration, his pronouncement actually accomplishes or effects the new relationship that it declares. By his declaration, Jesus constitutes a new family, mother and son. From the beginning, the Gospel of John has employed the metaphor of kinship to characterize the believer's new relationship to God.[25]

The clause "he took her into his own" expresses[26] not so much the beloved disciple's care for the needs of a frail, elderly woman—she has, after all, other adult children to perform their filial duties towards their mother (2:12; 7:3), though it is possible that they have become estranged[27]—but rather the creation of the new family of God, with distinct covenant overtones. These two disciples now belong together and form the basis of the fictive family.

---

25. R. Alan Culpepper, *The Gospel and Letters of John*, IBT (Nashville: Abingdon, 1998), 234; see also Margaret Wesley, *Son of Mary: The Family of Jesus and the Community of Faith in the Fourth Gospel*, ACTMS (Eugene, OR: Wipf & Stock, 2015), 273, 280–84.

26. Most translations add the word *home* here (e.g., NRSVue, NJB, NIV), but the Greek literally says "into his own things" (*eis ta idia*). The phrase parallels 1:11: "he came to his own."

27. See Wesley, *Son of Mary*, 267–68.

154 John

The mother of Jesus may also play a particular role in this account within the family of God. Not only is she never named in this Gospel, but she is also addressed here and at Cana as "woman" (*gunai*, 2:4). This is an unusual appellation from a son to his mother. Does this factor give added significance to her place within the new family formed at the foot of the cross? Some would argue that she recalls the figure of Eve, the first woman, who is also "the mother of all the living" (Gen 2:18–25; 3:20).[28] If so, something similar would apply to Mary the Magdalene, who is also addressed as "woman" (20:13, 15) by the angels and the risen Jesus when she meets him in the garden.[29] Both women are significant figures in the new family of God and, if there is also an association with Eve, their roles emphasize the restoration of kinship in the events of Jesus's death and resurrection.

The words of the risen Jesus to Mary the Magdalene, as she moves towards full Easter faith and prepares to proclaim the resurrection message to the other disciples, are significant in this respect: "I ascend to my Father and your Father and to my God and your God" (20:17). Both the continuity and the distinctiveness are equally important here. God is the Father and God of all the disciples, but God is first and foremost the Father and God of Jesus, the Son; there is a fundamental distinction at play. In other words, disciples become children of God by entering into the filiation ("sonship") of Jesus and sharing it. Because God is his Father, God can become the Father of the disciples; the ordering is of vital import. Disciples enter into a preexistent intimacy

---

28. Brendan Byrne, *Life Abounding: A Reading of John's Gospel* (Collegeville, MN: Liturgical, 2014), 318–19.

29. Dorothy A. Lee, "Mary Magdalene in Theological Perspective Across Gospel Traditions," in *Oxford Handbook of Mary Magdalene*, ed. Diane Apostolos-Cappadona, 2 vols (Oxford: Oxford University Press, forthcoming).

Birth and Family

and are granted a restored status that is dependent on their union with Jesus (17:20–23). This concept is similar to the Pauline notion of adoption, where the community of faith becomes the adopted sons and daughters of God through Christ (Rom 8:14–17).[30]

LOVE, FRIENDSHIP, AND ABIDING

The language of family in John's Gospel is the language of love, which is a key theme of this Gospel.[31] It is not mentioned explicitly in the prologue, yet its implication is there, as later texts in John make plain. The first explicit reference to love is in Jesus's conversation with Nicodemus where, after the latter's disappearance from the narrative, Jesus speaks of God's love for the world and God's desire that it escape condemnation (3:16–17). This is not primarily a description of the depth of divine love but rather the way in which God's love manifests itself: in the giving over of the Son to mortal flesh. This is, for John, a self-giving love which is also vulnerable in that it leaves itself open to rejection. The same love is evident at the beginning of the Last Supper, where Jesus's love for his own (*hoi idioi*) leads him to wash the disciples' feet as a sign of his self-giving love on the cross (13:1, 5). The Father's love, along with that of the Son, will come upon the disciples and make its home in them through the presence of the Spirit-Paraclete (14:21, 23).

Behind the divine love for the world and for the disciples

---

30. On adoption in the ancient world, see F. F. Bruce, *The Epistle to the Galatians: A Commentary on the Greek Text*, NIGTC (Exeter, UK: Paternoster Press, 1982), 197–98. Note that daughters are equally included in this language as heirs of Christ.

31. For further details on this theme, see Francis J. Moloney, *Love in the Gospel of John: An Exegetical, Theological, and Literary Study* (Grand Rapids; Baker Academic, 2013).

156 John

stands the love between Father and Son, which is—as we have seen—the source of the fictive family in this Gospel. The love and intimacy which thrive between God and Jesus form the basis of his ministry: its origin, inspiration, and sustenance (3:35; 5:20; 10:17; 14:31; 17:26). That love is also shared in and beyond the covenant community. It is a boundless love that flows over into the life of creation, even to the unbelieving world. Although John does not say so explicitly, the love which God has for an alienated realm is by implication the same love with which God created it in the first place. That love is not only given to the disciples but it is also to be shared, as is the divine love within the Trinity. Authentic love, in this sense, is not possessive or exclusive but free and overflowing. It flows from God and back towards God in an ever-circling stream.

A number of disciples are explicitly associated with Jesus's love because love lies at the essence of discipleship. The beloved disciple is the most obvious character. He is loved by Jesus and reclines beside him at the Last Supper, having the seat of honor beside his host and able to converse with him on intimate terms (13:23–26; 19:26; 20:2; 21:7, 20). Jesus loves Martha, Mary, and Lazarus (11:5, 36), and they clearly love him in return as his disciples. And Simon Peter is rehabilitated three times by the risen Jesus (paralleling his threefold denial, 18:17, 25, 27) with the language of love, which will lie at the basis of his leadership and eventual martyrdom (21:15–19).[32] Through Jesus's death and resurrection, the family is "refractured and reconfigured."[33]

Part of the language of love in John's Gospel is that of

---

32. It is important to note that the two verbs for love at 21:15–19 (*phileō*, *agapaō*) represent stylistic variation and are equivalent terms, as they are throughout the Gospel (Barrett, *Gospel According to St John*, 584).

33. Wesley, *Son of Mary*, 256–86.

friendship, as we saw earlier in this chapter.[34] In the ancient world, close friends could be seen as part of the family. The sense, therefore, is not that of acquaintances but of intimate friends and beloved companions, with whom all things are shared. In the extended paraphrase of the parable of the vine, Jesus speaks of his disciples as "no longer slaves" (*douloi*) but "friends" (*philoi*, 15:15). While obedience is still asked of them, it is an obedience based on friendship, not servility: the disciples are not kept in the dark but the divine knowledge is shared with them (15:13–15). This whole section is bounded on either side by the command to love each other (15:12, 17); this love is grounded in Jesus's love for his disciples. Although the love command is not new in biblical faith (see Lev 19:18), Jesus becomes the model, inspiration, and ongoing source of love. In that sense, the commandment has a "new" or fresh dimension in its christological focus (13:34).

To live in this love means to abide (*meno*), a verb that signifies more than just "remaining," which is a rather weak translation of a rich Johannine concept.[35] The parable of the vine, which brings this language to a climax in the Gospel, is about resting in love, both with God and within community. The fourth evangelist has spoken elsewhere of abiding throughout the Gospel: the Spirit's abiding on Jesus (1:32–33), Jesus's word abiding in the disciples (5:38), abiding through eucharistic participation (6:56), abiding in the light (12:46), and especially abiding in love (15:9–10). This abiding is not passive but dynamic and fruitful, as the parable indicates

---

34. See Gail R. O'Day, "I Have Called You Friends" (Waco, TX: Center for Christian Ethics at Baylor University, 2008), https://ifl.web.baylor.edu/sites/g/files/ecbvkj771/files/2022-12/friendshiparticleoday.pdf.

35. Sherri Brown, *Come and See: Discipleship in the Gospel of John*, BSCBA 16 (New York; Paulist, 2022), 76–92.

(15:4–7).[36] The Johannine language of abiding parallels the Pauline notion of the divine indwelling in the believing community (see Rom 8:9–11; 1 Cor 3:16; 2 Cor 6:16).

REFLECTIONS

There are several implications that flow from this discussion of birth and family in the Gospel of John. We might well imagine that in the ancient (and parts of the modern) world, where belief in Christ might lead to ostracism from the family and kinship group, the fictive family plays an essential role. The emphasis on the household of God, the family of the church, also has much to offer the modern Western context, where the wider family has in many ways broken down and almost disappeared. Families have been nuclear for decades now and are increasingly isolated from the wider family network of support. Single parents whose partners have abandoned the family are forced to struggle for employment, education for their children, and financial security in a world where food provisions and accommodation are increasingly out of the reach of those who are poor. The extended family, as the ancient world knew it, is not there to provide a safety net.

Nuclear families can easily find themselves isolated, lacking the underpinning support and sociality of the wider kinship network. The prevalence of divorce and the increase in domestic violence make these small units even more precarious, both financially and emotionally. In these contexts, the notion of a broader sense of family in the church that is both stable and inclusive and not based on genealogical

---

36. For further details on abiding and friendship in John, see Lee, *Flesh and Glory*, 88–109.

relationships can play a vital role in providing the support and social interaction that wider kinship networks once theoretically provided.

Yet seeing the fictive family only as a substitute for the absence or insufficiency of blood kinship networks does not do justice to Johannine theology. John's Gospel, like so much else of the New Testament, offers deep connections that are outside of blood or marital relations. They offer a broad and inclusive sense of kinship that crosses all kinds of barriers which the family cannot bridge: class, wealth, status, gender, race, and other barriers. The family of God is the intimate and inclusive connection between human beings of all kinds, regardless of status or context. This is a breathtaking vision of humanity united under God the Creator, possessing a new and radical sense of covenant in and through the person of Jesus Christ, who stands at the crossroads of the family of God: bringing it down to earth and raising it up to heaven.

John's understanding of the renewal of identity in the family of God thus makes a vital connection between human beings and their Creator. It makes possible the link to the mystery that lies in and beyond our reality; it connects mortality to divinity and does so in a profoundly personal way in relationship with God through Christ and in the power of the Spirit. This connection gives the possibility of a new identity that has the capacity to undergird all other forms of identity, providing a solid foundation that can weather the storms of mortal life.

This new reality, moreover, is based on love and not on the pragmatic need for survival. Love is the motivation, the means, and the goal of created life. That goal is reclaimed in Christ for all human beings and, indeed, beyond them for the whole creation. John's Gospel offers a vision of love, a love not able to be generated by human efforts, which will inevitably fail, but a love that comes freely and generously from God through incarnation, resurrection, and cross. It is a costly love that God bestows on creation, vulnerable and life-giving. This love within the fictive family transcends even death itself, so that human beings are connected not just within time but also across time, beyond death itself.

John's vision of kinship and community based on love is the only hope for a world that is divided and distorted, increasingly lonely, full of hatred and violence, and painfully disconnected. It deals definitively with sin and evil, promising a world without greed, selfishness, deceit, tragedy, and violence. It offers forgiveness and wholeness along with justice and truth,[37] overpowering evil with the gift of reconciliation in community. It overcomes the divider, the ruler of this world, who holds the unbelieving world in the grip of disunion and untruth. This vision takes effect in the person of Jesus Christ: his incarnation, his life and ministry of love, his sacrificial death on the cross, and his life-giving resurrection.

But this is not a remote and distant vision for the fourth evangelist. Through the incarnation it is already a reality, with a capacity to transform, not only death at the end but also mortality in the present moment, through birth in the Spirit. This rebirth is profoundly spiritual but is also grounded in material reality. It stems from a love that is political as well as spiritual, social and covenantal as well as personal, and concerned with social injustice as well as individual sin. Through relationship with Christ, rebirth gives access above all to the life of the blessed Trinity in the here-and-now, whose reconciling love reaches into the darkened world with forgiveness, intimacy, and abiding love.

---

37. For further details on the theme of social justice in John, see Kathleen P. Rushton, *The Cry of the Earth and the Cry of the Poor: Hearing Justice in John's Gospel* (London: SCM, 2020).

FURTHER READING

Akala, Adesola Joan. *The Son-Father Relationship and Christological Symbolism in the Gospel of John*. LNTS 505. London: Bloomsbury, 2014.

Byrne, Brendan. *Life Abounding: A Reading of John's Gospel*. Collegeville, MN: Liturgical, 2014.

Coloe, Mary. *Dwelling in the Household of God: Johannine Ecclesiology and Spirituality*. Collegeville, MN: Liturgical, 2007.

Moloney, Francis J. *Love in the Gospel of John: An Exegetical, Theological, and Literary Study*. Grand Rapids: Baker Academic, 2013.

Wesley, Margaret. *Son of Mary: The Family of Jesus and the Community of Faith in the Fourth Gospel*. ACTMS. Eugene, OR: Wipf & Stock, 2015.

CHAPTER 8

Law and Revelation

The law was given through Moses; grace and truth came through Jesus Christ. (1:17 NIV)

Our final chapter deals with two further themes in the Gospel of John emerging from the prologue that will complete our survey. Law and revelation are related and significant themes in the Fourth Gospel. They overlap in that the law itself is a consequence of divine revelation, particularly in relation to the Torah (Pentateuch), the first five books of the Old Testament. The Gospel of John is deeply embedded in the Old Testament and the entire Johannine narrative is indebted to its core feasts and symbolism. The law, in particular, is associated with Moses in this Gospel, and the two terms (*law* and *Moses*) are interchangeable. Moses is considered in the biblical world as the author of the Torah, and therefore the references to him are not so much to his life story as to the text itself. In that sense, we are talking not just of the law but also, more broadly, of Scripture itself (that is, the Old Testament). Moses, in this literary sense, plays a key role in the unfolding of revelation in the Johannine Jesus; something similar can also be said of other biblical authors such as Isaiah (1:23; 12:38–41). Indeed, revelation is so central a concept that the Johannine Jesus is sometimes

162

Law and Revelation 163

described as "the Revealer" in this Gospel because, as we will see, the disclosure of God's being and purpose is the goal of his life, death, and resurrection.[1]

The role of the law in the Fourth Gospel requires careful consideration in a study of Johannine themes. It is too easy to read John in a quasi-Pauline fashion in which law and grace are set over against each other in opposition (though this view is unfair to Paul's more intricate understanding of the law's goodness and limitations).[2] The ongoing place of Moses and the law has considerable significance in Johannine theology. References to the law, moreover, may sometimes be a compressed way of speaking of "the law and the prophets" (1:45; cf Matt 7:12; 22:40), so we are speaking more generally of the whole Old Testament. The theme of Moses and Scripture is closely linked to the role of that group of characters who appear in hostile contexts and are named *Ioudaioi* ("Jews"), which is itself an area of considerable controversy. Both Moses and the Old Testament are linked to the theme of revelation, which undergirds the theology of the Gospel and its presentation of Jesus. In this chapter, therefore, we are surveying the same mountain as we have in previous chapters but from a different angle. This new perspective will overlap with other themes we have already explored, including the role of Scripture but hopefully enabling a more complete portrait of John's intricate thematic unity.

---

1. For further details on revelation in John, see Gail R. O'Day, *Revelation in the Fourth Gospel: Narrative Mode and Theological Claim* (Philadelphia: Fortress, 1986), esp. 33–48.

2. The complex place of the law in Paul is neatly summed up by Brendan Byrne: "For all its own intrinsic holiness (Rom. 7:12), the impotence of the law to deal with sin led to its being a negative rather than a positive factor in the quest for salvation" (*Paul and the Economy of Salvation: Reading from the Perspective of the Last Judgment* [Grand Rapids: Baker Academic, 2021], 228).

BACKGROUND TO LAW AND REVELATION

Moses is first introduced explicitly at 1:17 as the agent of the law given by God on Mount Sinai ("*through* Moses"). Yet it is not the first reference to the Old Testament. The opening verses of the prologue are concerned with creation and imply the events narrated in Genesis 1–3. The disclosure of the incarnation employs language and imagery that also suggest the exodus period: the place of the tabernacle and the tent of meeting where Moses regularly meets with God, both associated with the terrifying manifestation of divine glory.[3]

The law is given on Mount Sinai as a gift of divine revelation, associated with the formation of the community of God's people and grounded in the covenantal formula with its obligations on both sides: "I will be their God and they will be my people" (e.g., Jer 32:38; Ezek 14:11; Zech 8:8). The giving of the law is the key event in salvation history for later generations, its implications drawn out in the prophetic writings of Scripture. For the first five books of the Bible, the narrative is one of covenant disclosure and covenant failure, the people of God reverting to idolatry, rebellion, and lack of trust in God's providential care. Their inability to keep the law and the resultant consequences form the backdrop for the Torah narratives. That there is something wrong—though not with the covenant itself—is part of the implications for the Johannine community and the "new thing" that takes place in Jesus. That new development is already foreshadowed in the Old Testament itself (see Jer 31:31–34).

Of some significance is the more immediate historical context of Judaism. The second century BCE saw a harsh

---

3. Janet Soskice, *Naming God: Addressing the Divine in Philosophy, Theology and Scripture* (Cambridge, UK: Cambridge University Press, 2023), 15–22 (8–39).

Law and Revelation 165

persecution of Jewish beliefs and the law was itself forbidden under the Syrian king Antiochus IV. His desire to unite his empire under Hellenism led him to desecrate the temple with a statue of himself as the great god, Zeus, and to forbid circumcision, the keeping of the Sabbath, and the observance of Jewish dietary laws. The resultant rebellion under the Jewish leader Judas Maccabeus, the expulsion of the Syrian overlords, and the founding of a Jewish ruling dynasty gave a new impetus to protecting the law and a new determination to retain and cherish it, no matter what.[4] The law lay at the core of Jewish identity and, with the destruction of the Jerusalem temple at the end of the Jewish War, Torah came to have a singular focus for Jewish identity. Christians in the first century played a part in cultivating this identity.

The Jewish philosopher Philo, who flourished in Alexandria in the first century CE, was deeply influenced by Greek philosophy, particularly Plato. As a devout Jew attentive to Greek philosophical ideas, he saw Moses as the first great philosopher and lawgiver. His *Life of Moses* presents Hebrew wisdom as superior to all others, and he endeavors both to defend Moses against pagan detractors and to reconcile Judaism and Hellenism. His first book is a kind of biography of Moses, while the second deals with Moses as lawgiver, as well as priest and prophet.[5] For Philo, Moses's laws are "better in fact than any that have ever arisen among either the Greeks or the barbarians."[6] These laws, he argues, are enduring, immortal, comprehensive, humane, and God-given: they are the result of divine revelation and are admired even outside

---

4. David A. deSilva, *An Introduction to the New Testament: Contexts, Methods & Ministry Formation*, 2nd ed. (Downers Grove: IVP Academic, 2018), 11–26.

5. Philo, "Life of Moses," in *Philo*, trans, F. H. Colson, vol. 6, LCL 289 (Cambridge, MA: Harvard University Press, 1935), books I and II.

6. Philo, "Life of Moses," III.12.

the Jewish faith.[7] This claim is not made for Greco-Roman laws and legal systems.

Nevertheless, law played an important role in the Greco-Roman world. One of the great Greek lawgivers was Solon of Athens (c. 630–560 BCE), who introduced a fairer economic system of law that limited the power of the aristocracy and gave a greater say in politics to all (male, free) citizens in Athens. His reforms of the legal system included both political and family laws.[8] He also revised the earlier, harsh system of law to make it more humane, although it continued to exclude women and slaves from citizenship and therefore from full protection under the law.

The Romans, likewise, had developed systems of law and justice over the centuries. Initially, Roman laws applied only to Roman citizens, but a new system later emerged that covered non-citizens to a certain extent. Under the Roman Empire, law and justice were ultimately in Roman hands under the jurisdiction of Roman magistrates, though concessions to local autonomy existed in some contexts and there was considerable diversity of practice. Yet the Roman emperor had final authority, granting legal exemptions and privileges to those whose social class made it affordable:

> According to the beneficial ideology—which advertised power relations of mutual benefit to both ruler and ruled—emperors were the ultimate bestowers of gifts and

---

7. Philo gives an excellent example in the fourth commandment: "who has not shewn his high respect for the sacred seventh day, by giving rest and relaxation from labour to himself and his neighbours, freemen and slaves alike, and beyond these to his beasts? For the holiday extends also to every herd, and to all creatures . . . It extends also to every kind of trees and plants . . . All such are set at liberty on that day, and live as it were in freedom . . ." ("Life of Moses," IV.21–22.)

8. For further details on this, particularly around family legislation, see Susan Lape, "Solon and the Institution of the 'Democratic' Family Form," *CJ* 98 (2002–2003): 117–39.

largesse, as well as dispensers of justice . . . [P]etitioners throughout the Roman provinces . . . looked to the emperors and imperial officials for decisions.[9]

Despite Roman claims for universal law across the empire, local contexts would also make use of their own systems of law alongside those of Rome. For example, in the Roman province of Judaea the Sanhedrin had some, though limited, authority for dispensing justice among Jewish people. The fact that Jesus was tried and convicted by Roman authority and executed by the Roman method of crucifixion, even with the connivance of the high priest and certain members of the Sanhedrin, indicates where power finally lay.

LAW AND REVELATION IN THE PROLOGUE

In the prologue, a contrast is implied between the law and Jesus: "the law was given through Moses; grace and truth became through Jesus Christ" (1:17). It would be easy to add the conjunction "but" between these two clauses, though no hostile distinction is actually made between them. They are placed side by side without explicit connection. This represents a gap that the implied reader needs to fill in order to answer how the two are related. The existence of a connection is clear. The verbal form "was given" (*edothē*) in the first clause is a "divine passive": that is, the passive voice presents God as the giver. We could paraphrase it as "God gave the law through Moses." In other words, the law itself is a form of revelation, the anterior form to that given in Jesus. The same verb is not used in the second clause: the "grace and

---

9. Caroline Humfress, "Law's Empire: Roman Universalism and Roman Practice," in *New Frontiers: Law and Society in the Roman World*, ed. Paul du Plessis (Edinburgh: Edinburgh University Press, 2013), 83 (73–101).

truth" simply "became" through Jesus Christ, just as the Word "became" flesh (1:14).

Note that this is the first mention of Jesus's name in the prologue. We have moved from Logos-Sophia to Son and now to the full name "Jesus Christ." Jesus follows on from Moses; indeed, the evangelist will later make it plain that the law itself points to Jesus and that without the law we would have no framework nor any symbolic structure by which to understand Jesus. Moses is not only the precedent for Jesus; he is also necessary for the revelation in Jesus, the Messiah. The reference to Moses is positive, therefore, since he, like Jesus himself, belongs under the umbrella of revelation.

The last verse of the prologue contains the only explicit reference to revelation in this section and it uses an unusual verb: the divine Son, who rests in the Father's embrace (lit. "lap" or "womb," a tangible image), has "exegeted" (*exēgeomai*) God (1:18). This verb has the sense of explaining or drawing out the meaning; the basic metaphor is to "lead or draw or bring out," though it is normally translated "reveal."[10] It implies an outward movement from within the palpable intimacy of Father and Son, a movement already intimated in the giving of the law and the Scriptures yet brought to completion in Jesus. In presenting him as the Revealer, "the Evangelist gives us not the teaching of Jesus, but his life and teaching as a unity."[11] Therefore, both Moses and Jesus are revealers in their life and teaching and their revelation comes from God, but Jesus's revelation represents God's *self*-revelation—and that makes all the difference.

---

10. See Rudolf Bultmann, *The Gospel of John: A Commentary*, ET (Oxford: Blackwell, 1971), 81–83. According to Bultmann, the verb "from earliest times was used in a technical sense for the interpretation of the will of the gods by professional diviners, priests and soothsayers" (83).

11. Bultmann, *Gospel of John*, 83.

LAW, SCRIPTURE, AND REVELATION IN THE GOSPEL NARRATIVE

Something "more" is unquestionably given in the Johannine Jesus in the prologue, but there are other possibilities for this "more" than a simplistic notion of replacement. The Johannine Jesus does not replace Moses and the Old Testament Scriptures in this equation.[12] On the contrary, Moses and Jesus are divine gifts, and both are manifestations of the same gracious and life-giving divine word: "The law was a gift from God, and the reference to Moses [at 1:17] ensures that the covenantal gift of Torah echoes through this proclamation."[13] A more Johannine solution to the issue is that the revelation received in Scripture has a further revelatory role beyond its own context. In John's Gospel, Scripture both points to and conveys Jesus in the same way that a symbol does.

The narratives following the prologue make reference to the fulfillment of Scripture in the events of Jesus's ministry: either in its foreshadowing or its realization. Thus, John the Baptist's message fulfills the words of Second Isaiah as the comforting voice in the wilderness (1:23; see Isa 40:3), yet he claims that he is not the returned figure of Moses—"the prophet"—nor is he associated with Elijah (1:21, 25; see Deut 18:15–18). Only Jesus fulfills the law and the prophets, and he is recognized as such by Philip and then by Nathaniel,

---

12. See Dorothy A. Lee, "The Significance of Moses in the Gospel of John," in *Creation, Matter and the Image of God: Essays on John* (Adelaide, Australia: ATF, 2020), 137–54. For the opposite view, that Moses (and therefore Judaism) is replaced by Jesus (and thus Christianity) throughout John's treatment of Moses, cf. John Ashton, *The Gospel of John and Christian Origins* (Minneapolis: Fortress, 2014), 22–61.

13. Sherri Brown and Francis J. Moloney, *Interpreting the Gospel and Letters of John: An Introduction* (Grand Rapids: Eerdmans, 2017), 191.

170   John

to the latter's initial astonishment (1:46). Similarly, in the
cleansing of the temple, the words of the Scriptures are ful-
filled in Jesus's action: so much so that his own prophecy
about his body is given the same status as, or at least parallel
to, Scripture (2:17, 22; Ps 69:9). The Bread of Life narrative
is based in part around the scriptural quotation "He gave
them bread from heaven to eat," which Jesus then qualifies
in terms of his own advent with the first of the "I am" sayings
(6:31–35). It is not always easy in John to pinpoint the exact
source of these Old Testament "quotations,"[14] but they serve
the purpose of setting Jesus's ministry firmly within a scriptural framework. In the Tabernacles narrative, the focus is
more exclusively on debate around Moses and the role of
the law as well as Abraham, both of whom attest beforehand
to Jesus (7:19, 22–23, 51; 8:17, 52–58). A similar conflict is
present in the story of the man born blind, which is in part a
tussle over whom Moses belongs to: the Jerusalem authorities
or Jesus (9:28–33). That conflict persists throughout Jesus's
ministry, John's point being that the law is on Jesus's side and
not over against it, as the authorities want to claim.

There are several words for "revelation" across the Gospel.
The more familiar language of *apokalupsis/apocaluptō* is
largely absent, except once in a quotation from the Greek Old
Testament (12:38; Isa 53:1). This language is more obviously
associated with the book of Revelation, where *apokalupsis*
("apocalypse," "revelation") is the first word (Rev 1:1), introducing both the series of visions which John the Seer sees and
the divine words he hears through the Spirit. Several other
terms are used in the Fourth Gospel: most commonly the verb
phaneroō (1:31; 2:11; 7:4; 17:6; 21:1 [2x]) and its closely related

---

14. In the case of 6:31, there are several possible OT sources for the quotation: Exod 16:4; Pss 78:24–25; 105:40; and Neh 9:15.

Law and Revelation 171

form *emphanizō* (14:21, 22); both mean "reveal" or "make manifest." The verb "make known" can also be used with the sense of revelation (*gnōrizō*, 15:15; 17:26 [2x]); similarly, the verb "show" (*deikvumi*) in some contexts is synonymous, having a similar sense of revelation (e.g., 10:32; 14:9; 20:20).

The wedding at Cana is the first explicit reference to revelation outside the prologue. It concludes with the evangelist's summary of the significance of this event, the first of Jesus's miracles in the Gospel: "Jesus did this as the beginning of the signs (*semeia*) in Cana of Galilee and he revealed his glory (*ephanerōsen*), and his disciples believed in him" (2:11). This first event has an important feature in displaying the significance of what John calls the signs and works (*erga*) of Jesus's ministry. There seems no clear distinction between these two terms (see 6:29), and John uses them more or less interchangeably to speak of Jesus's actions and teaching, which have been given to him by the Father to complete (e.g., 3:2; 4:34; 5:36; 9:4; 14:10). Only once does Jesus use the term *wonders* to speak of his miracles (*terata*, 4:48).

What Jesus reveals in the first miracle is not primarily his power over nature—although by virtue of being the Word he possesses that divine authority—but at a deeper level his own identity and the significance of his ministry. "Glory" refers back to the incarnation at 1:14 and its revelatory intent. In this narrative, Jesus discloses his own nature as the divine Son sent by the Father, bringing to birth the messianic age and the life of the world to come. He is indeed "the good wine kept till last" (2:10), and this miracle leads to believing for the disciples. Jesus's work or works are part of his divine commission, and the focus is revelatory. It shows forth the divine glory and the eschatological (future) life of heaven, which his creative power draws into the present.

The fifth of the "I am" sayings expresses this theme most

cogently, emphasizing Jesus's identity and the present moment: "I am the resurrection and the life. The one believing in me, even if they die, will live, and everyone living and believing in me will never ever die" (11:25–26a). Martha both expresses and represents the faith of the community in her decided reply: "Yes, Lord, I have come to believe that you are the Christ, the Son of God, the one coming into the world" (11:27). In this narrative, Jesus also uses the language of glory (11:4, 40).

As with Martha, the appropriate response to the revelation of the signs and works is not so much amazement but rather believing (11:28). We have already seen something in chapter 6 of the importance of believing in John's understanding of discipleship. But it is significant that Jesus speaks of faith itself as a work (*ergon*) that corresponds to the works which Jesus does: "This is the work of God," Jesus says to the crowds after the feeding, "that you believe in the one whom [God] has sent" (6:29). The first resurrection narrative concludes with the theme of believing as the right response to Jesus's signs, in words that echo Martha's confession of faith at 11:27: "These [signs] are written that you may believe that Jesus is the Christ the Son of God, and in believing you have life in his name" (20:31). These words sum up the purpose of the Gospel and of Jesus's divinely given commission: to bring people to faith so that they receive the gift of eternal life.

The motif of revelation throughout Jesus's ministry is explicit in the "feasts of the Jews" section of the Gospel (5:1–10:42). Here Jesus reveals himself, as we have already seen in chapter 5, as the fulfillment of the temple and its feasts and rituals. These are already the objects of divine revelation in the Torah and, far from being discarded with the advent of Jesus, now take on an additional revelatory role. They point symbolically to Jesus as the fulfillment of all that the temple and its activities represent. Thus, Jesus is the fulfiller of the

Sabbath, possessing the same divine exemption as the Father and receiving the uniquely divine authority of giving life and making judgement on the Sabbath (5:19–23). Far from nullifying the commandment, John's Sabbath Christology gives it a new revelatory dimension. In this sense, Jesus can claim that Moses (and therefore the law) will condemn Jesus's opponents: "Do not think that I will accuse you to the Father; the one accusing you is Moses in whom you have hoped. For if you believed Moses you would have believed me; for he wrote about me" (5:45–46).

The same is true for the feasts which follow: Passover, Tabernacles, and Dedication (John 6–10). In each case, Jesus is "the personification and the universalization of the celebration" for each of the rituals:[15] bread, water, and light. The notion of replacement is a feature of Jesus's detractors, who claim to stand for Moses over against Jesus (9:28–29). In terms of metaphor, the feasts themselves in their Old Testament understandings are necessary to understand the Johannine Jesus:

> Jesus transforms the signs and shadows of what was done in the Temple for Israel. Jesus is the life-giver and judge . . . and the bread from heaven . . . the living water, the light of the world, the revelation of the one true God, the messianic Good Shepherd . . . The Johannine story does not abandon the symbols.[16]

Once again law, Scripture, and revelation are closely linked and essential through their interplay in manifesting the Johannine Jesus.

---

15. Francis J. Moloney, *Signs and Shadows: Reading John 5–12* (Minneapolis: Fortress Press, 1996), 205.

16. Moloney, *Signs and Shadows*, 206.

LAW, SCRIPTURE, AND REVELATION AT THE LAST SUPPER

The Last Supper is bounded on either side by the twin panels of footwashing and prayer, which both carry the theme of "making God known" (13:1–38; 17:1–26).[17] The overarching theme is clearly that of revelation. Across these chapters is the double revelation of who Jesus is in relation to his departure—his return to the Father in glory—and who the disciples are as a community in the absence of Jesus. The God whom Jesus reveals in the bookends of the Last Supper is the God of love and intimacy, and Jesus's washing of the disciples' feet signifies union with him in his sacrificial and saving death,[18] providing a model of love and service for one another. In the prayer, it is Jesus's protective oneness with the Father which ensures the disciples' unity.

Though there are few explicit details about law in this section, two references to Scripture address the tragic loss of Judas Iscariot (13:18; 17:12; Ps 41:9). There are also frequent references to Jesus's commands, which have a parallel force, especially given that Jesus's words, as we have seen, have an equivalent status to Scripture (13:34; 14:23; 15:12, 14, 20; 17:6).[19] These commands are to be guarded and obeyed, not just for individual Christians but for the integrity of the Christian community as a whole. They are not optional extras but intrinsic to believing identity. This link between the words of Scripture and Jesus's own words underlines the ongoing relevance of the Old Testament and the law

---

17. Francis J. Moloney, *The Gospel of John*, SP (Collegeville, MN: Liturgical, 1998), 370–91, 458–81.

18. On the footwashing as symbolic of the crucifixion, see John Morgan-Wynne, *The Cross in the Johannine Writings* (Eugene, OR: Pickwick, 2011), 157–62.

19. See chapter 3.

for understanding the Johannine Jesus and the Johannine community.

Love and unity are revealed through the Last Discourse in the coming of the Holy Spirit in this Gospel, who is named "the Paraclete" as one dimension of the Spirit's work (elsewhere revealed as the source of life, 3:6, and reconciliation, 20:22–23). Different English translations opt for "Comforter" (KJV), "Counselor" (RSV), "Advocate" (NRSVue, NIV, REB), "Helper" (ESV, NASB), and "Companion" (CEB). Only the RNJB decides to go with "Paraclete," recognizing that no single translation captures the complexity of this term. In this sense, the Paraclete relates intimately to both the Father and the Son: comforting, reminding, bearing witness, convicting and judging, and teaching (14:16–17, 26; 15:26–27; 16:7–11).[20] Indeed, Jesus himself is the first Paraclete, since he promises "another Paraclete" on his departure (14:16; see 1 John 2:1). The overall message in the revelation of the Paraclete is that the community need not feel bereft or abandoned in the (temporary) absence of Jesus.

Revelation language appears in several contexts in the Farewell Discourse. Philip asks that the Father be revealed and Jesus's reply makes it clear that he is himself the revelation of the Father (14:8–9). Oddly enough, Jesus speaks of revealing himself to the disciples but not to the world (14:21–22). In the light of God's love for the world, revealed in the incarnation and on the cross (3:16–17), this seems a strange if not contradictory statement. Yet it makes sense within John's understanding of the *kosmos, in its negative sense,* as the realm of darkness and unbelief: "to pray for the *kosmos* would be almost an absurdity, since the only hope for

---

20. See Marianne Meye Thompson, *John: A Commentary*, NTL (Louisville, KY: Westminster John Knox, 2015), 318–22.

176   John

the *kosmos* is precisely that it should cease to be the *kosmos*."[21] None of this contradicts in any way God's love for the created world nor God's loving self-disclosure to all human beings.

Perhaps the most explicitly revelatory part of the Last Supper is Jesus's Great Prayer at its conclusion, with the theme of "making God known." We saw in chapter 7 that this prayer is an *anabasis*, an ascent to God that prefigures and speaks directly into the situation of Jesus's death and departure. Here he stands face to face with God, as he has from before creation (1:1–2; 17:24). The language of glory is particularly apt in the opening verses of the prayer, as it is the key term for understanding both incarnation and cross (17:1): it represents a mutual glorification—or revelation and exaltation—in which the Son glorifies (reveals and exalts) the Father and the Father glorifies (reveals and exalts) the Son. Behind this theme lies the core unity bringing together Father and Son in eternal amity and concord (17:24). Jesus can "make known" (*gnōrizo*) the Father to his disciples precisely and only because he himself intimately "knows" the Father (*ginōskō*).

The Prayer also reveals the ongoing identity of the community through knowledge of Jesus as "the one whom you have sent" (17:3), through the protective love he has for his own, and through the unshakeable unity believers share with the Father in love. Jesus has revealed to them God's name, which covers and shields them (17:6, 26). In other words, the Prayer reveals as much about the community as it does about God and Jesus. It reveals its identity as those loved and guarded as they are sent into the unbelieving world, it reveals the firm grounds of their security in an insecure and

---

21. C. K. Barrett, *The Gospel According to St John: An Introduction with Commentary and Notes on the Greek Text*, 2nd ed. (London: SPCK, 1978), 506.

Law and Revelation

vulnerable context, and it reveals their unceasing attachment to Jesus and through him to the Father. There is no direct reference to the Spirit-Paraclete in this prayer, but the Spirit's work is presupposed from beginning to end. The Paraclete is the one who will enable the unity to bind together the believing community, present and future, to keep it safe and to hold it in the divine circle of love. The Spirit ensures the continuity of the work of revelation, making God known in an ongoing way in the worshipping life, the interior love, and the outgoing witness of the community.

LAW, SCRIPTURE, AND REVELATION IN THE PASSION

The theme of revelation continues, and indeed intensifies, in the passion narrative of the Gospel (18:1–19:42). At first glance, the figure of Moses and the law which accompanies him seem to be missing from this narrative section. Nor is there any explicit language of revelation, as we have already encountered it. But to assume that neither theme is present in the story of the passion would be a mistake: it would mean reading the passion without any reference to what has gone before. John has carefully set up our understanding of the passion in previous narratives so that we will grasp its significance: most immediately in the Last Supper with its focus on Jesus's departure, but also further back in the narrative of Jesus's ministry, especially in references to his being "lifted up" or "exalted" (since the verb *hupsoō* can have both meanings, 3:14–15; 12:32). The cross is the climax of God's self-revelatory love in Jesus:

> For John, it is inevitable that the cross will be revelatory.
> It reveals supremely who Jesus is in his oneness with the

178   John

> Father . . . . It reveals his love for those he came to save . . .
> and, is, therefore, also a mirror to the love of the Father
> for the world.[22]

Previous allusions to the cross make it clear that this event represents, above all, the reciprocal glorification and exaltation of the Son and the Father. Jesus is glorified in his *anabasis*, his return to God, to the realms of glory; in this sense, the cross for him is a kind of ladder by which he departs to the place from whence he came. God is glorified in this event because the cross reveals the true, divine nature as consisting of radical life-giving and self-sacrificing love. As the revelation of glory, the crucifixion is tied in the closest possible way to the incarnation, outlining the contours of salvation in this Gospel. The cross is the direct consequence of the incarnation and the expression of God's vulnerable and life-giving love; both are equally revelatory and both are redemptive.[23]

John uses the language of "cleansing" as well as "life-giving" to refer to the cross, and it is symbolized and foreshadowed in the footwashing. The primary meaning of Jesus's actions (which readers often miss) is that of union and communion with him through his sacrificial death: "Unless I wash you," Jesus says to Simon Peter in response to his objection, "you have no part [or share] with me" (*meros*, 13:8). Only in the light of Easter will the true significance of the footwashing be revealed (13:7). The extended meaning of love and service within the community is a secondary implication of the footwashing arising from the core sense of union with

---

22. Morgan-Wynne, *The Cross*, 183.

23. John Behr sees the prologue itself as "a paschal hymn" implicitly connected to the cross (*John the Theologian and His Paschal Gospel: A Prologue to Theology* [Oxford: Oxford University Press, 2019], 245–70).

Jesus (13:12–17). Similarly, in the parable of the vineyard Jesus speaks of the branches being "cleansed"—though we usually translate it as "pruned"—by the Father to enable them to flourish (15:2). Jesus's death in this sense is revealed as life-giving by its cleansing from sin.

The main events on the cross carry the cleansing and life-giving meaning of the cross with a significant degree of irony.[24] The crucifixion is revealed as an enthronement in a paradoxical context of utter degradation and shame. The more the soldiers and authorities mock and deride, the stronger the irony of their unintended disclosure of Jesus's kingly nature. The purple robe and crown of thorns, along with the soldiers' mockery and abuse (19:1–3), and the taunting of Pilate against his Jewish adversaries (19:14–15, 19–22), all emphasize the core irony, in which Jesus's true identity is unveiled precisely in its annihilation. Here the light shines in the darkness and the darkness has failed to extinguish it, an interplay that has continued uninterruptedly since creation (1:5).[25] This same irony has already been seen in the earlier meeting of the Sanhedrin, when Caiaphas ironically prophesies that "it is expedient for us that one person should die on behalf of the people." John assiduously explains its meaning to the reader (11:50–52).

The ironical symbolism of the cross is evident from the main events that take place in John's account. The division of Jesus's clothing and the lots cast for the seamless robe point

---

24. For further details on Johannine irony, see Paul D. Duke, *Irony in the Fourth Gospel* (Louisville, KY: Westminster John Knox, 1986). O'Day sees irony as "a revelatory mode" (*Revelation*, 31–32).

25. On the close theological link between creation, incarnation, and resurrection in John, see John Painter, "'The Light Shines in the Darkness . . .' Creation, Incarnation and Resurrection in John," in *The Resurrection of Jesus in the Gospel of John*, ed. Craig R. Koester and Reimund Bieringer, WUNT 222 (Tübingen: Mohr Siebeck, 2008), 21–46.

to the unity which endures even in dissolution, division, and death (19:23–25a). The presence of the four holy women with the beloved disciple and the gifting of the mother and disciple to one another point to the formation of the community out of the death of Jesus, as we have seen in chapter 7 (19:25b–27). The same is true for Jesus's thirst, which signals his approaching death but also reminds the reader of Jesus's readiness to carry out the will of God. In his actual death Jesus breathes out the Spirit with his dying breath (*pneuma*, 19:28–30). The climactic moment of revelation is the flow of blood and water, sacramental symbols of birth and new life issuing from the death of Jesus; the event is caused ironically by the supposed piety of the Jerusalem authorities, who do not want dead bodies to remain on the cross for the Sabbath and Passover (19:31–34).

A further element is the theme of the fulfillment of Scripture, which appears throughout the passion story. On three occasions, beginning with the arrest and ending with the piercing of Jesus's side, the evangelist points to the realization of Scripture: in the dividing of Jesus's garments (19:24; Exod 28:32; Ps 22:18), in his thirst (19:28; Ps 69:21), and in the testimony to the piercing of his side (19:36–37; Exod 12:46; Num 9:12; Zech 12:10). This motif emphasizes Jesus's obedience to the Father and his readiness to take the divine path of suffering on behalf of sinful, enslaved humanity in order to give them life. It is an astonishing act of liberating love and grace.

To sum up: the cross as the climax of the Gospel discloses the revelatory meaning of salvation for John. It is essential for obtaining eternal life, and it underscores Jesus's identity, thus revealing the love of Father and Son. It signifies the judgement of the world and God's triumphant victory over "the ruler of this world" (*tetelestai*, "it is accomplished," 19:30). For those who believe, it effects union with Jesus and therefore with the Father through the Spirit.[26]

LAW, SCRIPTURE, AND REVELATION IN THE RESURRECTION

The resurrection narratives make only one allusion to Scripture and several references to revelation. The two disciples who run to the tomb after the summons of Mary the Magdalene do not understand the scriptural necessity of Jesus's resurrection (20:9). No indication is given as to which Scripture is in mind at this point: perhaps it is a more general and unspecified sense of the fulfillment of the divine will as revealed in the past to Israel. Whatever the Old Testament text may be, it is an odd statement following on from the beloved disciple's apparent believing at the sight of the head-cloth and folded grave clothes (20:8). Yet he communicates nothing of his believing either to his companion or to Mary, whom we now find weeping for the first time outside the tomb (20:11). The only sense to make of this apparent contradiction is that the beloved disciple has an inkling of what has happened but it is not sufficiently strong to enable him to speak of it: "It probably is believing that Jesus, as he had said he would, has returned to the Father."[27] Here the beloved disciple contrasts with Mary the Magdalene, who confidently proclaims the message once she has fully grasped it (20:18).

Three times in these narratives, John speaks of Jesus revealing himself to the disciples. The first is in the display of his wounds, which paradoxically fill the disciples not with dismay but with joy: the scars are the assurance of Jesus's

---

26. Morgan-Wynne, *The Cross*, 132–57.
27. David F. Ford, *The Gospel of John: A Theological Commentary* (Grand Rapids: Baker Academic, 2021), 999.

identity and risen presence with them, his conquest of death, and the enduring impact of his saving work for them through the cross (*deiknumi*, 20:20).[28] In this sense, Thomas is right to demand to see and touch the wounds, these paradoxical symbols of salvation, even though this is also the expression of his lack of faith (20:24–28). Jesus does display his wounds, and his final beatitude is proclaimed to those who do not have the luxury of such seeing but who depend for their faith on the revelation to Mary the Magdalene and Thomas—the first "apostolic" Christians.

The second resurrection narrative in Galilee uses more explicit language of revelation. Jesus manifests or reveals himself to the seven disciples by the sea (21:1). This scene is concerned with the revelation of the life of the church: its success in mission and its porous boundaries, symbolized by the almost-torn net, along with the nurturing and sustaining presence of the risen Jesus through the gift of the Spirit (21:1–14; see 20:19–23). The final scene with the two disciples, Simon Peter and the beloved disciple, ensures the church's leadership through reconciliation and martyrdom (21:15–19) and through the writing of the Gospel (21:24–25). Therefore, in the resurrection narratives, as in the passion, the language of revelation accompanies the theme of the fulfillment of Scripture to emphasize the events of Jesus's death and resurrection as integral to the divine plan of salvation.

"THE JEWS" IN JOHN

A related issue in Johannine scholarship has been the place and interpretation of the group of characters designated as

---

28. Dorothy A. Lee, "The Significance of the Wounds of Jesus in the Fourth Gospel," *Review & Expositor* 120 (2023): 114–26, https://doi.org/10.1177/0034637323119660.

hoi Ioudaioi in the Fourth Gospel. There is considerable controversy over this question:[29] whether John's Gospel is embedded in Judaism and positive towards it (e.g., 4:22) or whether the language fits the stereotype of antisemitism—"the Fourth Gospel seems to be at once the most Jewish and the most anti-Jewish of the gospels."[30] Christianity in the latter view is seen as rising from the ashes of Judaism, the negative portrayal of Jewish people in the Gospel confirming its distancing, if not inimical, attitude to Jewish custom and belief.[31] In the Tabernacles narrative, for example, hostility to this group is at its most stark (8:31–59), with the Johannine Jesus accusing "the Jews" of no longer being children of Abraham but rather of the devil (8:44); the narrative concludes with their attempt to stone Jesus. Elsewhere Jesus speaks of "your law" when in debate with the authorities, which seems to set him apart from his Jewish roots (8:17; 10:34).

For some, this portrayal of Jewish people—along with a number of other New Testament texts—signals the roots of Christian antisemitism, which resulted in the ongoing persecution and alienation of Jewish people in Europe, particularly during the Middle Ages. Eventually, it led to the Holocaust and the murder of millions of Jewish people before and during the Second World War. It is generally allied to a form of supersessionism that takes the view that Judaism and the Jewish people have been supplanted in God's election and covenant in favor of Christians. This view is often accompanied by a

---

29. For an overview of the debate, see Tom Thatcher, "John and the Jews: Recent Research and Future Questions," in *John and Judaism: A Contested Relationship in Context*, ed. R. Alan Culpepper and Paul N. Anderson, RBS 87 (Atlanta: SBL, 2017), 3–38.

30. Thatcher, "John and the Jews," 6.

31. Adele Reinhartz, "The Jews of the Fourth Gospel," in *The Oxford Handbook of Johannine Studies*, ed. Judith M. Lieu and Martinus C. de Boer (Oxford: Oxford University Press, 2018), 121–37.

184   John

disparaging of the Old Testament as representing a God of
wrath against the God of grace depicted in the New Testament.

These views have been contested by very different ways of
reading John's Gospel. One view, for example, argues that the
Greek term *hoi Ioudaioi* (often translated "the Jews") should
more accurately and consistently be translated "the Judaeans,"
referring primarily to those inhabiting the geographical location in and around Jerusalem. This solution is attractive. It
makes sense, for example, of John 11 and the presence of
Jewish mourners (probably women) comforting Martha and
Mary for the loss of their brother (11:31). However, it is also
true that conflict with this same group takes place in Galilee
(6:52). Another view is that the term "the Jews" in its hostile
sense—which, it is important to remember, represents only
a minority of references—is a shortcut for those members of
the Jerusalem priestly hierarchy who actively oppose Jesus.
After all, almost all the characters in the Gospel are Jews who
do not belong among Jesus's antagonists.[32]

There is a further consideration in this debate. For a good
deal of the twentieth century, Johannine scholarship assumed
that Christianity and Judaism had definitively parted company following the Jewish War and that Christians by the time
of the writing of John's Gospel had formed an autonomous
religious grouping of their own, with only historical links
to the parent faith. Indeed, some have argued that John's
community, presumably in Ephesus, was separated even from
other Christian groups, forming a sectarian community isolated from everyone else.[33]

---

32. For a view of "the Jews" from the perspective of social identity theory, see
Christopher A. Porter, "Will the Real *Ioudaioi* Please Stand Up?," in *The Enduring
Impact of the Gospel of John: Interdisciplinary Studies*, ed. Robert A. Derrenbacker Jr.,
Dorothy A. Lee, and Muriel Porter (Eugene, OR: Wipf & Stock, 2022), 62–80.

33. E.g., Wayne A. Meeks, "The Man from Heaven in Johannine
Sectarianism," *JBL* 91 (1972): 44–72.

Law and Revelation

More recent study of the Fourth Gospel has questioned this assumption, not only of John's arising from a sectarian community but also of this community being definitely separated in its self-understanding from Judaism.[34] Instead, it is more likely that the Johannine community sees itself as heir to the traditions and sacred texts of Judaism, although in some tension with the synagogue community. This self-identification need not rule out Gentile adherents, since Judaism was in some traditions open to Gentile engagement and participation. If this is so, then "the Jews" in John's Gospel cannot refer to all Judaism, and still less to all Jewish people, but in adversarial contexts refers to those who reject Jesus from within the ruling class in Jerusalem. In that sense, it is probable that the disagreements are intramural between two groups in the one faith tradition rather than between two different religions. John's Gospel in this sense is not antisemitic: "It cannot be claimed that the Johannine narrative disparages Judaism as a religious faith . . . If anything, references to Jewishness and to 'Israel' convey pervasively positive associations."[35]

REFLECTIONS

This chapter has challenged a number of assumptions sometimes held by Christians. In the first place, it contests the

---

34. Jörg Frey argues that the parting of the ways was gradual: "the separation between synagogal Judaism and Jesus followers was a rather incoherent process, one that happened not at one particular moment . . . that differed from group to group and from place to place" ("Toward Reconfiguring Our Views on the 'Parting of the Ways': Ephesus as a Test Case," in *John and Judaism: A Contested Relationship in Context*, ed. R. Alan Culpepper and Paul N. Anderson, RBS 87 [Atlanta: SBL, 2017], 238 [221–39]).

35. Paul N. Anderson, "Anti-Semitism and Religious Violence as Flawed Interpretations of the Gospel of John," in *John and Judaism: A Contested Relationship in Context*, ed. R. Alan Culpepper and Paul N. Anderson, RBS 87 (Atlanta: SBL, 2017), 287 (265–311).

186 John

equation that law equals bad and grace, apparent in Jesus, equals good. The identity of the Johannine Jesus, on the contrary, is grounded in the Old Testament, which is the result of divine revelation in this Gospel. Indeed, Moses, the law, and the Old Testament Scriptures are necessary, in John's worldview, to understand the Johannine Jesus; they function, in effect, as christological symbols. This means that the Old Testament traditions have a vital role to play in Christian life and worship. It is true that these older traditions also possess their own identity, independent of Christian, messianic interpretation. But, in the end, for Christians the two testaments belong together and each is to be read in the light of the other.

Secondly, this chapter also challenges the antisemitism found in some branches of Christianity, either implicitly or explicitly. If the Fourth Gospel is read aright, with awareness that the Johannine community does not see itself as separate from Judaism or the faith of Israel, there is no justification for Christian antisemitism. "The Jews" refers in the negative sense to certain of the Jerusalem authorities—excluding such figures as Nicodemus and Joseph of Arimathea—and certainly not to all the Jewish characters, who comprise the majority of figures in the Gospel.

How these distinctions can be carried forward in English translation is another question which is perhaps more difficult to answer. Reading Saint John's passion story on Good Friday, as many churches do, can hardly fail to give the impression of a supersessionist and antisemitic interpretation of the Gospel. The reiteration of the phrase "the Jews" in the translation of the passion narrative is problematical for the reader unaware of the context and subtleties of interpretation. It is one thing to study such texts with full awareness of the wider Gospel and broader implications; it is another issue to ask how they are to be used in the context of Christian worship. Real assistance is given in some English translations sensitive to the complexities of interpretation around these issues, such as the CEB and the NIV, which mostly translate *hoi Ioudaioi* as "the Jewish leaders." Another possibility is "Judeans," but, even so, this rendering should make it clear that it is certain of the leaders who are under attack, not the ordinary folk.[36]

Thirdly, the discussion on revelation reminds us of the importance of grasping the saving and life-giving significance of the cross and resurrection. John's view overthrows dominating understandings of how power is to be exercised. Salvation comes to us through vulnerable and sacrificial self-giving, not overpowering force or manipulation. But this spirituality is also material in the Gospel, emphasized by the emphatic bodiliness of Jesus's resurrection and the presence of his wounds; it points forward to Christian belief in the resurrection of the body, not only for Jesus but also for us.[37] That, too, is to be the shape of the church in its mission and evangelism, offering a God whose glory is apparent in loving self-giving—a glory that assures us of the defeat of sin and death—and who draws us into intimate communion with God and with one another.

Related to this is the significant awareness that it is not only the cross—the death and resurrection of Jesus—which saves in the Fourth Gospel, but also behind it the incarnation itself. The gulf between creation and God, widened by sin and

---

36. See Kathleen Troost-Cramer, *Jesus as Means and Locus of Worship in the Fourth Gospel: Sacrifice and Worship Space in John* (Eugene, OR: Pickwick, 2017), 115–45.

37. For further details on the bodily nature of the risen Christ in John 20, which is neither a crude, physical resuscitation nor a spiritualized reality, see Sandra M. Schneiders, "Touching the Risen Jesus: Mary Magdalene and Thomas the Twin in John 20," in *The Resurrection of Jesus in the Gospel of John*, ed. Craig R. Koester and Reimund Bieringer, WUNT 222 (Tübingen: Mohr Siebeck, 2008), 153–76.

death, is crossed in the Son's taking on of flesh. The incarnation reaches the fullness of revelation in the crucifixion, where the arms of Jesus open wide to embrace and draw all people and, indeed, all living things into the trinitarian circle of love (12:32).[38] In his human life and ministry, as much as in his dying and rising, the Johannine Jesus forges a new humanity ("Behold, the man!," 19:5), a new sense of covenant, and a new awareness of what it means to be a creature made in the divine image, obedient to and abiding in the Father and open to loving others. This realized vision means the restoration of human beings to their true destiny as children of God and the restoration of all creation to God. Jesus is the center of that salvation: the Revealer sent from God. He shows us who God is for us and who we are to be for God and for one another.

FURTHER READING

Behr, John. *John the Theologian and His Paschal Gospel: A Prologue to Theology*. Oxford: Oxford University Press, 2019.

Byers, Andrew J. *John and the Others: Jewish Relations, Christian Origins, and the Sectarian Hermeneutic*. Waco, TX: Baylor University Press, 2021.

Duke, Paul D. *Irony in the Fourth Gospel*. Atlanta: John Knox, 1985.

Kittredge, Cynthia Briggs. *Conversations with Scripture: The Gospel of John*. CS. New York: Morehouse, 2007.

Morgan-Wynne, John. *The Cross in the Johannine Writings*. Eugene, OR: Pickwick , 2011.

O'Day, Gail R. *Revelation in the Fourth Gospel: Narrative Mode and Theological Claim*. Philadelphia: Fortress, 1986.

---

38. On "all things" as the possible original text of 12:32 rather than "all people," see Dorothy A. Lee, "Jesus' Spirituality of [Af]filiation in the Fourth Gospel," *Religions* 13 (2022): 647.7 (fn. 12), https://www.mdpi.com/2077-1444/13/7/647?type=check_update&version=1.

Subject Index

Aaron, 94–95
Abel, 120
abiding, 61–62, 155–58
Abraham, 26, 45, 120, 170
active principle, 50
adoptionism, 33
Akhenaten (Egyptian pharaoh), 72
amanuensis, 3
Andrew, 2
anguish, 148–49
animals, liberation of, 103–4
Annas, 107, 121
Antiochus IV, 70, 165
antisemitism, 186
antithesis, 18
Apology (Plato), 49–50
Apuleius, 72
Arian heresy, 24
Arianism, 28–29
Aristotle, 141, 144
Arius, 28–29
ark of the covenant, 95, 97
Artemis, 7, 99–100
Artemisium, 7
Asklepios, 73
Aten (Egyptian sun god), 72
Athanasius, 29, 30
Athens, Greece, 166
Augustine of Hippo, 24, 77

Babylon, 95
Basil, 29
bearing witness, 127–30, 136. *See also*
    witness/witness theme
Becker, Ernest, 89

Becoming, 55–56
Being, 55–56
believers, missional life of, 35–36
believing/believing theme
    as ambiguous, 132
    in discipleship, 132–34
    Old Testament background of,
        118–20
    overview of, 117–18, 131–35
    in prologue, 122–23
    reflections regarding, 135–37
    as response to divine revelation,
        131, 172
    Roman background of, 120–22
    by Samaritan woman, 131
    as spectrum, 132
    spirituality of, 137
    teaching and learning process in,
        132–33
    trial motif and, 123–26
beneficial ideology, 166–67
biographies, defined, 12
birth/birth theme
    imagery of, 80, 123, 145–50
    joy in, 148–49
    as miracle, 77
    overview of, 139–40
    parable of the woman in labor
        and, 148
    reflections regarding, 158–60
blindness, 68–69, 73, 74, 81–83, 106
blood, 149–50
Bread of Life, 38, 63, 106, 170
bronze serpent, 152
Brown, Raymond E., 13

189

190 John

Caiaphas, 107, 121, 179
Chalcedonian Declaration, 29
Cana to Cana cycle, 14, 58, 78, 100–105
Cappadocians, 29, 30
cave, allegory of, 71–72
characterization, 18
childbirth. *See* birth/birth theme
children, family role of, 143. *See also* family/family theme
Christianity, 9, 183, 184, 186
Christology, 93
Chrysostom, John, 24
church
  bearing witness by, 136
  defined, 34
  evangelism by, 66
  history of, 35
  imagery of, 135
  mission of, 136
  overview of, 34–36
  as temple of the Holy Spirit, 113
Cicero, 120, 144
cleansing, 178
Clement of Alexandria, 40
climate change, 42
cloud, symbolism of, 94
cognitive stage of text interpretation, 19
community
  in the church, 34
  identity of, 176
  love in, 156, 160
  temple and glory in, 112–13
  unity in, 177
cottage industry, 143
Council of Nicaea, 29
covenant, 164
creation
  darkness and, 55
  dominion of humanity over, 47
  ethics and, 42
  life and, 88
  light and, 55, 69, 88
  overview of, 69
  rejection in, 122–23
  salvation and, 76–77
  Stoic doctrine of, 50
  threats to, 89–90

Wisdom and, 47, 54
Word and, 45, 53, 54
cross/crucifixion
  bronze serpent imagery and, 80
  as climax of the Gospel, 180–81
  Eucharist and, 63
  family and, 152–53
  as fulfillment, 59–60
  Great Prayer and, 176
  incarnation and, 188
  law and revelation and, 177–81
  Passover and, 35
  symbols/symbolism of, 86–87, 130, 179–80
  temple and, 107–10
Cyril of Alexandria, 24

darkness, 55, 68–69, 77–78, 106
David, 26, 144
death, desire for, 89
Deborah, 118
diction, 18
disciples
  as children of God, 154–55
  defined, 132–33
  Jesus as revealing to, 181–82
  love of, 156
  mission of, 10–11
  overview of, 134
  sending out of, 6
  trial motif and, 124–25
  witness of, 128–29
  women as, 134
discipleship
  abiding and, 61–62
  believing in, 132–34
  collegial nature of, 136
  love and, 156
  overview of, 132–33
  words of Jesus and, 58–59
Domitian (Roman emperor), 99
dualism, 68, 93

Easter, 13
Eastern Church, 41
education, 143
electricity, 90
Eliot, T. S., 66
Enoch, 120

Subject Index

environment, 89–90
Ephesus, 7–8, 99, 184
Epidauros, Greece, 73
Esau, 101
eschatology, 34–36
Essenes, 121
eternal life, 59, 87–92
ethics, 40–42, 60–61
Eucharist, 35, 63
Eusebius, 5
evangelism, 66
evil, blindness metaphor for, 73
exile, 95
extramission, 74

faith, 132. *See also* believing/believing
theme
false witness, 119
family/family theme
abiding and, 155–58
in the ancient world, 140–44
birth imagery and, 146 (*See also*
birth/birth theme)
challenges of, 158
children in, 143
crucifixion of Jesus and, 152–53
father in, 141
friendship and, 155–58
of God, 139, 159
hierarchy of, 141
hospitality in, 144
incarnation and, 152
isolation in, 158–59
of Jesus, 152–54
love in, 155–58
mother in, 141
overview of, 139–40, 150–55
reflections regarding, 158–60
renewal of identity in, 159
slavery and, 141, 142, 143
transition to, 146
Farewell Discourse, 16, 17, 31, 107–8,
125, 129, 151–52, 175–76
Father-Son imagery, 139, 150–51,
155–56. *See also* God; Jesus
Feast of Tabernacles, 105, 106
Feast of the Dedication (Hanukkah),
70, 82
feasts, 81–82, 105–7, 172–73

feminine imagery, 39
festivals, 81–82
fictive kinship, 144, 159
filiation, 39
first naivety, 18–19
fishing, 135–36
Flavian dynasty, 99
flesh/body, 38, 42, 93–94, 110–12
footwashing, 13, 35, 108, 174
forensic imagery, 119, 120, 123–26
foreshadowing, 18
forgiveness, 188
Four Gospels, overview of, 23–24
friendship, 140, 144, 155–58

glory/glory theme
community and, 112–13
flesh/body and, 110–12
of God, 97, 178
in Great Prayer, 176
human response to, 97
in incarnation, 102
of Jesus, 171, 178
overview of, 93–94
reflections regarding, 114–16
in the temple, 96–97
wedding at Cana and, 102
God
adoptionism and, 33
as center of John, 25–28
as Creator, 45
dwelling place of, 93–94 (*See also*
temple/temple theme)
as Father, 39, 150
glory of, 97, 178 (*See also* glory/
glory theme)
imagery regarding, 37, 56
Jesus's subordination to, 30
as life-giving, 77, 150
mindfulness of, 137
mission of, 130
of the Old Testament, 27
as origin of goodness, 80–81
as origin of light, 80–81
ruling power of, 47
as self-giving, 26
self-revelation of, 102
as source of life, 70–71, 150
as sustainer, 70–71

192 John

on trial, 119
Wisdom and, 48
wisdom of, 53–54
word of, 45, 53
wrath of, 184
goodness, 73, 80–81
good news, 75
Gospel of John
audience for, 8–11
authorship of, 1–6
bearing witness, 127–30
as biography, 12
as Book of Glory, 13
as Book of Signs, 13
dating of, 6–8
as dramatic narrative, 12
ethics in, 40–42
genre of, 11–12
God as center of, 25–28
imagery of, 37–39
inconsistencies of, 16–17
language of, 37–39
law, Scripture, and revelation in,
169–73
literary devices in, 18
mission focus in, 10–11
as narrative, 18
narrative fluidity in, 17–18
narrative outline of, 13–19
overlap in, 21
personal message of, 136–37
spirituality in, 40–42
Synoptic Gospels as compared
to, 24
themes of, 21
as theo-centric, 25–28
title of, 23–24
translations of, 21–22
venue of, 6–8
Gospel of Mark, 9–10
grace, 127, 167
Great Prayer, 108, 113, 176–77
Greco-Roman world
hospitality in, 144
as influence to Judaism, 8–9, 51
law in, 166
temples in, 98–100
Wisdom and, 49–51
witness in, 120–22

Word and, 49–51
Gregory Nazianzus, 29, 38
Gregory of Nyssa, 29

Hanukkah (Feast of the Dedication),
70, 82
Hasmonean dynasty, 121
healing, 13–14, 58, 79, 81, 106
Hellenistic Judaism, 51, 143, 165
heresy, 24
Herod the Great, 95–96
high priesthood, 121
Holocaust, 183
holy of holies, 96. *See also* temple/
temple theme
Holy Spirit
in Last Discourse, 175
as life-giving, 63, 106
maternal terms for, 147–48
overview of, 31–34
as Paraclete, 31, 175
power of, 11
spirituality and, 41
titles for, 175
work of, 177
Homer, 71, 73
hospitality, 144

"I am" sayings
on Bread of Life, 170
on light and life, 68, 75–76
Martha and, 83–84
overview of, 40
on resurrection and the life,
171–72
on truth, 127
identity
of community, 176
in family/family theme, 159
in family of God, 159
of Jesus, 34, 38, 40, 52–53, 94, 103,
104–5, 106, 186
new, 145
in Word/Word theme, 53
ignorance, blindness of, 82–83
Iliad (Homer), 71
imagery, 18, 37–39. See also specific
imagery
incarnation of Jesus, 26, 29, 102, 152,

Subject Index

160, 164, 168, 176, 187–88. *See also* Jesus
indwelling, 61–62
injustice, 61
intromission, 74
Irenaeus of Lyons, 2
irony, 18
Isaiah, 97
Isis (Egyptian goddess), 72–73
Israel. *See also* temple/temple theme
  accusations from, 119
  failures of, 164
  light and life to, 69, 70
  as people of God, 135
  wanderings of, 70

Jacob, 101–2
James, 3
Jerusalem, 98, 106, 121. *See also* Israel
Jesus. *See also* Word/Word theme
  abiding in, 61–62, 157
  adoptionism and, 33
  arrest of, 121
  ascension of, 152
  authority of, 26
  as Bread of Life, 38, 63, 106, 170
  as Bridegroom, 128
  Cana to Cana cycle of, 14, 58, 78, 100–105
  centrality of, 65, 115, 188
  cleansing of the temple by, 102–3, 170
  commands of, 60
  crucifixion of, 35, 59–60, 63, 80, 86–87, 107–10, 152–53, 176, 177–81, 188
  as divine gift, 169
  as divine Wisdom, 62–64
  divinity of, 24, 28, 53
  as embodiment of the temple, 105–6
  emotions of, 84
  Farewell Discourse of, 16, 17, 31, 107–8, 125, 129, 151–52, 175–76
  filiation of, 39
  flesh/body of, 110–12
  focus on, 27
  forgiveness from, 188

  as fulfillment, 59–60, 65–66, 169, 172–73
  as Gate, 135
  glory of, 171, 176, 178
  as Good Shepherd, 85, 135
  Great Prayer of, 108, 113, 176–77
  healings of, 58, 79, 81
  as hospitable Wisdom, 62–64
  humanity of, 24, 38–39
  in "I am" sayings, 40, 68, 75–76, 83–84, 127, 170, 171–72
  identity of, 34, 38, 40, 52–53, 94, 103, 104–5, 106, 186
  incarnation of, 26, 29, 102, 152, 160, 164, 168, 176, 187–88
  in Jerusalem, 16
  judgment against, 126
  as Lamb of God, 108–9, 152
  Last Supper and, 17, 35, 107–10, 155, 174–77
  Lazarus and, 83–87
  life through, 152
  as Light of the world, 82, 86, 91, 106, 130
  as Living Water, 106
  love of, 155, 157
  maleness of, 38–39
  ministry of, 78, 171
  miracles of, 171
  mission of, 64, 130
  narratives of, 14
  Nicodemus and, 75, 79–80, 147, 155
  opposition to, 122
  overview of, 28–31
  as personification of feasts, 173
  power of life in, 81
  prayer of, 33
  as Rabbi, 133
  as resurrection and the life, 171–72
  resurrection of, 59–60, 64, 83–87, 181–82
  return of, 148
  as Revealer, 162–63, 168, 188
  as sacrifice, 109
  Samaritan woman and, 36, 58, 63, 78, 104, 128, 131
  as Shepherd, 110
  sonship of, 39

194 John

subordinationist passages regarding, 29–31
as Teacher, 133–34
testimony of, 129, 130
threat to, 14
titles of, 40
travels of, 78
trial of, 123–26
as true Vine, 135
as truth, 127
at wedding at Cana, 58, 62–63, 77, 78, 101, 171
words of, 44–45, 57–62
worship and, 33, 104–5, 115–16
Jewish War, 8, 121
Jews, in John, 182–85, 186–87
John (apostle), 1–3
John of Ephesus, 6
John the Baptist, 2, 11–12, 55, 78, 122, 123–24, 127–28, 136
Jonathan, 144
Joseph, 120
Josephus, 8–9
joy, 79, 148–49
Judaism
    Christianity and, 9, 183, 184
    feasts and festivals in, 81–82, 105–7, 172–73
    Hanukkah in, 70, 82
    hellenization of, 51, 143
    historical context of, 164–65
    hospitality in, 144
    as influenced by Greek ideas and culture, 8–9
    leadership groups in, 121–22
    temple background in, 94–98
Judas, 59
Judas Iscariot, 174
Judas Maccabeus, 70, 165
judgment, 80, 91, 118–19, 126
Junia, 6
justice, 121

kingship, 75
kinship, 140–44, 158–59, 160. *See also* family/family theme

ladder imagery, 101
lamb, symbolism of, 108–10

language, of John, 37–39
Last Discourse, 175
Last Supper, 17, 35, 107–10, 155, 174–77
law courts, 120–21
law/law theme
    background to, 164–67
    gift of, 45, 118, 164, 167
    in Gospel narrative, 169–73
    in Greco-Roman world, 166
    Jews and, 182–85
    at the Last Supper, 174–77
    overview of, 162–63
    in the passion, 177–81
    in the prologue, 167–68
    reflection regarding, 185–88
    in resurrection, 181–82
    as revelation, 167–68
    in Roman Empire, 166–67
    tablets of, 95
Lazarus, 5, 21, 77, 83–87, 108, 156, 184
learning, 133
Levites, 123–24
Lewis, C. S., 67
Library of Celsus, 7
life/life theme
    birth imagery and, 80
    creation and, 88
    God as source of, 77, 150
    in "I am" sayings, 75–76
    Jesus as, 152, 171–72
    Jewish and Greco-Roman thought regarding, 69–74
    in John's narrative, 74–76
    joy and, 79
    light and, 70, 71
    modern references to, 88–89
    in the Old Testament, 69
    overview of, 68–69
    in prologue, 76–78
    reflections regarding, 87–92
    restoration of, 78–81
    resurrection and, 83–87
    water as, 79, 104
    in Word, 76
Life of Moses (Philo), 165
light/light theme
    access to, 72
    blindness and, 68–69, 81–83

Subject Index

creation and, 55, 69, 88
darkness at war with, 77–78, 106
God as origin of, 80–81
in "I am" sayings, 75–76
Jesus as, 106
Jewish and Greco-Roman thought
    regarding, 69–74
in John's narrative, 74–76
judgment and, 80, 91
life and, 70, 71
love and, 91
in the Old Testament, 69, 70
overview of, 68–69
in prologue, 76–78
reflections regarding, 87–92
salvation and, 70
sight and, 81–83
sources of, 90–91
subordinate symbols of, 86
symbolism of, 55, 71
as taking for granted, 90
loquaciousness, 66
Lord's Supper, 63
love
    command of, 60
    ethic of, 60–61
    in Father-Son imagery, 155–56
    of Jesus, 155, 157
    in Last Discourse, 175
    light and, 91
    overview of, 155–58, 159–60
Lucretius, 74

Marcion, 27
Martha, 36, 83–84, 129, 156, 172, 184
Mary (mother of Jesus), 36, 152–54
Mary of Bethany, 36, 42, 84, 156, 184
Mary the Magdalene, 16, 36, 154, 181
materialism, 88–89
Maximus the Confessor, 30
medicine, 89
meditation, 137
men, subordination to, 30
Metamorphoses (Apuleius), 72
Middle Platonism, 50
mindfulness, 137
monotheism, 72
mortality, 55–56, 80
Moses

as agent of the law, 162, 164
appointment by, 118
ark of the covenant and, 95
bronze serpent and, 80
as divine gift, 169
glory of God and, 97
as icon, 120
as philosopher, 165
revelation of Jesus and, 168
salvation and, 26
Ten Commandments and, 45
in tent of meeting, 94
Mount Olympus, 71
Mount Sinai, 45, 95, 118, 164
music, 66

Naomi, 144
narrative fluidity, 17–18
Nathaniel, 101, 169
Nicene Creed, 24, 29, 34
Nicodemus, 75, 79–80, 147, 155

Odyssey (Homer), 71
Old Testament. See also Scripture
    Index
    blindness in, 73
    canon of, 27n5
    embeddedness of, in John, 162
    glory theme in, 96–97
    God of, 27
    life theme in, 69
    light theme in, 69, 70
    references to, 26–27
    temple/tabernacle in, 94–98
    words of Jesus and, 59
    Word theme and, 45–49
oppression, 61
Origen, 24, 27, 30
orthodox theology, 24

Palestine, 121
Papias of Hierapolis, 5
parable of the sheepfold, 82
parable of the vine, 157
parable of the vineyard, 135, 179
parable of the woman in labor, 148
paradox, 18
parallelism, 18
passion narrative, 107–10, 177–81

196   John

passive principle, 50
Passover, 35, 108
Paul, 8
perichoresis, 30
persecution, 70, 125
personification, of Wisdom/Sophia,
    48
persuasive speech, 120
Pharisees, 7, 121–22, 123–24
Philip, 169, 175
Philo of Alexandria, 8–9, 50, 165
Pilate, 75
Plato, 49–50, 51, 71–72, 74, 165
Plutarch, 12
Pontius Pilate, 121, 125–26, 127, 179
pool of Bethesda, 81
Pool of Siloam, 105–6
prologue, of John. *See also* Gospel
    of John
    believing in, 122–23
    law in, 167–68
    light and life themes in, 76–78
    Logos and Sophia in, 52–57
    reference to truth in, 127
    revelation in, 167–68
    temple/temple theme in, 100–105
    witness in, 122–23
prophets, word to, 46

Rahab, 120
rebirth, 160. *See* birth/birth theme
recognition, 18
redemption, 53
rejection, 122–23
religion, 65
Republic (Plato), 71–72
restoration, 78–81, 145–50, 188
resurrection of Jesus, 59–60, 64,
    83–87, 181–82. *See also* Jesus
revelation/revelation theme
    background to, 164–67
    believing as response to, 131
    in Gospel narrative, 169–73
    Jews and, 182–85
    at the Last Supper, 174–77
    law as, 167–68
    overview of, 162–63
    in the passion, 177–81

    in the prologue, 167–68
    reflection regarding, 185–88
    in resurrection, 181–82
    words for, 170–71
reversal, 18
Ricoeur, Paul, 18–19
Roman Empire, 96, 98, 121, 166–67
royal official, 58, 79
Ruth, 144

Sabbath, 81, 124, 143
Sadducees, 121
Salome, 1–2
salvation, 70, 76–77, 112, 153, 188
Samaritan woman, 36, 58, 63, 78,
    104, 128, 131
Sanhedrin, 121, 167, 179
Sarah, 26, 45, 120
scribe, 3
Scripture, 18–19, 169–73, 180. *See
    also* Gospel of John; Old
    Testament
second naivety, 19
Second World War, 183
Septuagint, 8
sheep imagery, 109–10, 135
Sheol, 71
Shepherd, 110
sight, 73, 81–83
silence, 66–67
Simon Peter, 2, 3, 6, 12, 64, 87, 129,
    133, 156, 178
sin, 69
slavery, 141–42, 143
Socrates, 49–50, 66
Solomon, 95
Solon of Athens, 166
soul, 71
spirituality, in John, 40–42, 137
Stoics, 50–51
subordinationist view, 29–31
Suetonius, 99
suffering, 148–49
symbolism, 18, 37
Synoptic Gospels, 9–10

tabernacle, 94, 95. *See also* temple/
    temple theme

Subject Index

Tabernacles narrative, 82, 145–46, 183
taxation, 98, 121
technology, 89
temple/temple theme
  background of, in Judaism, 94–98
  Cana to Cana cycle and, 100–105
  church as, 113
  cleansing of, 102–3, 170
  community and, 112–13
  destruction of, 7, 95, 96, 98, 114,
    121
  in Ephesus, 99–100
  feasts and, 105–7
  glory in, 96–97
  in Greco-Roman cities, 98–100
  Jesus as embodiment of, 105–6
  Last Supper and, 107–10
  liberation of animals from, 103–4
  overview of, 93–94
  passion and, 107–10
  in the prologue, 100–105
  rebuilding of, 95
  rededication of, 70
  reflections regarding, 114–16
  renovation of, 95–96
  structure of, 96
  symbolism of, 103
  water in, 96
Ten Commandments, 45
tent of meeting, 94
Teresa of Ávila, Saint, 137
Tertius, 3
Tertullian, 30, 31
testimony, 129. *See also* witness/
  witness theme
text interpretation, three-stage
  process of, 18–19
Theophilus, 12
Thomas, 5, 16, 84, 86, 129, 182
Timothy, 8
tone, 18
Torah, 162, 165
Tractates, 24
trial imagery, 119, 123–26
Trinity, 30, 31–32, 37. *See also specific*
  persons
truth, 127
Tutankhamen, 72

unity, 175, 177

vision, 74

water
  in birthing, 149–50
  in healings, 106
  imagery regarding, 63
  Jesus as, 106
  as life, 79, 104
  symbolism of, 79, 96, 106
  in the temple, 96
wedding at Cana, 58, 62–63, 77, 78,
  101, 171
wellness industry, 89
willful rejection, blindness of, 82–83
Wisdom/Sophia
  in creation, 47, 54
  feminine imagery regarding, 39
  of God, 53–54
  Greco-Roman world and, 49–51
  hospitable, 62–64
  as host, 48
  imagery regarding, 56
  personification of, 48
  in the prologue, 52–57
  reflections for today regarding,
    64–67
  as water, 63
  Word and, 44, 47
witness/witness theme
  bearing, 127–30
  of the disciples, 128–29
  of Jesus, 129, 130
  of John the Baptist, 127–28
  Old Testament background of,
    118–20
  overview of, 117–18
  in prologue, 122–23
  reflections regarding, 135–37
  Roman background of, 120–22
  of the Samaritan woman, 128
  trial motif and, 123–26
women, 30, 134, 141, 142
Word/Word theme (Logos)
  creation and, 45, 53, 54
  divine identity and, 53
  Greco-Roman world and, 49–51

hospitable Wisdom and, 62–64
imagery regarding, 56, 66
life and, 76
mortality and, 55–56
Old Testament and, 45–49
overview of, 44–45
in the prologue, 52–57
reflections for today regarding,
64–67
Wisdom and, 44, 47

words of Jesus and, 57–62
World War II, 183
worship, 33, 35–36, 99, 104–5,
115–16
wounds, symbolism of, 111–12

Year of Jubilee, 143

Zebedee, 1, 3
Zeus, 165

Scripture Index

OLD TESTAMENT

Genesis
1. 76
1–3. 164
1:1 52
1:1–2:3. 45
1:1–2:4a. 76
1:3 . . . . 69, 76
1:14–19 76
1:26–27. . . . . . .47, 135
1:27 . . . . .135, 147
2–3 69
2:18–25 154
3:20. 154
12–25. 120
28:12–17 101

Exodus
12:46 180
13:21–22 70
16:4 170
17. 119
18:24–26 118
20:1–2 45–46
20:2–17 45
20:3 115
20:16 119
23:1–2 119
25:9 94
25:10–22 95
26. 94
27:1–8 94
28:32 180
33:18–23 97
40:6 94

Leviticus
4:7 94

16:1–19 95
19:14 73
19:18 . . . . . .60, 119, 157
21:18–19 73
25:8–17 143

Numbers
9:12 180
21. 80
21:4–9 152

Deuteronomy
5:6–21 45
5:20 119
6:5 119
10:1–5 95
10:19 60
18:15–18 169
19:15 . . . . .119, 129
19:16–19 119
28:29 73

Ruth
1:16–19 144

1 Samuel
4:19–22 97
18:1–4 144

2 Samuel
6:6–11 95

Nehemiah
9:15 170

Job
9. 119
40–41 119

Psalms
6:5 71
23. 135
26:8 97
27. 70
36:9 70
41:9 174
69:9 . . . . . . .59, 103, 170
69:10 LXX 59
69:21 180
78:24–25 170
80:6–18 135
105:40 170
145:15–17 47
146:8 73

Proverbs
8:1–6 48
8:22–23, 27, 29b–31 . .48
9:1–6 62
22:18 180

Ecclesiastes
3:19–21 71

Isaiah
1:11–17 119
5:1–7 135
6:1–8 97
6:2 102
29:9 73
29:18 73
35:5 73
40:3 169
40:4 76
42:16 73
43:10 76
43:26 119

199

200 John

46:4 76
53:1 170
55:11 58
56:7 102

Jeremiah
31:8 73
31:31–34 164
32:38 164
42:5 119

Lamentations
4:14 73

Ezekiel
1:4–25 24
14:11 164
34 135
47:1–11 96
47:1–12 106
47:8–10 136

Daniel
7:13 102
12:2 71

Amos
5:21–24 119

Micah
1:2 119
2:1–2, 12 46
3:9–11 119

Habakkuk
2:4 120

Zechariah
8:8 164
12:10 180
14:8 96

Malachi
1:8 73
3:5 119

NEW TESTAMENT
Matthew
1:1–17 12

1:1–25 52
6:22–23 74
7:12 163
17:24–27 98
22:40 163
27:56 2

Mark
1:1 12
1:14–15 52
8:22–25 68
8:38 102
9:2–9 82
10:46–52 68
11:15–17 102
13:26–27 102
14:22–25 109
15:40 2

Luke
1:4 12
1:26–38 53
8:2–3 6
10:1–12, 17–20 6
21:20–24 98
24:50–51 152

John
1–20. 3
1:1 . . . . 44, 52, 108
1:1–2 . . . .25, 29, 32, 52,
        76, 151, 176
1:1–5 . . . . 54, 122
1:1–12:50. 14
1:1–18 . . . . .14, 19
1:1–51 14
1:3 . . . . 42, 54, 82
1:4 68
1:5 . . . . .55, 77, 179
1:6–8 123
1:6–13 . . . . . 54, 55, 123
1:7 . . . . .117, 122
1:9 . . . . 123, 127
1:10–11 123
1:11 145
1:11–12 122
1:12 145
1:12–13 . . . . . . .34, 123,
        135, 139

1:13 . .110, 123, 146, 148
1:14 . .13, 32, 34, 38, 45,
       55, 93, 100, 102,
      111, 127, 137, 150,
          152, 168, 171
1:14–18 . . . . 54, 55, 100
1:15 123
1:15, 29, 36 128
1:16 127
1:17 . . . . . 127, 162, 164,
          167, 169
1:18 . . . . .29, 32, 56, 57,
          108, 168
1:19–12:50. 13
1:19–28 123
1:19–51 . . . . 14, 134
1:21, 25 169
1:23 . . . . 162, 169
1:29 . . . . 35, 108
1:29–34 33
1:31 170
1:32–33 157
1:35 2
1:35–42 11
1:36 108
1:38 133
1:45 . . . . 132, 163
1:46 170
1:51 101
2:1–4:54 . . . .13, 14, 58,
          78, 101
2:1–11 . . . . . . 14, 36, 62
2:1–12 . . . . 78, 134
2:3 78
2:4 . . . . 149, 154
2:4a 78
2:4b 78
2:5 . . . . 58, 78
2:10 171
2:11 . . . . . . .13, 63, 102,
          170, 171
2:12 153
2:12–25 14
2:13 108
2:13–3:21 78
2:13–22 102
2:14–16 33
2:16 151
2:17 . . . . .59, 170

Scripture Index

201

2:18 124
2:18–21 33
2:18–22 103
2:19 . . . . 59, 103
2:21 103
2:22 . . . . .59, 170
3:1–21 147
3:1–36 14
3:2 171
3:3 . . . . .75, 147
3:3–8 32
3:4 147
3:5 . . . . .75, 147
3:5–6 83
3:6 . . . . . . 110, 147, 175
3:6–8 147
3:10 79
3:11, 32 130
3:14 80
3:14–15 . . . . . 152, 177
3:15–16 77
3:16 . . . . 26, 80, 130
3:16–17 . .37, 60, 155, 175
3:17 . . . . 26, 80
3:19–21 80
3:20–21 147
3:22 147
3:22–36 78
3:30 . . . . 128, 136
3:32 130
3:32–33 129
3:33 127
3:35 156
4:1–42 . . . . . 14, 78, 104
4:5–6 104
4:6–15 104
4:7–23 63
4:10 106
4:20–26 104
4:21 104
4:22 . . . . . . 9, 104, 183
4:23 104
4:23–24 104
4:24 127
4:25 104
4:26 . . . . . 75, 104, 131
4:28–29 36
4:28–30 63
4:29 131

4:29–30 128
4:34 . . . .11, 26, 130, 171
4:35–38 123
4:39–42 . . . . .128 36
4:41–42 58
4:42 105
4:43–54 14
4:46–54 . . . . . 13–14, 79
4:48 171
4:50 58
4:51–53 58
5. 81
5–10 . . . . . . .13, 81, 105
5:1 . . . . 13, 16
5:1–10:42 . . . . . .14, 172
5:1–47 14
5:2–9a 14
5:16 124
5:17 151
5:18 . . . . 29, 132
5:19–21 150
5:19–23 . . . . . . 26, 173
5:20 156
5:21–23 81
5:24 59
5:26 83
5:28–29 34
5:31 129
5:32, 37 129
5:35 127
5:36 . . . . 129, 171
5:36–37 . . . 11, 130, 150
5:38 . . . . .61, 157
5:39, 45–47 129
5:45–46 . . . . . . 132, 173
6. 35
6–10 173
6:1 16
6:1–15 63
6:1–71 14
6:4 108
6:29 . . . . . . 11, 130, 131,
171, 172
6:29, 44, 57 . . . . 11, 130
6:31 170
6:31–35 170
6:32 151
6:35 . . . . 40, 63, 106
6:35, 48, 51 63

6:39 34
6:41, 48, 51 38
6:42 38
6:51 . . . . 32, 63
6:51–56 111
6:51–58 . . . . 35, 63
6:52 184
6:53–56 63
6:55 127
6:56 . . . . 62, 157
6:63 . . . . 32, 110
6:67, 70 6
6:67–71 134
6:68 129
7:1–8:59 14
7:1–52 . . . . 82, 105, 132
7:3 153
7:4 170
7:7 130
7:10 16
7:15 . . . . 124, 133
7:16 . . . . . . .11, 130, 133
7:19, 22–23, 51 170
7:30–32, 45–49 124
7:37 106
7:37–38 . . . . . . 106, 113
7:39 . . . . 32, 63, 83, 106
7:50–52 124
7:53–8:11 105
8:12 . .40, 68, 75, 82, 106
8:12–59 . . . 82, 105, 132
8:14 . . . . 129, 130
8:15 110
8:15–16 126
8:16–18 . . . . 11, 130
8:17 . . . . .170, 183
8:20 149
8:24, 28, 58 75
8:26 127
8:31 . . . . 61, 132
8:31–33 59
8:31–36 146
8:31–59 183
8:32, 45–46 127
8:39, 41 132
8:44 . . . . 126, 183
8:48 . . . . 124, 132
8:51 59
8:52 132

8:52–58 170	11:25–26a 172	13:30 87
8:58–59 124	11:27 . . . . 129, 172	13:31–14:31 15
8:59 . . . . . . 61, 105, 132	11:28 172	13:34 . . . . . .60, 157, 174
9. . . . . 68, 81, 105	11:31 184	13:34–35 41
9:1–7, 35–41 124	11:33, 35, 38 85	13:35 130
9:1–41 14	11:39 84	14. 16
9:3 . . . . 83, 106	11:41–42 152	14:1 131
9:4 . . . . .11, 130, 171	11:43 84	14:2 62
9:5 . . . . 40, 75, 82	11:47–53 . . . 61, 85, 121	14:6 . . . . . . 40, 113, 127
9:6–7 106	11:48 . . . . 103, 132	14:8–9 175
9:7 . . . . 11, 130	11:48–53 124	14:9 171
9:14 124	11:49–50 107	14:10 171
9:22 . . . . : 124	11:50–52 179	14:16 175
9:24 132	12:1 108	14:16–17 175
9:24–34 . . . . .61, 124	12:1–8 . . . . . . 36, 42, 84	14:17 . . . . . . 31, 62, 127
9:28–29 . . . . . . 132, 173	12:3 84	14:21 . . . . 155, 171
9:28–33 170	12:9–11 85	14:21–22 175
9:35–38 106	12:12–19 15	14:22 171
9:39–41 . . . . . . 82, 106	12:20–36 15	14:23 . . .41, 60, 62, 155,
10:1–18 . . . . 61, 135	12:21 152	174
10:1–21 . . . . 82, 110	12:23 . . . . 78, 149	14:24 . . . . 11, 130
10:1–42 14	12:27 149	14:25–31 125
10:7 40	12:31 . . . . .81, 112	14:26 . . . . 62, 175
10:11 40	12:32 . . .80, 112, 177, 188	14:28 29
10:16 10	12:35–36 81	14:31 . . . . 16, 156
10:17 . . . . 85, 156	12:37–50 15	15:1 . . . . 16, 40
10:17–18 . . .32, 86, 104,	12:38 170	15:1–8 41
110	12:38–41 162	15:1–9 61
10:18 151	12:42 124	15:1–16:4a 15, 17
10:20 124	12:44 131	15:1–17 135
10:25 . . . . 129, 130	12:46 157	15:2 179
10:30 29	12:49 . . . . . 11, 130, 150	15:3 61
10:30–33 124	13–17, 20–21 14	15:4–7 158
10:31–39 14	13:1 . . . .13, 60, 79, 108,	15:7 61
10:32 171	149, 155	15:8 . . . 42, 61, 133, 151
10:34 183	13:1–17:26 . . . . . 15, 108	15:9 62
10:39 . . . . .61, 124	13:1–21:25. . 13, 15, 107	15:9–10 157
11:1–12:11 . .15, 84, 108,	13:1–30 . . . . 15, 35, 108	15:10 42
134	13:1–38 174	15:11 61
11:1–12:50 14	13:2–30 13	15:12, 14, 20 174
11:4, 40 . . . . . 108, 172	13:5 155	15:12, 17 157
11:5, 36 156	13:7 178	15:12–17 61
11:9–10 87	13:8 178	15:15 . . . . .157, 171
11:15 84	13:12–17 179	15:18 59
11:16 84	13:13 133	15:18–16:4 125
11:17–27 36	13:18 . . . . .59, 174	15:26 . . . . . 31, 105, 127
11:21–27 132	13:19 75	15:26–27 . . . . . 129, 175
11:25–26 . .34, 40, 68, 83	13:23–26 156	16. 16

Scripture Index

16:2 124
16:4b–33 ....15, 17
16:7–11 175
16:8 31
16:8–10 130
16:11 126
16:13 .. 32, 41, 127, 134
16:13–14 31
16:21 148
16:22, 33 125
16:22–23 34
17............... 151
17:1 ....149, 176
17:1–26 ... 15, 108, 113, 174
17:2 111
17:2–3 113
17:3 .....127, 132, 176
17:6 .. 131, 170, 174, 176
17:12 59
17:14 57
17:17 58
17:20 174
17:20–23 ..... 135, 155
17:21 ..... 11, 130, 150
17:21–22 113
17:23 130
17:24 ..33, 135, 151, 176
17:26 .....156, 171, 176
18:1–11 15
18:1–19:42..... 15, 107, 108, 177
18:3 86
18:5, 8 75
18:6 86
18:9 59
18:10 12
18:12–19:16a....... 15
18:13–14, 19–23 ... 107
18:15–16 5
18:17, 25, 27 156
18:18 87
18:19 14
18:19–24 125
18:20 107
18:28 109
18:28–19:16a...... 125
18:36 75

18:37 .... 75, 129
19:1–3 179
19:5 188
19:7 132
19:13 126
19:14–15, 19–22 ... 179
19:16b–42........ 15
19:23–25a 180
19:24 .... 60, 180
19:25–26.......... 36
19:25–27.......... 42
19:25b–27........ 180
19:26 156
19:26–27......... 152
19:26–27, 35–37 2
19:28 ..... 26, 60, 180
19:28–30......... 180
19:30 .... 86, 181
19:31 109
19:31–34......... 180
19:34 .....111, 113, 149
19:34–37......... 32
19:35 128
19:36 109
19:36–37...... 60, 180
19:37 152
19:38, 40 110
20:1–18 .... 15, 16
20:1–21:25......... 15
20:2 156
20:7 85
20:8 181
20:9 .... 60, 181
20:11 .... 85, 181
20:12 110
20:13, 15 154
20:16 133
20:17 .... 112, 154
20:17–18 36
20:18 181
20:19–23....... 15, 16
20:20 .. 86, 103, 171, 182
20:20, 25–27......111
20:22 .... 11, 32
20:22–23..........175
20:23 .... 61, 130
20:24 .... 6, 134
20:24–29 ...... 15, 16

20:25–28......... 86
20:27 .... 86, 103
20:28 ....32, 57, 91, 129
20:30 13
20:30–31.... 12, 15, 16
20:31 ....131, 172
21............3, 16, 17
21:1 170
21:1–8 64
21:1–14 .... 15, 16, 136
21:2 3
21:7 .... 2, 128, 156
21:9 87
21:9, 15–19 17
21:9–14 64
21:15–19 ... 15, 64, 156
21:18–24 17
21:19 .... 112, 133
21:20 156
21:20–24 ...... 15, 64
21:22 133
21:23 2
21:24 ...... 2, 35, 128
21:25 15

Acts
1:9–11 152
3–4 3
12:1–2 3
19:23–40......... 100
19:35 99

Romans
7:12 163
8:9–11 158
8:14–17 155
16:7 6
16:22 3

1 Corinthians
3:16 158
3:16–17 113

2 Corinthians
6:16 158

Hebrews
9:1–5 95

John

11	120

2 Peter

1:4	134

1 John

2:1	175
3:2	137

3 John

6, 9	135

Revelation

1:1	170

4:6b–11	24
20:19–23	182
20:24–28	182
21:1	182
21:1–14	182
21:15–19	182
21:24–25	182

ANCIENT SOURCES
Sirach

15:3	62
24:19–21	62
24:21	48
46:19	119

Wisdom

1:6	119
3:1–9	71
7:27–28	48
9:1–4	47